PARADOX OF ORGANIZATIONAL CHANGE

PARADOX OF ORGANIZATIONAL CHANGE

Engineering Organizations with Behavioral Systems Analysis

by
Maria E. Malott, PhD

CONTEXT PRESS
Reno, NV

Paradox of Organizational Change:
Engineering Organizations with Behavioral Systems Analysis

Paperback pp. 216

Distributed by New Harbinger Publications, Inc.

Library of Congress Cataloging-in-Publication Data

Malott, Maria E.
[Paradoja de cambio organizacional. English]
Paradox of organizational change : engineering organizations with behavioral systems analysis / by Maria E. Malott.– 1st American ed.
p. cm.
"Paradoja de Cambio Organizacional, was published in Spanish by Editorial Trillas ... 2001"–P.
ISBN-13: 978-1-878978-42-4 (pbk.)
ISBN-10: 1-878978-42-X (pbk.)
1. Organizational change. 2. Interbehavioral psychology. 3. Behavioral assessment. 4. Behavior modification. 5. System analysis. I. Title.
HD58.8.M2453 2003
658.4'063–dc21

2003006930

---

933 Gear Street, Reno, NV 89503-2729

Printed in the United States of America

Cover design by Omar Mora Mora and Dr. Javier Pucheta Garcipiña of the Art Institute of the *Universidad Veracruzana.*

ACKNOWLEDGMENTS

The first edition of this book, *Paradoja de Cambio Organizacional*, was published in Spanish by *Editorial Trillas* (Malott, 2001b). The Spanish edition would not have started – or developed – without the consistent support of my friend and colleague A. Daniel Gómez Fuentes. Daniel directed the Research Master's Program of Applied Psychology to Education at the *Universidad Veracruzana* in Mexico. The program, founded in 1965, has won national recognition for combining research and applications in behavior analysis.

The Spanish version was conceptualized in 1993 when Daniel offered me the opportunity to participate in his master's program as an on-going guest instructor. The objective? To teach students and Veracruz's business leaders about organizational behavior management, using the reality-based applications I was conducting in the United States and abroad. The original idea was to combine this teaching effort with the development of a textbook on organizational change.

Daniel, the faculty and students of the program – over a period of almost 10 years – consistently offered me the most wonderful, welcoming support and feedback via numerous drafts and versions of the Spanish edition. More than 400 seminar participants in Mexico contributed with their input and experience. Participants from all types of industries – manufacturing, hotel management, service, construction, retail, insurance, state government, education, and health – verified the cross-business applicability of the principles and methods of organizational change presented in this book.

In addition, Dr. Marco Wilfredo Salas Martínez and A. Daniel Gómez Fuentes directed master's theses on the application of components of this book to enhance higher education systems. Elvia Molina Candiani (1997), Mauricio Eliseo Aguirre Serena (1998) and Sergio Ezequiel Alvarado Ruiz (2000) worked on improving the productivity of the university's administration. Marco Antonio Nava Bustos (2001), Alberto Francisco Alarcón Urdapilleta (2001), Karla Lavarreda Martínez (2001) and Ruth Serrano Solís (2001) worked on changing administrative processes of the *Universidad Pedagógica Veracruzana*. The work was also supported by other faculty: Joaquín Rosas Garcés, José Arturo Pérez Medellín, Pilar González Flores and Oralia Gómez Fuentes coordinated the logistics of my many trips to Mexico with the support of administrative personnel; Enrique Zepeta García, Alejandro Reyes, José Luis Colorado and Raúl Rosas López provided technical support for all seminars; Dr. Javier Pucheta Garcipiña, director of the Art Institute of the *Universidad Veracruzana*, and graphic designer Omar Mora Mora designed the book's original covers.

The faculty of the master's program helped transcribe the first seminars and conferences. They also edited initial versions of some chapters, with the help of A. Daniel Gómez Fuentes, Dr. Marco Wilfredo Salas Martínez, Joaquín Rosas Garcés, Jerónimo Reyes Hernández and Noemí Ramos. Full drafts of the Spanish edition were reviewed by Dr. Guillermo Yáber and Dr. Elizabeth Valarino from the *Universidad Simón Bolivar* in Caracas, Venezuela; Coral García Asarola, from *Universidad Católica del Uruguay* in Montevideo, Uruguay; Marco Antonio Nava Bustos, Alberto Francisco Alarcón Urdapilleta, Karla Lavarreda Martínez, María Elena Martínez Ponce, Martha Elsa Libreros Fernández, Rafael Cortéz Rodríguez, Dinorah Arely Escudero Campos, and Laura Patricia Medrano Herrera from the *Universidad Veracruzana*. Armando Maldonado, editor from *Editorial Trillas,* was also most helpful with the final edition.

The actual work of each case illustrated in the book is based on a real application of a systematic effort of organizational change. Each case has taken, in reality, anywhere from eight months to five years. I fictionalized and simplified the real cases to protect the confidentiality of my clients and to make the reading user-friendly. Without direct personal experience of changing organizations, I would have not been able to learn how to implement real change. I am in debt to my clients from all industries who trusted in my ability to help their organizations. Many of them challenged and enriched my perspective of change. I am especially thankful to Dick Varnell, Dora Lezovich, Peter Heinz, and Doug Bylsky from retail; Jon Eickhoff and Dr. Susan Eickhoff from manufacturing; José Iguina from pharmaceutical; Franc Laux from automotive; Mari Lou Cazers from foods; and Bertie Borrel from service.

The current English edition has undergone considerable revisions and improvements from the Spanish edition. I am most thankful to my mentors who inspired and nurtured my professional growth: Dr. Richard W. Malott and Dr. Dale M. Brethower, from *Western Michigan University*, and Dr. Sigrid S. Glenn, from the *University of North Texas*. They reviewed sections of this edition and spent countless hours helping me analyze complex organizational change endeavors from the conceptual perspectives of behavior analysis, systems analysis and cultural design.

I am fortunate to have had the collaboration of numerous colleagues who volunteered their time and effort to review this English edition. My most sincere appreciation goes to Lori H. Miller, a doctoral student of *Western Michigan University*. Lori reviewed each chapter carefully, gave excellent input, applied the model presented in this book in her doctoral research, and provided consistent encouragement. Lori has taught me much about what it is to be a mentor. Pam Skelton, from Airways Airlines, also made significant contributions with her editing and provided the perspective of an organizational change consultant by using the concepts presented in the book across various industries. Dr. Ramona Houmanfar, from the *University of Nevada,* Reno, was an extremely diligent editor and used a draft of this edition in a systems analysis class with her graduate students: Janice Doney, Scott Herbst, Heidi Landaburu, Kristen Maglieri, Charna Mintz, Horacio Roman, Jennifer Thomas, and Kevin Williams. Ramona and her students provided careful revisions and made sure the terminology used was consistent with various behavior analysis domains – such as experimental, clinical and organizational behavior management. Dr. Mark Dixon and Dr. Ruth Anne Rehfeldt, from *Southern Illinois University,* also provided encouragement. Thomas Breznau, from the *L. Lee Stryker Center*; Dora Lezovich, from *Meijer, Inc.*; Allen Bullard, from *Dollar General Corporation*; and Mark S. Repkin, from *Certif-A-Gift* offered careful and insightful input from the business client's perspective. And last, but not least, Thea Rozetta Lapham – professional journalist and editor from *Lapham & Associates* – who enhanced the quality of the writing in considerable ways.

May this work awaken your curiosity and sense of inquiry, generating the enthusiasm you need for managing organizational change.

TABLE OF CONTENTS

LIST OF FIGURES

LIST OF TABLES

Chapter 1
The Paradox

CHAPTER 1
THE PARADOX

Nothing stays firm forever; as the seasons turn, everything vanishes like morning dew (Sonnet 60).

William Shakespeare (1564–1616)[1]

Paths Over the Sea

I was 21 years old when I met Dr. Leona Montoya in my first professional job at a human resources institution. She would often chide the management of public and private organizations for leading without developmental strategies and consistently failing to implement long-term change processes.

I have observed many of Dr. Montoya's impressive interactions with a variety of audiences. She was my role model of a professional woman: cultivated, educated, critical, constructive, and productive. Dr. Montoya received her doctorate from *Sorbonne University* in Paris, traveled around the world and often published about organizational change.

On one occasion, she visited my institution. She was looking for someone to give her a ride home when we met in an elevator. Without hesitation, I offered my assistance.

Where do you live? she asked me.

When I responded, she said, *That is in the opposite direction of my home!*

It doesn't matter, it's a pleasure to help you, I replied.

As I drove, I asked Dr. Montoya about her life, education, and accomplishments. With each answer, my admiration for her grew more and more. Inwardly, I sighed. My accomplishments were nothing in relation to hers. Respectfully, I said:

Dr. Montoya, you must feel so proud of your achievements.

What achievements? I have accomplished nothing, she answered.

Astonished, I replied, *How could you say NOTHING? What about your contributions, your writing, your travels, your...*

She interrupted me. *Those things do not matter. They are transient. My contributions do not last. When I leave, what I have built will not continue.*

After a brief silence, she kept going. *My son is an architect. He builds physical structures that last over time. But, me? The structures I build fall apart in a short time – nothing remains.*

[1] *English poet and dramatist.*

This was the only conversation I ever had with Dr. Montoya. To this day, she has no idea that our dialogue remained deeply etched in my thoughts. It is ironic that she believed her contributions were short-lived because her apprehension became my professional challenge.

Contradiction 1: Dynamic vs. Constant

Although my conversation with Dr. Montoya was several years ago, her words still remain true. I have toiled to find an answer to the question she framed for me in our brief encounter: Can one create lasting changes in evolving organizations?

The first contradiction in the paradox of organizational change is dynamic vs. constant. In this book, we will see that although the environment is continuously changing, the processes accounting for the change remain constant.

> *Concept 1-1. Dynamic vs. Constant Contradiction – the environment where change occurs is dynamic, as it evolves over time. But the process of change is constant because the dynamic relationship between behavior and environment is always present.*
>
> *Concept 1-2. Change – the product of alteration, variation, or modification*[2].
>
> *Concept 1-3. Change Process – a series of actions that result in alteration, variation, or modification.*

The Greek philosopher Heraclitus[3] said, "We do not bathe twice in the same river." Organizations are constantly changing in one direction or another. The traditional approach to change implies that the river is always the same. Organizational change consultants usually produce "something," and when they achieve "that something" they get paid. They believe that the product of change is the "thing," the project, or the program they generated. But they miss a fundamental point: The product of change cannot be understood as something static or permanent. The moment that we manage to produce the thing, the project, or the program, we have to review, adapt, and alter it.

The poet Antonio Machado[4] illustrated the ephemeral nature of change efforts in his poem "Cantares." Following are some excerpts:

[2] *Encarta, 2003.*

[3] *Heraclitus (540?-475? AC) was a Greek philosopher who believed that the world was in constant change. He was borne in Ephesus, today's Turkey. He was one of the founders of metaphysics. (See Khan, 1979.)*

[4] *Antonio Machado Ruiz (1875-1939) was a Spanish poet and member of the freedom movement known as "the generation of 1898." His "Complete Poems" were published in 1917. (See Machado, 1969.)*

Journeyer, it is your tracks
that make the trail, nothing more;
Journeyer, there is no trail,
in going, it is brought forth.
Journeying, the path arises;
only when you turn and glance
do you see the path – once taken,
never to be taken twice.
Journeyer, there is no way,
only wakes you leave behind.
... All passes and stays but
our thing is to walk
to walk making roads over the sea.

Typical organizational change efforts are created with the intention of long-term success, yet they are often transient like paths over the sea. Once completed, the organization – like the sea – remains essentially the same.

For many years, I heard the same ideas, saw the same mistakes and felt the frustration and discouragement generated by failure to succeed in change. People grow tired of projects, programs, and initiatives because they do not last despite the fact they start with much enthusiasm and become the ongoing chat of the organization. Eventually, people stop taking these change efforts seriously and the initiatives stop. All will soon be forgotten. Then someone will identify the same unsatisfied need and launch a similar initiative under a different name with a new package.

Is it worth it to invest so much energy if – in the end – there is little impact? Why invest so much time in something that, by its very nature, will not last? How can we create initiatives that adapt to constant changes and endure? Can we create initiatives that build on the successes and lessons of the past rather than always starting from scratch?

Contradiction 2: Complex vs. Simple

The second contradiction of the paradox is complex vs. simple. The environment where change takes place is complex – affected by the interactions of many parts and behaviors. Change efforts cannot ignore such complexity if they are to be effective. In spite of this inherent complexity, we will see in this book that the process of change is simple. Its essential component is the behavior of each individual and that behavior's consequences.

Concept 1-4. Complex vs. Simple Contradiction – the environment of change is complex because it occurs in the midst of multiple and convoluted interactions. It is simple because there is only one essential process that accounts for the evolution of organizations – the functional relationship between the behavior and the environment.

One day, I was talking with Michigan architect Norman Carver, known for creating a unique style of contemporary architecture[5] that resembles the style of Frank Lloyd Wright. Norman integrates elegant architectural plans with the natural environment. He has designed and overseen the construction of more than 150 buildings.

Norman, you should be proud of your work.

What makes you think so?

Each home enhances its occupants' quality of life. And your structures are long lasting.

Hmm... I never thought about the lasting aspects of my work.

I told him the results of my efforts are vulnerable to drift. They depend on what people do. To my surprise, Norman said that he would have preferred his work to be less durable.

When I asked him to clarify what he meant, Norman replied, *on a few occasions, after seeing structures I designed 30 years ago, I asked myself: Did I build this? I would prefer to erase them out of my portfolio.*

Norman's constructions are part of a changing and complex world. When he started designing and constructing buildings 30 years ago, his work was affected by many variables and was constrained by the available technology, building regulations, construction materials, his experiences, and development.

Lifestyles and the domain of architecture are subject to ongoing changes and increased complexity. Oftentimes, a building can be adapted to accommodate new advances. Occasionally, however, the existing structure is too limiting; remodeling is too expensive and may offer few possibilities of success. In these circumstances, starting over again can be more cost-effective than renovation.

Organizations are more easily influenced by environmental changes than architectural projects, mainly because the success of an organization depends on what people do and the effects of their work. Not only is each instance of behavior unique, but it is affected by the dynamic interaction of a multitude of variables, such as the actions of other individuals, customer demands, and market changes.

Rigid organizational structures that do not adapt to evolving complexity do not last. They are closed systems. Biology teaches us the need for interaction with the environment. A cell dies if it does not respond to the changing complexity in its surroundings. Likewise, as an organization evolves, so must its internal structures.

> *Concept 1-5. Closed System – group of interrelated components that do not interact or evolve with changes in the environment. Closed systems eventually die.*

The Shaker community in the United States was a closed system. In 1774, a portion of the Shakers, who came from England, immigrated to New York. In the

[5] *For an appreciation of Carver's architectural style, see, 1981, 1987, 1993, 1995.*

beginning, there were nine members. By 1880, the Shakers had grown to 6,000 members with communities in Indiana, Ohio and Kentucky[6].

The Shakers believed in celibacy. Their behavior was governed by the Order of the Apostles whose principal idea was to separate the genders to prevent biological reproduction. These practices included having doors and stairs assigned by gender to avoid interactions between males and females.

In addition, the Shakers ignored the local social and legal systems. They accepted homeless children and incorporated them into the work force. Subsequently, they were accused of exploiting minors and failing to respect legal regulations.

The Shakers did not develop effective strategies to maintain their principles within the larger and complex society in which they lived. As a result, by 1900, the community had been reduced to 1,000 members. Today there are only a few members. The lesson? Closed systems die because they do not adapt to environmental complexity.

Contradiction 3: Chaotic vs. Orderly

In this book, we will see that although organizations are seemingly chaotic, unsystematic and unpredictable, the process of change is orderly and predictable. This contradiction is a third component of the paradox: Change is chaotic and orderly.

> *Concept 1-6. Chaotic vs. Orderly Contradiction – organizations are seemingly unpredictable, but the process through which they change can be systematic and predictable.*

In a conversation with Nicholas Mukomberanwa[7], a Zimbabwean sculptor, I asked, *How can you foresee the shape you give to the rock?* He replied, *I can't predict the final form that results from my carving. It is like pouring water on earth. Do you think that I can direct where the water goes? It works the other way around. It is the configuration of the rock that controls the shape of my sculptures, not my plan. The only predictable course is my carving style.* (Figure 1-1 shows a photograph of a Mukomberanwa sculpture.)

Organizational change usually means influencing, managing, and monitoring a course of action. But there are many uncontrollable events in an organization, making it seem chaotic. Many incidents occur without our influence and too many things changing all the time makes us feel out of control.

Mukomberanwa inspired in me a valuable insight: Although he did not control the final form of the sculpture, his carving process was orderly and predictable. His

[6] *See Stein (1994), who wrote a general history of the Shaker community, from its beginnings in the XVII century.*

[7] *Nicholas Mukomberanwa is known as one of the most skillful sculptors of Zimbabwe. See Guthrie (1989) for a description of his work.*

Figure 1-1. Sculpture of Nicholas Mukomberanwa

sculptures are the result of natural progression. Each carving stroke determines the next. The formation of the lakes, rivers, and mountains follows an analogous evolutionary process. Each drop of rain affects the configuration of the land, even when its contribution appears insignificant at any given time.

Organizational change can be analogous to Mukomberanwa's sculpting. The form evolves from the process. The analysis of the process should be one of the first steps and the rest can be built from there. Change efforts must conform to the organization's needs, allowing the result of each component of change to shape the next.

Change Process

Systems that consider and adjust for environmental dynamics, complexity, and chaos – referred to as open systems – have a greater chance of survival than those that are closed. For example, the likelihood of an organization's survival increases if it continuously adapts to fluctuations in the market, consumer trends, and technological advances.

Concept 1-7. Open System – a group of interrelated components that adapt to complexity, dynamics, and chaos in the environment.

A family is an example of an open system. Here, the dynamics change with economic and social demands, such as family members' jobs, the addition of children, and age-related physical changes. Although adaptation is fundamental, open systems do not last simply because they interact with the environment. More is needed.

Open systems change with time: they evolve. But why worry about controlling the evolution of systems? Wouldn't it be easier to let a system take its own course without intervention? Wouldn't it be more convenient to let it die due to its own failure to adapt? Why bother?

Letting organizations "go with the flow" is, of course, an alternative. But it is like letting a vessel drift in the sea, with the wind and current determining its direction. Letting processes drift is a poor option for organizational-change leaders.

We tend to treat change as if the "thing" to be changed is a closed system. We seem more comfortable if the department, process, or activity we want to change exists in isolation: thereby allowing us to bypass the complexity caused by interacting with other departments, processes, or activities. We place walls where there were none – "*my* department, *my* employees, *my* processes" – and create an illusion of simplicity and permanent results.

But if we contain change within artificial walls, our systems will likely die. "*My* department, *my* employees, *my* processes" are affected by internal and external events. Change needs to be viewed as part of a process within open systems. The result of change is dynamic, constantly evolving and complex. Organizations are convoluted, but the basic principles of change are not.

Paradox of Organizational Change

Organizational change is a paradox. The paradox consists of inherent contradictions. One contradiction is that change is dynamic, yet the process of change is constant – it remains the same. Another contradiction is that change is complex, but the process of change is simple. (In this case, "simple" means having few elements.) A third contradiction is that the change appears chaotic and uncontrollable, while the process of change is orderly and systematic. (See Table 1-1.)

Table 1-1. Paradox of Organizational Change

Paradox (Contradiction)	
Change Environment	**Change Process**
DYNAMIC (Change over time) COMPLEX (Having many parts) CHAOTIC (unsystematic, unpredictable)	CONSTANT (Not changing or varying) SIMPLE (Having only one part) ORDERLY (Systematic, predictable)

Concept 1-8. Paradox of Change – change involves contradictions between the environment where change occurs and the process of change: dynamic vs. constant, complex vs. simple; chaotic vs. orderly.

If organizations are dynamic, complex, and chaotic, can we affect the destiny of organizations? The answer is definitively YES. But to influence the course of organizations, we have to understand the paradox of organizational change. Chapter 2 presents an introduction to the constant, simple, and orderly aspects of the paradox.

Conclusions

Organizational change is paradoxical because it involves contradictions between the nature of the environment where change takes place and the process that causes the change.

The first contradiction is dynamic vs. constant. The environment where change occurs is dynamic as it evolves over time; however, the process of change is constant because the dynamic relationship between behavior and environment does not vary. Many organizational change initiatives are like paths over the sea: transient and short-lived, giving the impression that change efforts are in vain.

The second contradiction is complex vs. simple. The environment of change is complex and the process is simple. It is complex because it occurs in the midst of multiple and convoluted interactions. It is simple because there is only one essential process that accounts for the evolution of organizations. Its essential component is the behavior of each individual and that behavior's consequences.

The third contradiction is chaotic vs. orderly. The environment appears unsystematic and uncontrollable, yet the way that the environment change is systematic and predictable. In summary, the paradox of organizational change is the inclusion of seemingly contradictory change elements: dynamic vs. constant, complex vs. simple, and chaotic vs. orderly.

Review

1. Based on your own experience, give an example of:
    - Closed system
    - Open system
2. What does paradox of change mean?
3. Explain each apparent contradiction of the paradox with an example:
    - Dynamic vs. constant
    - Complex vs. simple
    - Chaotic vs. orderly

Chapter 2
Basic Principles

CHAPTER 2
BASIC PRINCIPLES

Water may flow in a thousand channels, but it all returns to the sea.

Anonymous Chinese proverb

The Magic Cylinder

Sunshine, let me show you a magic cylinder, said the grandmother.

The grandmother was named Moon Goddess nearly 100 years ago, following a pre-Inca tradition from the surroundings of Titicaca Lake – the highest lake in the world, located in South America between Peru and Bolivia.

Sunshine was seven years old. She was a beautiful, Native-American girl, with toast-colored skin, brown eyes, and straight black hair that cascaded to her waist. She wore a coat typical of ancient Inca royalty. It featured a geometric pattern of red and yellow tones, dyed with extracts from leaves, bark, and mud.

Reaching to the bottom of her woven, flax-made basket, Moon Goddess extracted a bronze cylinder. At one end was a small opening with a viewer and at the other end a metal drum. Tiny, dazzling gemstones – mixed with shimmering foliage – floated in oil between two pieces of glass nestled inside the drum.

Moon Goddess showed Sunshine how to use the bronze cylinder. She grasped it with her left hand, closed her left eye and looked through the viewer with her right eye: aiming the cylinder toward the sun and rotating the drum slowly.

Ah! Sunshine exclaimed with glee, when Moon Goddess passed the cylinder to her and she discovered its magic for herself. Inside, the young girl found a wealth of colors and symmetrical shapes. As she rotated the drum, new combinations gradually appeared. Again, Sunshine exclaimed *ah!* Moon Goddess watched silently, cherishing her granddaughter's curiosity and amazement.

Sunshine wondered about the endless designs she was seeing. *How many shapes are inside this magic cylinder?* she asked. Moon Goddess smiled tenderly. She knew the number of patterns was infinite, a concept her granddaughter was learning with every turn of the cylinder.

Moon Goddess unveiled the magic behind the cylinder by saying, *This is a kaleidoscope. Its magic has an explanation.* She then told Sunshine about Sir David Brewster, a Scottish scientist who accidentally invented the kaleidoscope in 1816 while performing experiments with light.

Taking the cylinder from the girl's hands, Moon Goddess explained that the reflection of the floating objects inside the drum produced the symmetrical colored shapes.

How? Sunshine asked.

Within the cylinder there were two mirrors, Moon Goddess said, *positioned at an angle. The size of the angle determines the number of symmetric shapes.* She then used her hands to illustrate the various degrees while explaining that a 45-degree angle produces eight symmetrical reflections, a 70-degree angle produces six and a 90-degree angle produces four. The combined movement of the gems and leaves with the mirrors generates infinite forms.

Moon Goddess concluded her unique lesson by saying that the magic of the kaleidoscope was even more spectacular than it had first appeared. The marvel came from the infinite combinations resulting from its unchanged elements. Simplicity and complexity coexisted inside the kaleidoscope.

Basic Concepts

Like the kaleidoscope, change generates dynamic, complex, and unpredictable combinations based on constant, simple, and orderly processes. Throughout this book, I will illustrate the constant, simple, and orderly aspects of the paradox discussed in the last chapter. In this chapter, I introduce the essentials which consist of the fundamental principle of environmental selection, the basic units of analysis, and the method for change.

Principle of Environmental Selection

To improve processes, organizations undergo countless attempts to change what employees do. Although change initiatives generate much enthusiasm and effort, people often end up doing the same thing that they did before. We try new strategies when finding that our previous attempts to change fail. If instruction does not result in effective change, we might invest in technology. If technology does not make a difference, we might promote our best workers to management positions. And, when everything else fails, we blame the employees.

Blaming employees is easier than recognizing that the system has problems or that we – as managers – are partly responsible for the failure to change. Accordingly, employees are accused of being dumb, unmotivated, irresponsible, and uncaring. This is called organizational victim blaming.

> *Concept 2-1. Organizational Victim Blaming – unjustly assuming that those who suffer the consequences of a poor functioning system are responsible for the system's flaws.*

Employees become enemies in the blaming game. There is no trust. We treat people like opponents and, in return, they regard us as adversaries. The open-door policy does not exist and fear of lawsuits makes it impossible to give employees honest feedback.

I have yet to meet an employee who likes to fail or who does not care about being competent. True, employees are not always able and willing; they may lack the right skills, knowledge, or motivation to do the job well. Unfortunately, we tend to conclude that their limitations are the problem without studying the system in which they work, understanding their jobs, or knowing what variables maintain their current behavior.

The underlying law or assumption in change is environmental selection. The strategies in this book are based on the belief that the environment affects what people do. This is the basic principle: The conditions that precede and follow our behavior affect how we behave in the future. This assumption helps us steer our efforts toward engineering processes that are more productive than blame, paranoia, and fear.

> *Concept 2-2. Environmental Selection – the underlying principle of change: the conditions that precede and follow the behavior of individuals affect how they behave in the future.*

Cultural Selection

Customer purchasing trends determine the product mix that retailers carry. Customer specifications define the goods manufacturers produce and customer demands control the service standards of their providers. In a way, customers ultimately initiate the change practices organizations pursue. Organizations that fail to adapt to the demands of their customers will not last. There is no alternative. Businesses have to generate enough sales to survive.

At a broader level, American anthropologist Marvin Harris[1] attempted to show the material basics of the survival of cultural practices. Through studies of specific societies, he showed that the economic basis of the culture shape cultural practices as well as people's beliefs and values. His position is known as cultural materialism. For instance, he provided an economic interpretation for the "sacred cow" tradition in India. Preserving cattle is an economic necessity. Cows are draft animals, particularly well-suited for farming, and scavengers of trash; dried cattle feces are also a major source of fuel. Consequently, the Indian population is better off economically by preserving cows than consuming them. Like organizational practices, cultural practices are the product of cultural selection. That is, practices are more likely to endure if they contribute to the survival of the group (or the customer's organization) through cost-effective production of essential material goods or services.

> *Concept 2-3. Cultural Selection – cultural practices that produce material gains for a culture tend to survive.*

[1] *See "Cultural Materialism" by Marvin Harris (1979). His books on cultural materialism include: "The Nature of Cultural Things" (1964); "Cows, Pigs, Wars and Witches" (1974); "Cannibals and Kings: The Origins of Cultures" (1977); "Why Nothing Works" (1981); and "The Sacred Cow and the Abominable Pig" (1986). For a compatible, compelling argument about cultural selection, see Diamond, 1997.*

The implication of cultural selection in organizational practices is widely recognized. We can check the newspapers for daily reassurance that the fate of organizations depends on their ability to meet customer needs in a cost-effective manner. Bankruptcy, mergers, reorganizations, layoffs, acquisitions ... all seem to be driven by the need to adapt for survival.

Behavioral Selection

I am puzzled by our general acceptance of environmental causes to explain organizations' performance and our refusal to use environmental causal explanations to account for employees' behavior. We attribute an organization's poor performance to external circumstances, such as increased competition, economic recessions, limited supplies, and weather conditions. But we attribute an employee's poor performance to inherent characteristics, such as his or her willingness and attitude. Why is it that when things go wrong we excuse organizations and blame employees?

Individuals are like organizations. Their environment influences their actions. There is comprehensive and exhaustive research demonstrating what is known as the law of effect. This law specifies that the relationship between behavior and its consequences affects the future likelihood of that behavior. Edward Thorndike[2] originally formulated the law in the following terms: *Under constant conditions, the future probability of the behavior increases when the behavior has been paired or followed by satisfaction; the future probability decreases when the behavior is accompanied or paired with aversive outcomes.* (Thorndike, 1911, p. 243.)

> *Concept 2-4. Law – affirmation of an invariable order or relationship that occurs under specific conditions.*
>
> *Concept 2-5. Law of Effect – under constant conditions, the future probability of the behavior increases when rewarding consequences follow it. The future probability of the behavior decreases when aversive consequences follow it.*
>
> *Concept 2-6. Behavioral Selection – behavior that produces rewarding consequences for the individual tends to reoccur.*

Although the law of effect was originally formulated in a monograph in 1898, it was not until the 1940s that it was accepted within the theoretical body of behavioral psychology, based on the work of B. F. Skinner and his followers[3]. For almost a century, the law of effect has been demonstrated in numerous applications

[2] *Edward L. Thorndike developed the law of effect for the first time in 1898 as part of his doctoral dissertation, titled "Animal Intelligence: An Experimental Study of the Associative Processes in Animals". In 1911, he published it as part of his book "Animal intelligence: Experimental Studies."*

[3] *Keller & Shoenfeld, 1950 (reprinted in 1995).*

with human and animal behavior. The philosophical foundation of the law of effect is essential for organizations to understand why behaviors occur and how to effectively change behavior. Behavioral and cultural selection are the basic mechanisms underlying organizational change[4].

Basic Units of Analysis[5]

Units of analysis are parts in which a system can be analyzed. We cannot successfully change an organization unless we understand its components: behavioral system, behavioral contingency, and metacontingency.

> *Concept 2-7. Units of Analysis – parts in which a system can be analyzed: behavioral system, behavioral contingency, and metacontingency.*

Behavioral System

A system is a group of interdependent elements that form an entity. A behavioral system is one formed by individuals interacting toward a common goal. Many different entities can be called a behavioral system; for instance, a family, a department, an institution, or a country.

> *Concept 2-8. Behavioral System – a group of interrelated elements that form an entity.*

Consistent with environmental selection, much of what happens in organizations depends on the world outside. The total performance system (TPS) was developed by Dale Brethower as an analysis tool that helps to illustrate how a behavioral system interacts with its environment[6].

TPS has the following components:

1. An ultimate mission, reason for which the system exists
2. Product that results from the system (either behavioral or aggregate product)

[4] *To take the environmental approach one step further, Charles Darwin – in his book "Origin of the Species" (published in 1859 and reprinted in 1979) – proposed environmental determinism in the development of biological structures. He argued that evolution of a species consists of gradual and continuous change in biological populations across many generations. Darwin suggested that changes are the result of natural selection. Natural selection is the differential preservation across generations of inherited traits that best fit the environment in which organisms live. Those that survive and pass their traits to the next generation tend to embody favorable natural variations.*

[5] *Malott (2001, May) presented a similar analysis to the one in this section.*

[6] *Brethower, 1972, 1982, 1993a, 1993b, 1995, 1999, 2000; Brethower & Smalley, 1998.*

3. Receiving system or customers who receive the product
4. Receiving system feedback
5. Processing system that transforms the resources into products
6. Processing system feedback
7. Resources needed to generate the product
8. Competition for resources and customers

Figure 2-1 shows the total performance system diagram.

Figure 2-1. Total Performance System

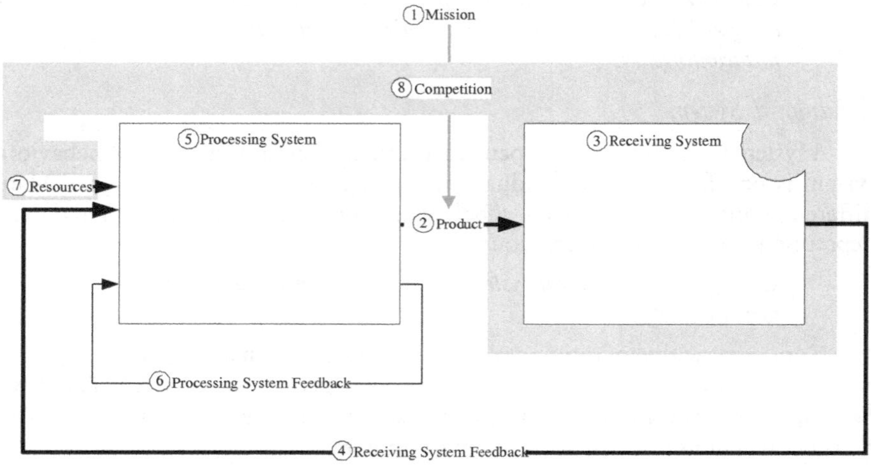

Concept 2-9. Total Performance System – an analysis tool of an organization which includes the mission, product, receiving system, receiving system feedback, processing system, processing system feedback, resources, and competition.

The numbers in Figure 2-1 indicate priority of analysis. Start with the mission and consider all of the other elements in context of that mission: the product, the receiving system and feedback concerning the product. Numbers 1– 4 should be analyzed *before* proceeding with numbers 5 – 8.

Let's use TPS to analyze an injection-molding factory that produces plastic parts.

1. *What is the ultimate mission of the system?* Increase sales and, ultimately, the market share of the clients' products.
2. *What is the product?* Plastic parts.
3. *Who is the receiving system?* Organizations from various manufacturing sectors that require plastic components to generate their products, such as those in telecommunications, technology, and health care.

4. What is the feedback from the receiving system? Customer's response regarding the sales price, product quality and timeliness of delivery.
5. What is the processing system? All activities and interactions of all departments that transform resources into plastic parts. For example, the production department receives the plastic, molds and trims it, and prepares shipments; the quality-control department examines samples of recently-molded products; the engineering department stops production to verify mold details; the sales department brings customers to observe production; the maintenance department stops production to adjust the presses; and the training department interviews workers at the plant to identify knowledge and skill deficiencies.
6. What is the feedback from the processing system? Information or data about the functioning of all the departments, such as cost, quality, and timeliness.
7. What are the resources needed? All that is needed to produce plastic parts: capital, presses, plastic, skilled workers, and molds.
8. Who is the competition? Other manufacturers of plastic parts that compete for customers and a skilled labor force.

See Figure 2-2 for a graphic representation of TPS.

Figure 2-2. Application of TPS to an Injection-Molding Manufacturing Company

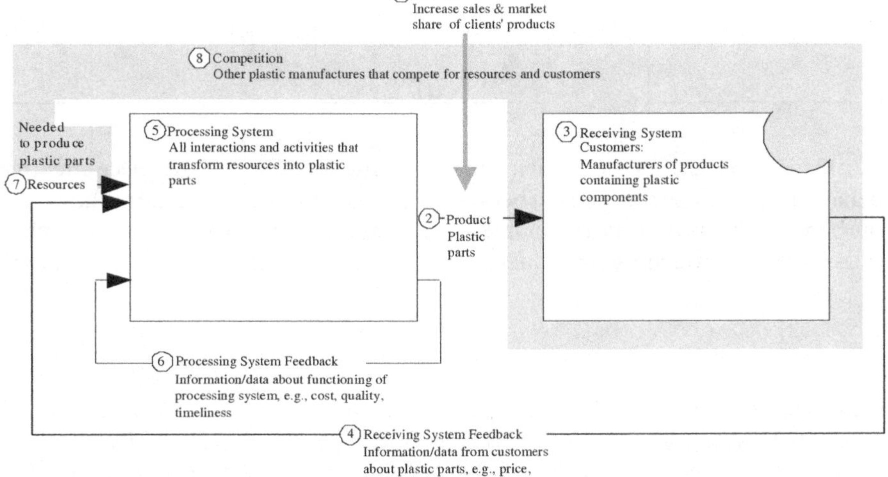

TPS provides the perspective of open systems that we discussed in the previous chapter. The factory will stop existing if customers no longer purchase the finished products. The receiving system determines the evolution and survival of the factory.

Since 1983, when I took my first class with Dr. Dale Brethower at Western Michigan University (Kalamazoo, Michigan), I have used TPS as an analysis tool. Because virtually everything around us is a system, TPS is an indispensable tool for generating objective overviews and identifying critical areas that need improving.

Behavioral Contingency

Since the underlying principle in behavior analysis is the environmental selection of behavior, our behavioral units of analysis are not just behaviors but relationships between behaviors and their environments[7] – which complicates organizational analysis.

The basic unit of analysis of behavior is called behavioral contingency. The behavioral contingency describes the relationship between a behavior and its consequences. Simply stated, the relationship affects the future probability of that behavior. If aversive consequences follow a behavior, the frequency of that behavior will decrease in the future. In contrast, if rewarding consequences follow a behavior, the frequency of that behavior is likely to increase in the future. Figure 2-3 shows a diagram of a behavioral contingency.

Figure 2-3. Behavioral Contingency

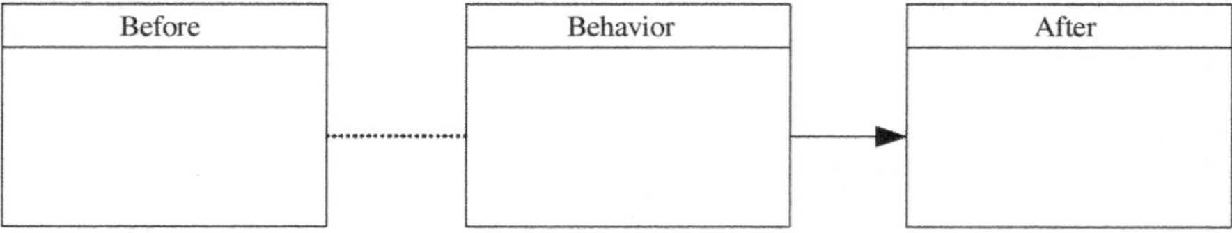

Figure 2-3 specifies the behavior and the consequence that takes place after that behavior occurs. The comparison between the before and after conditions shows that the behavior has produced a favorable or an unfavorable change. For instance, when the stove is hot, touching it produces a burn. Before touching the stove, there is no

[7] *Skinner (1953, 1957, 1974) defined operant behavior as the actions of the organism change as a function of the effects of its behavior in its environment. (Also see Lattal & Perone, 1998.) A multitude of operant behavior features have been studied experimentally. For instance, studies of stimulus discrimination, stimulus generalization, response generalization, schedules of reinforcement, and stimulus equivalences (See the Journal of Experimental Analysis of Behavior and the Journal of Applied Behavior Analysis.)*

burn; after touching it there is a burn. The transition from "before" to "after" is a change that is likely to reduce the future probability of touching a hot stove.

A similar lesson can be learned during a business meeting. If we give our personal opinion and our boss showers us with compliments, we are more likely to give our opinion again. Figure 2-4 illustrates both examples.

Figure 2-4. Examples of Behavioral Contingencies

Before	Behavior	After	
no burning	touch hot stove →	burning	The future probability of toughing the hot stove will decrease
no compliment	speak →	compliment	The future probability of speaking in meetings will increase

Metacontingency

Ignoring an organization's complexity is a mistake. An organizational process could easily involve hundreds or thousands of different behaviors. In addition, people participate in various organizational processes simultaneously. The contingencies that affect the behavior of individuals in one process influence the behavior of other individuals.

Organizational systems cannot be understood by analyzing individual behavioral contingencies because that would be impossible. It would take years to understand all of the behavioral contingencies in a system. We cannot change the organization by focusing solely on the behaviors of a few individuals. This would be like trying to purify only one cubic mile of water in the middle of the ocean.

The problem with relying on the analysis of behavioral contingencies is that the unit is too detailed. We would not attempt to study the circulatory system by analyzing the interaction of each cell with its surroundings in the heart, blood, and blood vessels. Instead, we would start with a larger unit of analysis, such as the performance of the heart. We can see if blood is pumped from the heart through the arteries or if blood is returned to the heart through the one-way valves of the veins. If the heart does not pump adequately, we might look into the artery's performance. Likewise, we use large units of analysis when we begin analyzing organizations.

Sigrid Glenn (1988) introduced the concept of metacontingency – a unit that facilitates handling behavioral complexity in organizations[8]. A metacontingency

[8] *Glenn, in press, 1986, 1988, 1991; Glenn & Madden, 1995; Glenn & Field, 1994.*

has three components: interlocking behavioral contingency, aggregate product, and receiving system demand.

Interlocking behavioral contingency

"An interlocking behavioral contingency involves the behavior of at least two participants, where any components of the behavioral contingency or the behavioral product of one participant interacts with elements of the behavioral contingency or product of other participants." (Glenn, 1988, p. 167). The metacontingency can be illustrated in an assembly line. The behavior of one individual is to trim excess plastic from a part. A second individual receives and then wraps the trimmed part. A wrapped part is received by a third individual who boxes it. The actions of one individual stimulate the actions of another. Figure 2-5 illustrates the concept of interlocking behavioral contingency in an assembly line.

Figure 2-5. Interlocking Behavioral Contingencies[9]

Before 1
Behavior 1
Person A
After 1
Before 2 (= After 1)
Behavior 2
Person B
After 2
Before 3 (= After 2)
Behavior 3
Person C
After 3

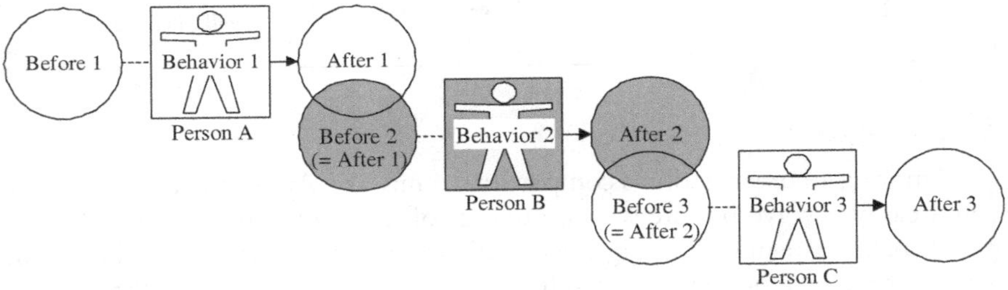

Concept 2-10. Interlocking Behavioral Contingency – involves the behavior of at least two participants, where any component of the behavioral contingency or product of one participant interacts with elements of the behavioral contingency or product of other participants.

The dynamics of organizations are not as linear as the preceding assembly-line example. Instead, they involve convoluted interlocking behavioral contingencies. For instance, the consequence of the behavior of one participant could serve as antecedent for the behavior of another; the behavior of one person could serve as consequence for another; the behavioral product of one person could serve as consequence for another[10]. Figure 2-6 shows examples of various types of interactions between contingencies and behavioral products of two participants in interlocking behavioral contingencies.

[9] *The diagram in Figure 2-5 is based on Glenn & Malott, 2001, May; Malott & Glenn, 2001, May.*

Figure 2-6. Example of Interactions Between Behavioral Contingencies

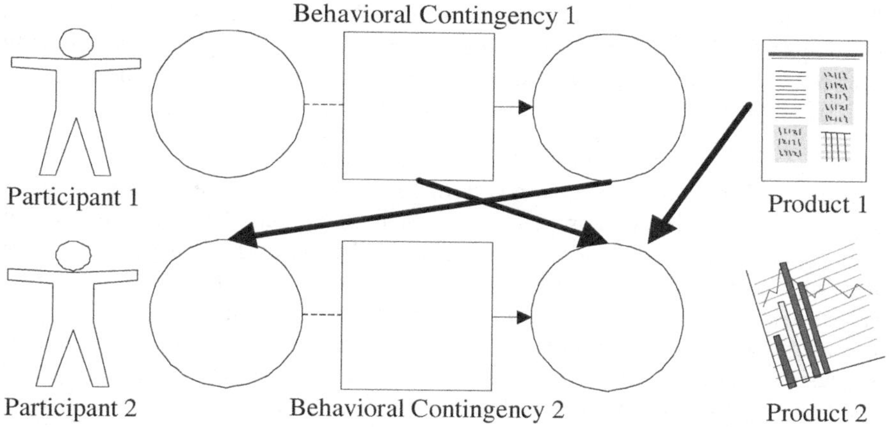

Behavioral Contingency 1

Participant 1

Product 1

Participant 2

Behavioral Contingency 2

Product 2

Aggregate product

Throughout this book, I define behavioral product as the evidence left behind after the behavior occurs and aggregate product as the overall result that compounds multiple behavioral products. For instance, a deposit slip is the behavioral product of a financial clerk's deposit transaction; a bank's transaction activity report is the aggregate product of all the individuals working in the bank. Because an aggregate product is generated by many individuals (for instance, a finished airplane), variations in the behavior of one individual alone typically do not have a considerable impact on the overall performance of the system.

Concept 2-11. Behavioral Product – results after the behavior occurred.

Concept 2-12. Aggregate Product – compounded result of multiple behavioral products.

It is impossible, impractical and unnecessary to study all behavior that occurs in organizations. To narrow down the set of interrelated behavior that makes a difference for an organization, we focus on interrelationships that generate relevant aggregate products for the survival of the organization[11]. If an aggregate product does not meet required standards, then we should study metacontingencies involving

[10] *In Chapter 6, we will see that the consequence of the behavior of one individual could serve as antecedent for another behavior of the same individual. However, relationships between environmental events of behaviors of a single individual are not interlocking contingencies because, by definition, interlocking refers to interactions between environmental events and behavior of at least two individuals.*

aggregate subproducts. For instance, we might examine the cost of running a restaurant as the aggregate product. If costs are not up to standard, we might analyze the metacontingencies that produce aggregate subproducts indispensable for sales – food preparation, service, purchasing, and billing. If billing generates too many financial reconciliation problems, we might look at smaller metacontingencies, such as bill generation, bill processing, and tipping.

Receiving system demand

A set of interlocking behavioral contingencies will continue to exist only if its aggregate product has demand from the receiving system. The receiving system demand determines survival of an organizational practice. Here lies the principle of cultural selection. For instance, a factory manufactures merchandise purchased by its customers. Without customer demand, the organization will die. The receiving system demand maintains a multitude of interlocking behavioral contingencies in all the organizational processes, such as production, shipping, and purchasing. Likewise, internal organizational processes survive only if there is receiving system demand. For instance, specific financial reporting will only be maintained if other departments ask for it. Figure 2-7 illustrates the components of a metacontingency.

Figure 2-7. Components of a Metacontingency

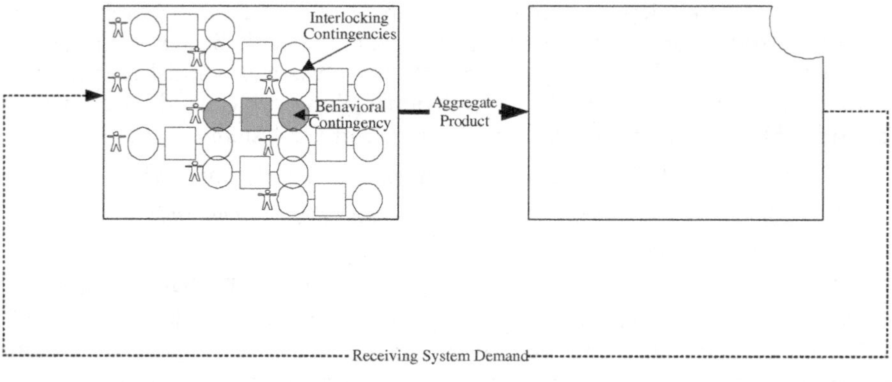

In summary, a metacontingency involves a conglomerate of interlocking behavioral contingencies containing the behavior of multiple individuals, which generates an aggregate product that has a demand.

[11] *Gilbert (1996) presented a similar perspective – we should focus on the behavior of a system only when the system is failing to achieve its product.*

Concept 2-13. Metacontingency – a conglomerate of interlocking behavioral contingencies containing the behavior of multiple individuals, which generates a product that has a demand.

Incidentally, Gilbert (1996)[12] defined performance as behavior and its product. For instance, the performance of a financial clerk consists of the clerk's actions (e.g., receiving money, entering data, and computing) and the product or evidence left after those actions (e.g., transactions processed). As in the metacontingency, performance should involve a product valued by its customers. In Chapter 7, we will see that the term "performance" is useful when referring to multiple behaviors of an individual and that individual's outcome.

Concept 2-14. Performance – behavior and its product.

In a behavioral system, individual behavioral contingencies are imbedded in interlocking behavioral contingencies of two or more individuals. Interlocking behavioral contingencies are parts of the organization's processing system. A processing system also includes the interaction of individuals with resources, such as information, data, equipment, technology, facilities, raw materials, and supplies. Figure 2-8 illustrates the relationship between behavioral contingencies, interlocking behavioral contingencies, metacontingencies, and the total performance system. Analyzing organizations without understanding such relationships can lead us to

Figure 2-8. Relationship Between the Processing System, Metacontingency, Interlocking Behavioral Contingencies, and Behavioral Contingency.

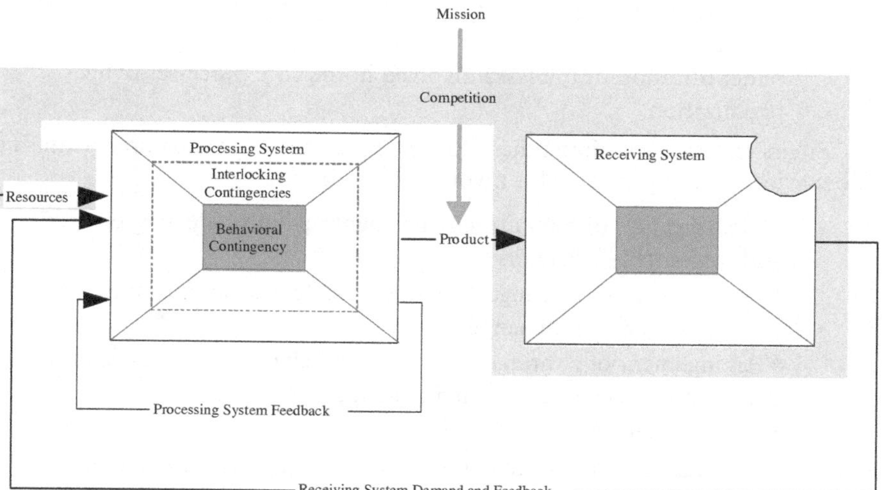

[12] *Thomas Gilbert made significant contributions in the area of engineering performance. See, Dean, 1999-a, 1999-b; Gilbert, 1996, 1999; T. B. Gilbert & M. B. Gilbert, 1999.*

focus on irrelevant aspects of the organization: a classic example of the blind leading the blind.

Method of Organizational Change

This book represents an attempt to depict an effective method to re-engineer organizations. The method is systematic and orderly. It is the outcome of nearly 20 years of efforts to comprehend and manage change in education, retail, service, manufacturing, government, and health industries. The method incorporates the basic concepts presented in this chapter of environmental selection and the basic units of analysis (behavioral system, behavioral contingency, and metacontingency). The method is illustrated in the Behavioral Systems Engineering Model shown in Figure 2-9.

The Behavioral Systems Engineering Model presented in Figure 2-9 is a summary of the information provided in this book. Each section of the model will be addressed in a separate chapter, with the exception of the behavior section which takes two chapters. The Behavioral Systems Engineering Model involves two components: analyzing behavioral systems with metacontingencies, and engineering and sustaining change with behavioral contingencies.

The analysis of behavioral systems evolves from most to least complex, until key behavioral contingencies are identified. The process involves the following:

- Analysis of the macrosystem in which the organization operates
- Assessment of the organization as a total performance system
- Transformation of the administrative structure in a functional organization where the output of some departments serves as the input for others
- Identification of the tasks involved in the core processes of the organization

Engineering and sustaining change are based on the design and implementation of behavioral contingencies. This involves the following:

- Identification of behavior-environment relations affecting desirable and undesirable behaviors
- Arrangement of contingencies to stimulate desirable front-line participants behavior change
- Arrangement of contingencies to affect behavior at all levels of management needed to maintain change
- Development of data control systems
- Constant adjustment of contingencies to ongoing organization dynamics

Those who work in the field of organizational change tend to have two different emphases: some who engage in systems analysis and others who engage in behavior analysis. Traditionally, system analysts criticize behavior analysts for investing too many resources in irrelevant behavior changes. Behavior analysts criticize the system

Figure 2-9. Behavioral Systems Engineering Model

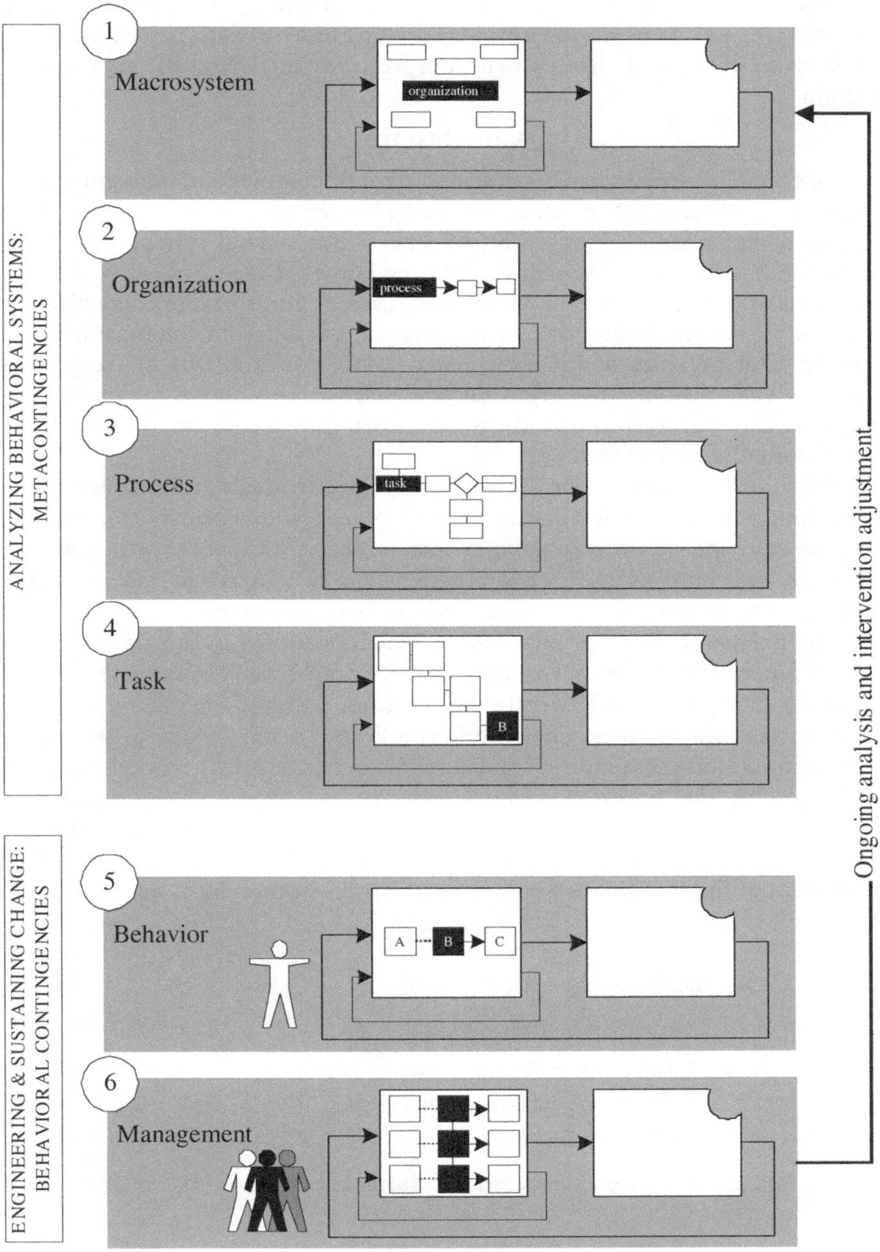

ANALYZING BEHAVIORAL SYSTEMS: METACONTINGENCIES

1 Macrosystem
organization

2 Organization
process

3 Process
task

4 Task
B

ENGINEERING & SUSTAINING CHANGE: BEHAVIORAL CONTINGENCIES

5 Behavior
A B C

6 Management

Ongoing analysis and intervention adjustment

analysts for producing superficial changes. Both are partly right. The Behavioral Systems Engineering Model attempts to bring these two perspectives together. Systems analysis and behavior analysis are both necessary and complementary. Systems analysis allows us to travel through the complexity of organizations and identify target behaviors worth improving for long-term survival; behavior analysis allows us to implement changes that improve how people and the organization perform.

Conclusions

Like a kaleidoscope, change generates infinitely complex and transient combinations of stable elements based on simple and orderly processes: the principle of environmental selection, basic units of analysis (behavioral system, behavioral contingency, and metacontingency), and a method of change.

Environmental selection implies that the causes of organizational practices are in the environment. When the consequence is rewarding for the organism, the behavior that precedes it will more likely recur – selection by consequences. Likewise, when the output of organizational practices contributes to the materialistic survival of the organization, the practices that generated them will more likely carry on – cultural selection.

Behavioral systems involve the interactions of individuals within an entity that generates a product. They include the mission, products, receiving system, feedback from the receiving system, processing system, feedback from the processing system, resources, and competitors. Behavioral systems can be analyzed in smaller units of analysis – the behavioral contingency and the metacontingency.

The Behavioral Systems Engineering Model presented in this book has two sections: analyzing behavioral systems with metacontingencies and engineering and sustaining change with behavioral contingencies. Systems analysis includes the study of metacontingencies in the following levels: macrosystem, organization, processes, and tasks. Engineering and sustaining change consist of designing and implementing interlocking behavioral contingencies for employees working in processes and the performance managers across multiple subprocesses and management levels. It also includes development of control systems and constant adjustment of the change intervention to the organization's dynamics.

Review

Define the following basic concepts:

- Environmental selection
- Total performance system (TPS)
- Behavioral contingency
- Metacontingency

What is the difference between cultural selection and behavioral selection?

List the components of the organizational change model.

Chapter 3
Macrosystem & Mission

CHAPTER 3
MACROSYSTEM AND MISSION

If you don't know where you are going, you will probably end up somewhere else.

Laurence J. Peter (1919–1988)[1]

John Wise

It was the 10th anniversary of the University of Saint Fernand. In the spotlight was John Wise, its founder. The university community took this opportunity to commend him for his contributions to education and for making Saint Fernand such an important town in the country.

John Wise was born in the San Joaquin village of Saint Fernand during a time when shortages of drinking water and electricity occurred on a regular basis. Only five of his 16 brothers survived childhood. John was determined and resourceful. He got his first job at the age of eight, harvesting coffee beans at the Coyoacal Hacienda.

His mother, Ann, came to the hacienda one day with the news: *They are going to open the school! The school will bring us out of ignorance, will help us improve, will open our road to the future!*

Working together, the mother and son picked coffee beans and saved enough money to buy schoolbooks. Throughout the next several years, John excelled at his studies. Then one day the dream came true: Ann bought a new dress and traveled to the capital to witness her son graduate with honors.

Who knew that John would later establish – and lead – the University of Saint Fernand?

John objected to establishments of higher learning that focused on sophisticated and theoretical discussions while the country's reality worsened. He challenged the educational system, saying that it had lost sight of its mission.

How could the university ignore the fact that 130 out of 1000 infants in Saint Fernand died at birth? Or that 23 percent of the population was malnourished? In spite of an abundance of resources, large numbers of people were dying of curable diseases. Twenty-five percent of the population was illiterate and 34 percent of the

[1] *Dr. Laurence J. Peter, Canadian writer, was a professor of education at the University of Southern California and the University of British Columbia. He co-authored the "Peter Principle", which says that "in the hierarchical administrative structure, people tend to be promoted to their level of incompetence" (Peter & Hull, 1976). He wrote several additional works, among them "Peter's Quotations: Ideas for Our Times" (Peter, 1993).*

children dropped out of school. Thirty-one percent of the adult population was unemployed.

The mission of the university isn't to get more research grants, isn't to enroll students, isn't to develop more programs, isn't to hire distinguished professors... The mission of the university is to improve the well-being of its community.

It was with his community's well-being in mind that John organized students, workers, and area professionals into teams designed to foster a reform of the educational system. As a result, Saint Fernand University began offering technical careers designed to have a positive impact on the quality of life and the administration of natural resources.

The university taught by doing[2]. Students learned by developing and maintaining basic community projects. For instance, they implemented an exceptional agricultural plan; reforested the region; bred livestock; built homes; rescued ancient crafts (baskets, ceramics, and painting); fought illiteracy; fostered primary and secondary education; and carried out preventive health-care programs.

Over the next 10 years, the University changed the lives of more than 10,000 peasants. Additionally, the alumni became increasingly valued in the job market, helping Saint Fernand attract students from elsewhere to come and study where people learned by helping the community[3].

Macrosystem

The University of Saint Fernand emerged and evolved within the larger system that contained it – the educational system. Organizations can be conceived as metacontingencies that belong to larger metacontingencies – their macrosystems. Before imbedding ourselves in the details of the organization, we ought to step outside and first look at the macrosystem.

> *Concept 3-1. Macrosystem – the system that contains the organization we are analyzing.*

Saint Fernand University is a component of the educational system, which contains smaller metacontingencies – special education, primary (K through 5th grades), middle (6th through 8th grades), technical, and higher education. The aggregate product of the education macrosystem consists of the production of skilled and educated individuals who can service the community – the receiving system. The community is formed by multiple metacontingencies as well, such as

[2] *Even though the fictional story of John Wise and Saint Fernand illustrates a model of an applied university, I do not believe that this the only valid model of higher education. Other models could be of value, such as those based on philosophical and theoretical orientations. See Johnson & Bell (1995) for an alternative model.*

[3] *In his book "Killing the Spirit," Smith (1990) writes about the degeneration of the American University because of the emphasis in research instead of teaching.*

the students, families, other disciplines, industries (manufacturing, service, and retail), government, and infrastructure (e.g., transportation, housing, and utilities). The demands from the community – the receiving system – shapes the evolution of the educational macrosystem.

Therefore, a component of the educational macrosystem is the University of Saint Fernand, that is, the organization we are primarily interested in. The aggregate product of the University consists of BA and MA graduates who are in demand by specific systems in the community. Figure 3-1 shows the relationship between the educational system and the University of Saint Fernand metacontingencies.

Figure 3-1. Relationship Between the Macrosystem and Organization Metacontingencies

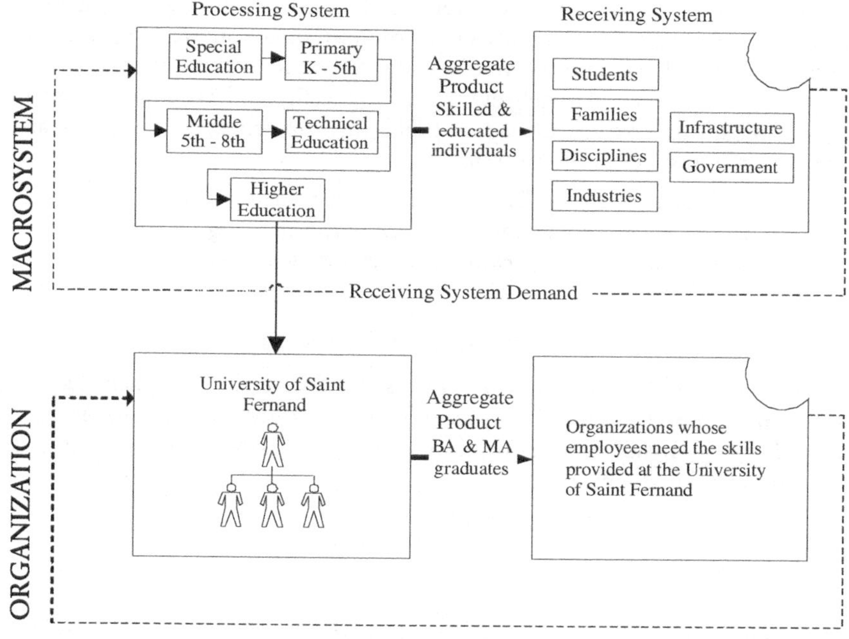

If we ignore details of the macrosystem, we will not understand current demands nor anticipate future ones. For instance, Saint Fernand's education programs resulted from the appreciation of the regions resources, opportunity for industrial development, infrastructure conditions, and information about the well-being of the community.

Furthermore, without the understanding of the macrosystem, it is not possible to know how the organization fits in with related systems. For example, the university had to consider the quality and level of education provided in primary, middle, and technical education. Knowing the demands and the performance the macrosystem's components is indispensable to set direction for the organization's long-term survival.

Mission

If we want to influence the destiny of an organization and ensure adaptation and long-term survival, we need to start with a clear perspective of an organization's mission. The mission needs to be operationalized in the context of the macrosystem that contains the organization.

Concept 3-2. Mission – the ultimate goal of the organization.

Natural systems do not have inherent missions; they just exist and evolve. Why do we need to create missions to lead organizations? Because without intervention, the evolution of organizations is unpredictable: they might become more or less complex, they might or might not adapt. Without direction, we cannot ensure that organizations will adjust or survive in the macrosystem where they operate[4].

The mission is a tool to help everyone – especially leaders – guide the evolution of organizations. Proactive leaders build mission-driven systems to facilitate adaptation and survival of the system at large[5].

Concept 3-3. Mission-Driven Organizations – define the ultimate mission of the organization in its macrosystem and design contingencies that facilitate the achievement of the intermediate and ultimate objectives.

Organizational Myopia

Unfortunately, organizations often lose sight of the dynamics of their macrosystem and their mission. To change an organization without understanding its macrosystem and ultimate mission is organizational myopia (Malott, 2001a) – to produce without realizing the purpose.

[4] *Establishing humanitarian missions is a goal worth pursuing when designing behavioral systems. B. F. Skinner (1953) said we should be concerned about a culture that does not convince its young that survival is a great value, because that culture will have less chance of survival. Creators of utopian communities and those who dream of ideal societies have identified the underlying principle as the well-being of humanity. Consult writers of cultural utopias, such as Bacon (1956), "New Atlantis"; Bellamy (1967); "Looking Backward, 2000-1887"; Campanella (1981), "The City of the Sun: A Political Dialogue"; More (1999), "Utopia"; Plato (2000), "The Republic"; Skinner (1976), "Walden Two"; Wells (1933), "The Shape of Things to Come".*

[5] *For further elaboration of goal-directed systems see M. E. Malott, 1992, 1998; R. W. Malott & M. E. García, 1987; Malott, Malott & Trojan, 2000.*

Concept 3-4. Organizational Myopia – to lose sight of the dynamics of the macrosystem and mission.

A form of organizational myopia is to confuse the product of the organization with its mission. This is the case when we believe that the mission of universities is to generate bachelor's and master's degrees, the mission of manufacturing businesses is to produce specific goods, and the mission of retail businesses is to sell specific consumer goods. These are the organizations' products and should not be confused with their missions.

The mission is the ultimate reason for the existence of the organization in the system that contains it. The mission of an organization tends to be more stable than its products. The products might change from time to time in order to accomplish the mission more effectively. For instance, in order to more effectively meet community needs, a university might create certificate programs with fewer requirements than bachelor's or master's degrees. Likewise, manufacturing companies might alter product lines and retail businesses might replace brick-and-mortar establishments with virtual stores on the Internet.

Losing sight of the macrosystem and mission may cause the organization to fail. The risks are generating incompatible strategies and falling into the activity trap (as I will describe next) – the side effects of which are costly and dysfunctional.

Incompatible Strategies

Imagine having your tire blow out in the middle of a four-lane highway. That's exactly what happened to me one day, as I drove to the airport in Detroit. I parked on the shoulder of the highway and dialed the Detroit-area emergency road service number from my cellular phone. A man answered. *Name?*

Sir, I am in an emergency situation. I need help.

Name?

Maria Malott.

Phone number? He insisted in an irritated tone.

After I told him my phone number, I explained what happened.

The man then informed me that they were all busy and there was no one to help, nor did he know when anyone would be available. When I insisted for help, he hung up: just like that!

Obviously, this man did not have a clue that his organization's mission was to save lives and prevent automobile accidents. Like the emergency road company, many organizations develop strategies that hurt customers or the community. These strategies are often incompatible with ultimate objectives.

Activity Trap

In his book, *The Activity Trap*, George Odiorme (1974) said people tend to fall into the activity trap when they loose sight of the mission. They invest energy in tactics without concern for the ultimate result.

Concept 3-5. Activity Trap – focus on the activity, losing sight of the mission.

Author Stephen Covey (1990) illustrates the activity trap in this anecdote: A group goes on an excursion. After a few days in the jungle, the leader climbs to the top of a tree and shouts *Stop! We have taken the wrong path*. The group responds, *don't distract us; we're advancing at a good pace.*

I experienced another example of the activity trap during a trip to Morocco, when 10 different guards checked my passport. They did it before I entered the departure gate at the Barajas airport in Madrid, while waiting at the gate, before boarding the airplane, when leaving the airplane in Casa Blanca, standing in line for customs, after leaving customs, before and after passing my suitcase through an automatic security system, while waiting to retrieve my suitcase, after manually inspecting my suitcase and before departing from the airport.

Even with all this checking, the guards reviewed the passport inconsistently. Each guard would flip through the pages until arbitrarily stopping at one, as if he had suddenly found something. Then he would return the passport to me. If I had asked them what they were looking for, I would probably have gotten different answers. To avoid offending an armed guard in a country unfamiliar to me, I abstained from questioning and observed their behavior. I concluded that their inspection system had fallen into the activity trap. The guards acted like they were reviewing the passport, but it was not clear that they knew what they were looking for.

Micro management is an expression related to falling into the activity trap. Micro means small. Micro management refers to the inability to delegate and the allocation of too much time checking on others rather than holding people accountable. We micro manage when we insist on checking every last detail of an activity that is the responsibility of someone else.

Concept 3-6. Micro Management – excessively checking on others' activities rather than delegating responsibilities and holding others accountable, losing sight of the main objective.

When we micro manage, we over-direct and inadvertently block progress toward the mission. When supervising each minute detail, we do not have time for the more important aspects of the organization: we do not have time to figure out how the activity contributes to the organization's mission.

Formulation of the Mission

The mission is a tool for establishing an organization's direction. Unfortunately, typical efforts to formulate the mission are often a waste of time. After much investment, the mission turns out to be nothing more than a theoretical and politically-correct statement. It becomes a public relations document used to avoid conflict with the public, customers, and employees.

Mission statements can become so convoluted that we must constantly re-read them to remember what is written; and when the mission is too complex or ambiguous, it does not lead to action. Martin Luther King, Gandhi and Mother Theresa did not have to double-check their mission statements to stay on track. Though it is possible that in hard times they might have been tempted to give up, their mission kept them going.

To avoid organizational myopia, it is useful to define the mission in the context of the system that contains the organization – the macrosystem. Figure 3-2 shows the basic questions in the analysis of the macrosystem.

Figure 3-2. Total Performance Systems of the Macrosystem

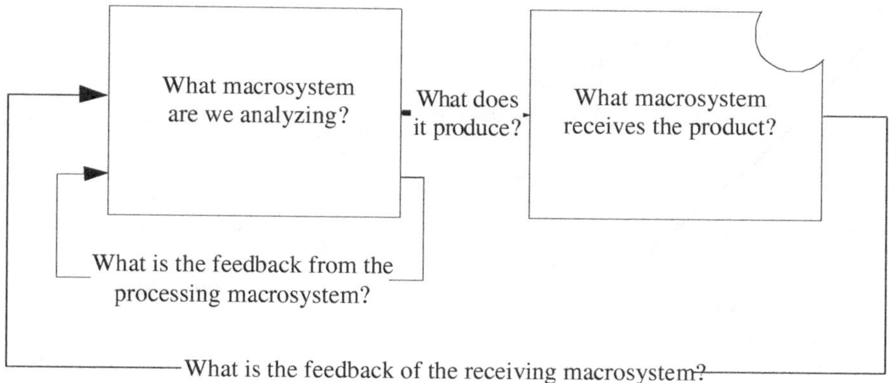

Let's use the example of the University of Saint Fernand to formulate its mission based on the analysis of the macrosystem. First, we need to answer the basic questions of the macrosystem that encompasses the University:

What macrosystem are we analyzing? The educational system that includes special education, K through 5th grade, 6th to 8th grade, technical, and higher education.

What does it produce? Skilled and educated human resources.

What macrosystem receives the product? The community (e.g., students, families) disciplines, industries, government, and infrastructure.

What is the feedback from the receiving macrosystem? Information concerning whether or not the alumni satisfy the needs of the receiving systems.

What is the feedback from the processing system? Information about the functioning of the education industry; for instance, cost and duration of education.

We should not confuse the total performance system analysis of the macrosystem with that of the organization. Figure 3-3 illustrates the differences between them.

Figure 3-3. Relationship Between the Total Performance System of the Macrosystem and the Organization

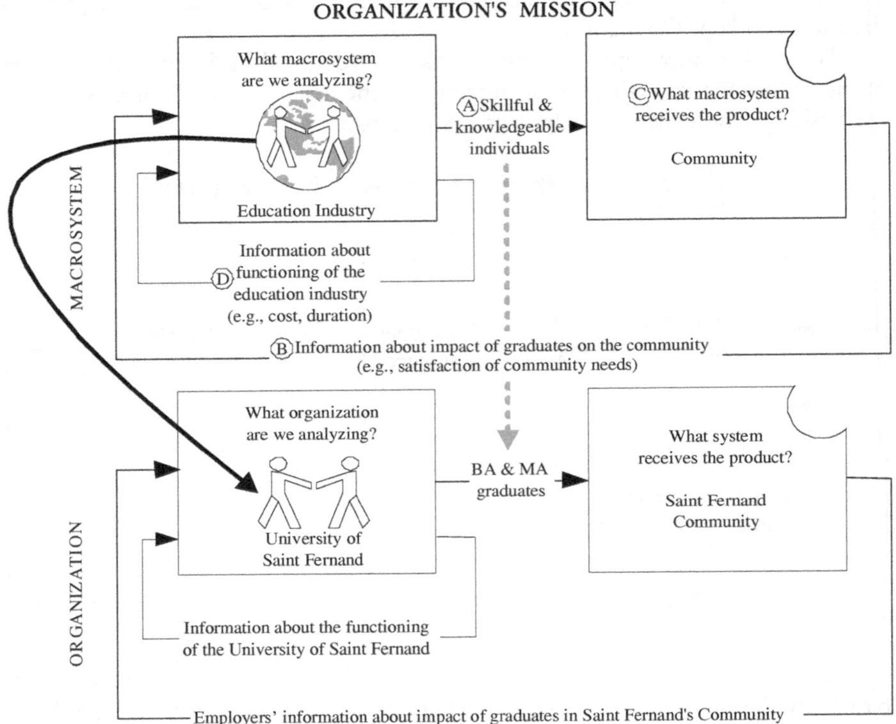

Based on the total performance system (TPS) of the education industry, we could state the mission of the University of Saint Fernand using the Guide for Formulating the Mission shown in Figure 3-4. According to the guide, the mission of the organization should be based on the macrosystem that contains it. The mission is to satisfy the needs of the system that receives the products of the macrosystem.

Figure 3-4. Guide for Formulating the Mission

MACROSYSTEM THAT CONTAINS THE ORGANIZATION

The mission of ______________________
(Organization being analyzed)

Is to ______________________
(A. Product of macrosystem)

that ______________________
(B. Feedback from the receiving system of macrosystem)

of ______________________
(C. Receiving system of macrosystem)

In ______________________
(D. Feedback from the processing system of macrosystem)

Concept 3-7. Guide for Formulating the Mission – the mission of the organization is stated in terms of the product, receiving system, and feedback from the receiving and processing systems of the macrosystem.

Figure 3-5 illustrates the application of the guide for formulating the mission to the University of Saint Fernand.

Figure 3-5. Mission of the Education System

MACROSYSTEM THAT CONTAINS THE ORGANIZATION
Education System

The mission of the University of Saint Fernand
(Organization being analyzed)

Is to produce skilled and educated individuals
(A. Product of macrosystem)

that meet the needs
(B. Feedback from the receiving system of macrosystem)

of its community, disciplines, industries, and government
(C. Receiving system of macrosystem)

In a cost-effective way
(D. Feedback from the processing system of macrosystem)

Figure 3-6 and Figure 3-8 show more applications of the guide to the mission formulations of a hospital and a clothing manufacturing company in Saint Fernand.

Figure 3-6. The Mission Statement of an Organization Belonging to the Health Macrosystem

MACROSYSTEM THAT CONTAINS THE ORGANIZATION
Health System

The mission of Saint Fernand Children's Hospital
(Organization being analyzed)

Is to provide treatment and prevent diseases
(A. Product of macrosystem)

that maintain good physical and psychological conditions
(B. Feedback from the receiving system of macrosystem)

of the population
(C. Receiving system of macrosystem)

In a cost-effective way
(D. Feedback from the processing system of macrosystem)

Figure 3-7 shows a graphic representation of the relationship between the macrosystem and the Hospital of Saint Fernand.

Figure 3-7. Relationship Between the Macrosystem and the Hospital of Saint Fernand

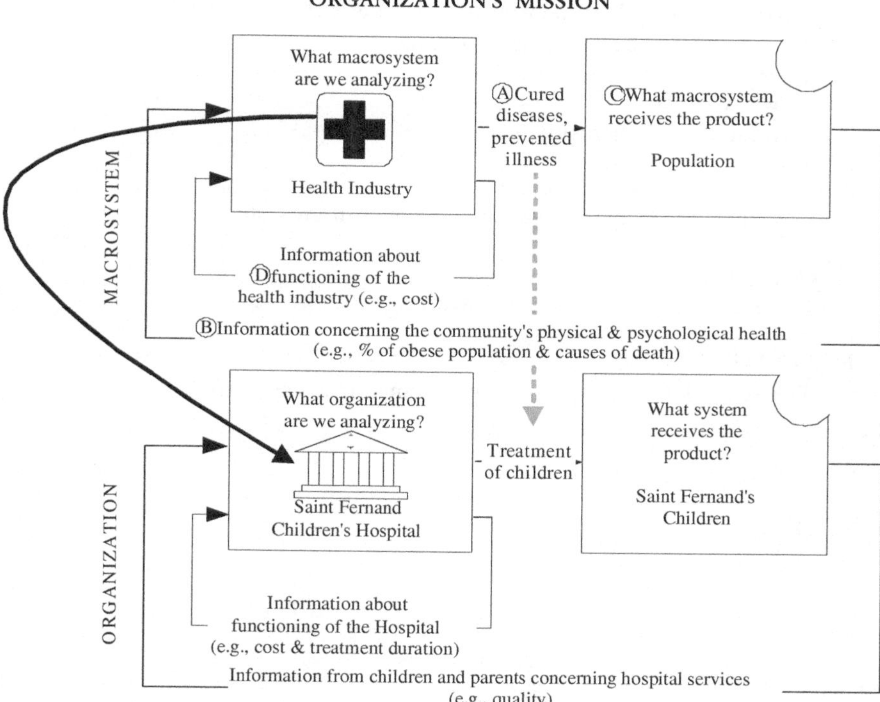

Figure 3-8. Example of the Mission Statement of an Organization Belonging to the Manufacturing Macrosystem

MACROSYSTEM THAT CONTAINS THE ORGANIZATION
Manufacturing System

The mission of Saint Fernand women's clothing manufacturing
(Organization being analyzed)

Is to make clothes
(A. Product of macrosystem)

that meets quality expectations
(B. Feedback from the receiving system of macrosystem)

of the population
(C. Receiving system of macrosystem)

In a cost-effective way
(D. Feedback from the processing system of macrosystem)

Figure 3-9 represents the relationship between the macrosystem and the textile manufacturing of Saint Fernand.

Figure 3-9. Relationship Between the Macrosystem and the Textile Industry of Saint Fernand

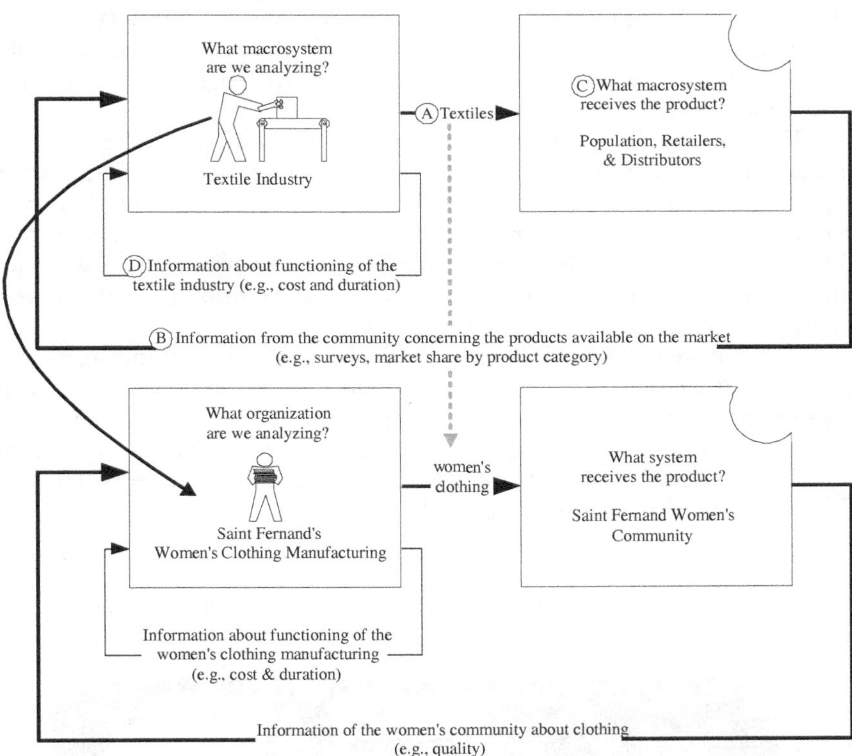

The mission ought to be simple and clear enough to facilitate action. Mission without action does not lead to change. But action without mission will lead to ineffectiveness, loss of resources, and frustration.

Conclusions

As presented in Chapter 1, change is paradoxical. On one hand, organizations are dynamic, complex, and chaotic; on the other hand, the process of change is stable, simple, and orderly – as described in Chapter 2 when introducing the Behavioral Systems Engineering Model. In this Chapter, the first component of the Model was described: the analysis of an organization ought to start by analyzing the macrosystem – or the metacontingency – that contains it. The macrosystem shapes the configuration of organizations. As implied in the fundamental principle of environmental selection, it imposes demands to which the organization has to adapt in order to survive.

The mission is the ultimate objective of the organization. It is the formulation of the activity directed to a specific purpose. It takes a conscious effort to create a mission. Organizations do not evolve consistently in order to reach a specific purpose; they do not have an inherent objective because they evolve based on the dynamics of existing contingencies. Therefore, an organization can adapt to its immediate environment and, at the same time, contribute to its long-term destruction or that of the macrosystem that contains it.

Unfortunately, many organizations suffer from myopia. Without a clear vision of their macrosystem it is hard to understand the mission. Without mission, organizations develop incompatible strategies and fall into the activity trap. To avoid organizational myopia, a guide was used to help formulate the mission based on the macrosystem containing the organization in question. Figure 3-10 shows the first systematic step of organizational change.

Figure 3-10. Level 1 of the Behavioral Systems Engineering Model

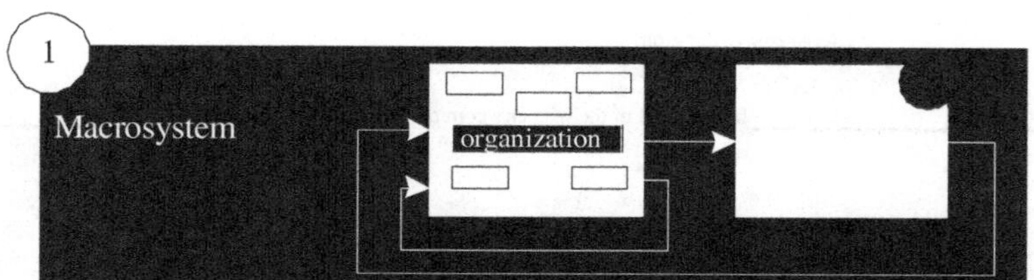

Review

Define the following concepts:

- Mission
- Macrosystem
- Mission-driven organizations

Organizational myopia

Describe two side effects of organizational myopia?

Formulate the mission of an organization using the guide in Figure 3-11:

Figure 3-11. Application of the Guide of Formulating the Mission

MACROSYSTEM THAT CONTAINS THE ORGANIZATION

The mission of ______________________
(Organization being analyzed)

Is to ______________________
(A. Product of macrosystem)

that ______________________
(B. Feedback from the receiving system of macrosystem)

of ______________________
(C. Receiving system of macrosystem)

In ______________________
(D. Feedback from the processing system of macrosystem)

Chapter 4
Organization

CHAPTER 4
ORGANIZATION

Too many bricklayers make a lopsided house.

Anonymous Chinese proverb

The Inheritance

Lia was exhausted. Looking up at the clock on the wall, she said, *Oh no! It's 2:15 a.m.!*

She was the owner of *Impact* – an advertising company specializing in print promotions. Six hours after everyone else had gone home, Lia was still working at the conference table: no breaks, no food, and piles of documents stacked everywhere.

The office's four lateral windows were open. As a storm approached, thunder reverberated in the halls and a suffocating humidity invaded the room.

She remembered the day her father asked her to step inside his office at *Impact* – and closed the door. As Lia studied her father's face, she saw the weariness there. Still, he looked at her with the same candor and respect he always had. Taking a deep breath, he came right to the point: *I have spent 35 years at Impact and I am tired. It's time for me to retire.*

That was three years ago. The once-thriving company was now on the verge of ruin. The tension was palpable, frustration was high and productivity was low. Highland, *Impact's* oldest and most important customer, was threatening to take its business elsewhere because of poor service.

Impact was on the brink of financial collapse. The company's top employees had already left and the rest of the staff was frightened. If *Impact* did not secure a loan – fast – layoffs would be inevitable.

Lia sat at the table and cried. What had she done to her father's dream? What had she done with the family inheritance? She couldn't stop thinking *What a failure! I have betrayed my father's trust.*

Suddenly, in the midst of her musing, heavy rain began to pour and a strong wind swooped through the office window: lifting documents off the table and scattering them around the room.

As she frantically tried to rescue the papers, Lia sobbed *Oh! no, the documents are getting wet!* Then she stopped and realized her own stupidity. *What am I doing?* She ceased picking up the papers and closed the windows.

The tempest continued outside, yet it became calm inside.

Collapsing into a nearby chair, Lia reviewed the incident. She observed herself picking up the papers while the windows remained open. *Impact worked the same way.*

We are desperately running from one place to another instead of stopping to "close the windows" and find effective solutions to our problems.

Encouraged by the revelation, Lia said to herself, *I was wrong! If there is no time, I should find the time – time to improve rather than to regret, to analyze rather than to cry.* She gathered her belongings, turned off the lights and went home. As she drifted off to sleep, Lia said, *Tomorrow will be a new day for me AND for Impact!*

Total Performance System

The next morning, Lia searched through handout materials from an organizational behavior management seminar she had attended. Included in the information was just what she needed: The Total Performance System (TPS) diagram (Brethower, 1972; O'Brien, Dickinson, & Rosow, 1982). This is a simple tool (introduced in Chapter 2) that provides a general overview of the organization and helps focus on the most critical areas for improvement. See Figure 4-1.

Figure 4-1. Total Performance System

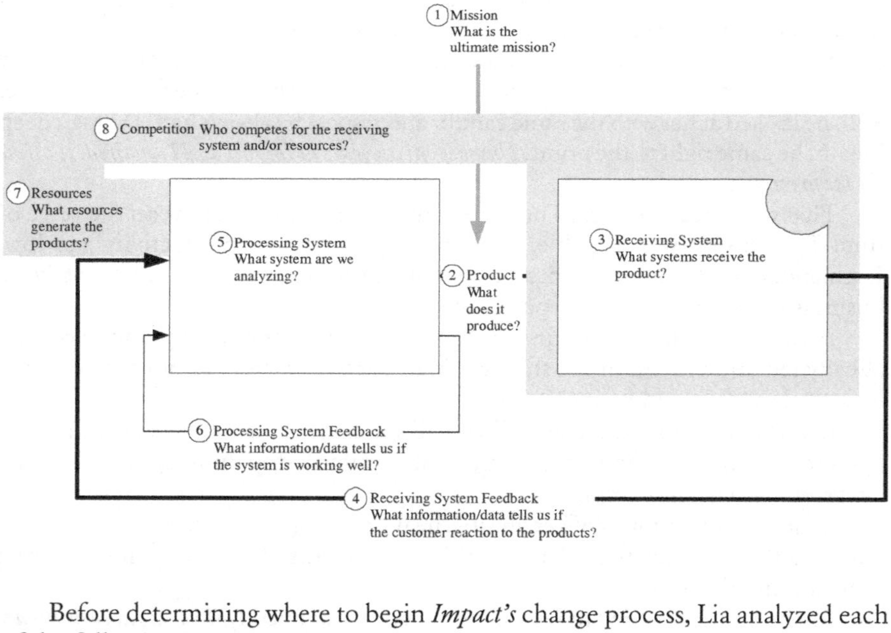

Before determining where to begin *Impact's* change process, Lia analyzed each of the following TPS components:

- Mission
- Products
- Receiving system
- Receiving system feedback
- Processing system

- Processing system feedback
- Resources
- Competition

Measures

In order to analyze an organization objectively, the TPS components should have measures that indicate performance in each area. First, Lia determined the measures, specifying the type, unit, and standard of each. The type is the nature of the measure (e.g., volume, quality, and cost). The unit is the expression of the measure; in other words, how it is quantified (e.g., number of hours or percentage of production). The standard describes the performance expectation based on past performance, the performance of competition, or specific values (e.g., 40 hours per week and 30 percent of the total production).

Concept 4-1. Basic Elements of Measurement – type of measure (nature of the measure), unit of measurement (expression of the measure), standard (quantitative performance expectation).

Organizations generally work with five types of measures: volume, quality, timeliness, duration, and cost. All system measures should have a standard or a goal with which to evaluate actual performance. The following examples are types of measures, units, and standards.

Volume

Volume involves quantity or rate. In *Impact's* case, quantity meant total number of graphic designs. Rate consists of quantity per unit of time: number of graphic designs produced in one week. In measuring graphic designs, number is the unit of measurement while the standard is the performance goal. For instance, Lia could expect 150 graphic designs per week based on past performance.

Concept 4-2. Volume – quantity or rate.

Quality

Quality refers to the precision or essential properties of the product. At *Impact*, the measure of quality was complex. Lia defined quality as the percentage of customer guidelines incorporated into the graphic design (unit). The designers did not understand the measure of quality; they believed that the more original the design, the better. But Lia established limits on how original the designs could be based on the parameters the customers established – the designs had to incorporate all customer specifications (standard). If the design does not incorporate guidelines established by the customers, the customers will not be satisfied with the product.

Concept 4-3. Quality – essential properties or precision.

Timeliness

Timeliness reflects the number of units (e.g., days, hours, minutes) past a customer's deadline. Lia's goal was for 95 percent of *Impact's* work to reach the customer on time (standard).

Concept 4-4. Timeliness – ability to meet deadlines.

Duration

Duration is the amount of time that it takes to finish a product – such as the number of hours (unit). For instance, a small graphic design project should not exceed more than 10 hours (standard).

Concept 4-5. Duration – quantity of time invested.

Cost

Cost refers to the dollars or effort invested in generating a product. If a designer invests 10 hours in a project, and he or she earns $50 per hour, the production cost is $500. Lia's goal was that actual costs averaged 95 percent of the projected cost estimated to determine the selling price (standard) of the products.

Concept 4-6. Cost – value defined in terms of money or effort invested.

Lia used the various types of measures described above when studying each of *Impact's* TPS components, as we will see next.

Components

What Is the Mission?

Lia always thought *Impact* existed to produce graphic designs. But now she was questioning that assumption: *Why produce graphic designs? What is the mission of Impact?*

Creating radio campaigns was *Impact's* primary focus 20 years ago. Customers comprised a variety of clients from the entertainment industry, including the musical group Santana. The company's name, *Impact,* was chosen because its products – the radio campaigns – impacted the market share of its customers. This became the company's competitive edge over the other four advertising agencies in town.

Impact was part of the advertising industry: that was the macrosystem in which it operated. Lia understood that the mission of the advertising industry was to increase sales and marketing in the business sector. This realization made it easier for her to understand that *Impact's* mission was much more than producing graphic designs. *Impact's* mission was to increase the market share of its customers. Lia needed to understand the advertising industry in which *Impact* operated and how its services distinguished it from other advertising companies in meeting market demands.

How would she know if *Impact* was achieving its mission? Lia realized she must measure the sales and market share of each customer's product. She would use dollars as the unit of measure. Lia knew the standard of this measure would vary with the product, company, or condition of the market; therefore, she did not define a precise dollar amount for the standard.

What Are the Products?

The products are what the organization produces for its customers; in other words, its aggregate results. *Impact* generates two types of product: graphic designs for print ads and marketing plans for customers.

Lia noticed the volume of *Impact's* graphic designs and marketing plans varied considerably, from one month to another. But she did not know if the variability was due to the complexity of the jobs or inefficient production. She decided to measure volume (type) in terms of rate: number of designs and marketing plans produced per week (unit). She classified the products as complex or simple, depending on their level of difficulty, and by type of industry: manufacturing, retail, or service.

After gathering the initial data and evaluating the implications, she would establish standards. Because she had not collected data in the past, she had no idea what to expect.

Lia understood the difference between *Impact's* mission and its products. Over the last 20 years, *Impact's* products had changed – from radio campaigns to graphic designs and marketing plans; however, its mission remained the same – to increase sales and market share of customer's products and services.

What Is the Receiving System?

Lia analyzed *Impact's* receiving system by the size of its customer organizations: small, medium, and large companies. Small companies sold less than \$5 million, medium-size companies sold between \$5 million and \$1 billion, and large companies had a gross income of over \$1 billion per year.

The unit of measurement was the percentage of annual sales by company size. *Impact* had two large customers, one in the retail industry and one in manufacturing. The two customers generated 95 percent of *Impact's* sales. The remaining five percent came from small businesses. *Impact* had no medium-size customer base.

> *Concept 4-7. Receiving System – customers who receive an organization's products and services.*

As we saw in chapter 2, the receiving system demand is what ultimately maintains the set of interlocking behavioral contingencies that form an organization. Analysis of the receiving system involves specifying strategies to reach the market of potential customers. The most successful approach in reaching *Impact's* target market were sales appointments with small companies and full-scale presentations to large companies.

> *Concept 4-8. Market Strategy – method of taking an organization's products and services to the potential market.*

Lia concluded that *Impact* had to diversify its market because too much of the company's income depended on its two, large customers. This type of financial dependency was a threat to *Impact's* long-term survival. Therefore, Lia defined the company's new standards as follows: 30 percent in sales to large companies and 70 percent in sales to medium-sized companies. She opted not to continue targeting small companies because they often couldn't afford the price of *Impact's* products and services.

What Is the Receiving System Feedback?

The receiving system feedback consists of information or data that reflect the customer's evaluation of the products and services. Lia used two feedback measures: quality and timeliness. She defined quality as the percentage of customer guidelines incorporated into the graphic designs, and timeliness as the percentage of orders received on time by the customers.

> *Concept 4-9. Receiving System Feedback – data or customer information that reflects the evaluation of the organization's products and services.*

Impact's unit of measure was the percentage of customers satisfied with the products. All of its customers (based on surveys) rated the quality of the company's products and services very highly.

Although quality was not a problem, timeliness of delivery was. The unit of measure was the percentage of projects shipped after the deadline. To her shock, Lia found that 73 percent of the company's projects were in the "delayed" category. Prior to collecting the revealing data, she – and her staff – had the impression that *Impact* was very timely. So Lia established a new standard: at least 95 percent of the work should be delivered on time.

What Is the Process?

The process consists of all the tasks that transform the resources into products and services. The process involves all the interlocking behavioral contingencies that ultimately generate the aggregate products – graphic design and marketing plans for the customers. *Impact* had several subprocesses, each one representing a smaller metacontingency. The most essential were capturing customers' concepts, designing the prototype and producing the ads. In addition, other support processes were needed: generating new business, managing existing customer accounts and monitoring finances.

> *Concept 4-10. Process – systematic tasks that transform an organization's resources into products and services.*

The organizational structure is part of the processing system. It consists of the administrative-reporting relationship between departments within organizations: graphically represented with an organizational chart. Although the organizational structure should facilitate the optimal function of the organization, it often gets in the way. This was the case at *Impact,* where there were 19 departments and only 75 employees. Lia had copied the organizational chart of a typical advertising company. Figure 4-2 shows the company's original organizational chart.

Concept 4-11. Organizational Structure – administrative-reporting between departments within organizations.

Concept 4-12. Organizational Chart – graphic representation of the organizational structure.

Figure 4-2. Impact's Summary of the Organizational Structure

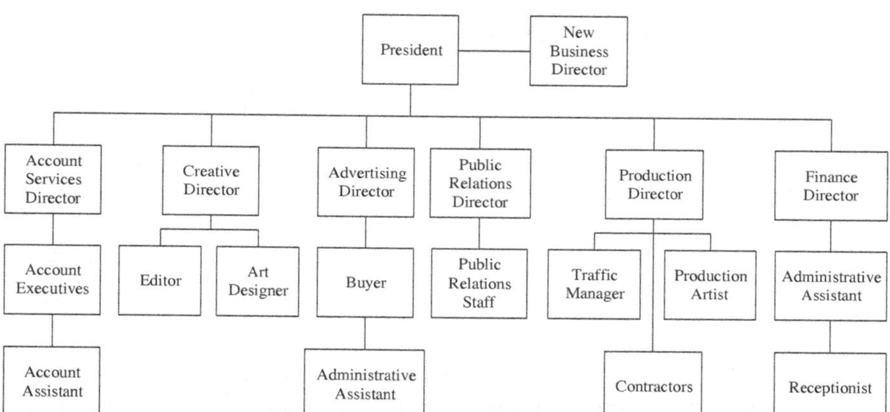

Seven departments reported to the president: New Business, Account Services, Creativity, Marketing, Public Relations, Production, and Finances. Each department was independent of the others; therefore, there were no clear processes to ensure an efficient and productive relationship between departments.

The departments of client organizations were non-integrated as well. Representatives from the various companies interacted with staff from *Impact's* Account Services, Creative, Advertising and Finance departments. They would all then, in and out of turn, provide *Impact's* Production department with direction. As a result, production often received conflicting messages from various sources. The company ended up investing four times the resources quoted in the original price. And – by implementing multiple, ambiguous, and contradictory directions – the Production department became inefficient and *Impact* had to set higher fees than those of its competitors.

Impact's organizational structure, as stated earlier and shown in the original organizational chart, did not facilitate the integrated work between its departments: instead, it got in the way of an efficient organization. By restructuring the company,

Lia created a plan whereby the output of some departments served as the input to others – and where the interaction between departments was clearly identified. (See Figure 4-3.)

Figure 4-3. Impact's Department-Function Organizational Chart[1]

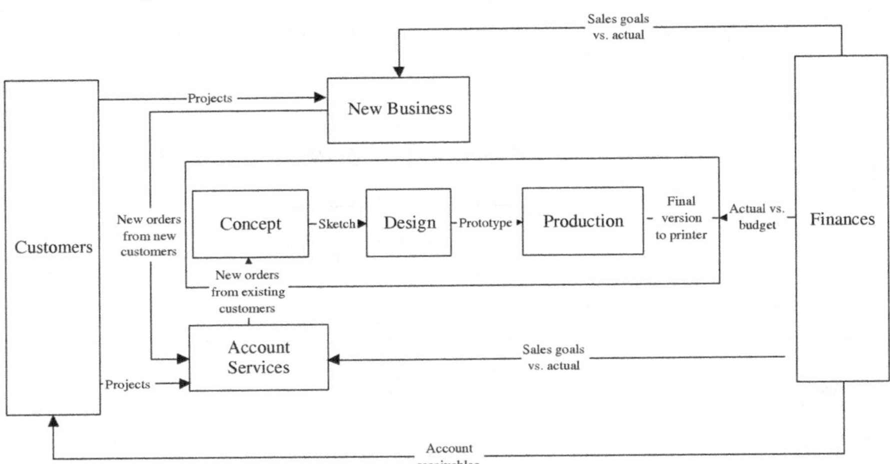

In the new organizational chart it was easier to appreciate the smaller metacontingencies contained within the larger metacontingency of the organization as a whole. For instance the "Concept" department involved all the interlocking behavioral contingencies that generated sketches – the aggregate product. Sketches were in demand by the "Design" department and it is that demand that should shape their characteristics and the interlocking behavioral contingencies that generate them.

Lia identified a department or metacontingency, involving the set of interlocking behavioral contingencies, their aggregate product, and the source of receiving system demand for each key function of the organization. The New Business department generated orders from new customers. The Account Services department generated new orders from existing customers, by ensuring that their current needs were met. Both existing and new orders were inputs to the Concept department, which generated a rough sketch that met customers' guidelines and needs.

The Design department transformed concepts into prototypes that the Production department used to generate ads. The Finance department let Concept, Design,

[1] *With the exception of the customer, Figure 4-3 represents the Processing System of Impact. It illustrates which departments interact with the customers.*

and the Production department staff know if processing costs met the budget: in addition to letting New Business and Account Services' personnel know if actual sales matched the company's goals. The Finance department also provided accounts receivable information to customers, such as timeliness and accuracy of payments.

The arrows on the new organizational chart showed the work relationship between departments – that is, the lines of receiving system demands. New Business would be the only department to interact with new customers. The Account Services department monitored customer accounts and provided clear specifications of customer needs and wants to the Concept department; Concept provided sketches to the Design department; Design provided the prototypes to the Production department; and Production provided ads to customers. By organizing *Impact* as a process, Lia simplified the number of departments and their interactions.

Lia's goal was to maximize the entire organization's effectiveness. However, if some departments outperformed others, *Impact* would not function properly. The maximization of one department could be detrimental to the entire system.

For instance, if New Business generated too many sales – and Account Services could not ensure the completion of those orders to the customer's satisfaction – repeat orders would be unlikely. Sometimes the maximization of subsystems must be controlled to optimize the whole. In order to optimize the results of a subsystem we tend to jeopardize the optimization of the whole system. This is what Heylighen (1992) called the sub-optimization principle.

> *Concept 4-13. Sub-Optimization Principle – optimization of a subsystem does not result in the optimization of the whole system.*

What Is the Processing System Feedback?

The processing system feedback consists of information that indicates how well the system functions. Among other indicators, Lia measured the cost of production. The unit of measurement was the percentage of production cost in relation to the estimated cost. Her standard was approximately five percent discrepancy between the real and estimated cost.

> *Concept 4-14. Feedback of the Processing System – evaluation of how a system functions.*

Lia learned that the cost of production was generally 30 percent higher than estimated, as each order generated a substantial amount of unnecessary work. *Impact* was losing money with each order it processed. It was clear to Lia that *Impact* was not designed to manage the interface between departments needed to efficiently produce quality products and services.

Which Resources Are Indispensable to Generate the Products?

Typically, organizations conclude prematurely that they need more resources, more equipment, more training, more employees, or more technology. Initiating the analysis of an organization by scrutinizing its resources can result in organizational myopia. Without access to critical information, a company might acquire resources it does not need. To complete the analysis, the organization must determine which resources it requires to generate the main products and services customers buy. These resources include personnel, services, information, materials, and equipment.

- **Personnel**: Managers and workers.
- **Services**: Contracted work that facilitates the organization's operations, such as photography and printing services.
- **Information:** Data or knowledge, for instance, production cost.
- **Materials:** Items needed to do the job, for example, electronic image libraries.
- **Equipment**: Tools needed to do the job, such as electronic systems and computers.

Concept 4-15. Resources – indispensable means to generate the organization's products; for example, personnel, services, information, materials, and equipment.

Lia measured various *Impact* assets. The most interesting to her were human resources. *Impact* replaced approximately 50 percent of its graphic designers each year. Consequently, Lia chose retention and percentage of employee retention, per year, as the units of measurements. Her goal? To hire high-quality employees and retain them – with minimal or no turnover.

Who Is the Competition?

In general, there are two types of competition: competition for customers and competition for resources.

- **Competition for customers:** Organizations that produce a higher quality of products and services, faster – and at a lower cost – typically get the largest share of the market. Therefore, it is important to analyze the organizations that compete for customers.
- **Competition for resources:** Organizations also compete for resources, in addition to customers: especially if resources are limited.

Impact did not have much competition for customers because it was the only advertising agency within 100 miles. Personnel, however, was a different story. Graphic designers from *Impact* were hired with better salary and benefit packages by the advertising departments of local manufactures and retailers.

Concept 4-16. Competition – organizations that offer products or services to the same potential customers and that use the same resources to generate their products.

Lia estimated that the region (within a 100-mile radius of *Impact*) needed about 500 trained graphic designers to satisfy market demand. However, the area had no training centers for graphic designers.

The lack of regional training institutions made working for *Impact* an excellent learning opportunity for aspiring designers. When the designers acquired enough experience, they sought better offers elsewhere. After a careful analysis, Lia concluded that the training cost was too high and that *Impact* would be financially better off by offering a competitive compensation package to its employees. The additional money spent on salaries and benefits was less than the cost of recruitment, selection, and training.

Value

The total performance system (TPS) analysis helped Lia identify the following critical areas for improvement:

- **Mission:** Initially, the company's mission was to produce graphic designs; however, Lia realized that such an assumption was shortsighted. Its ultimate mission was to increase the market share of its customers' products and services. The bigger picture gave her flexibility in considering future development strategies.
- **Receiving System:** 95 percent of *Impact's* orders depended on two, large customers. *Impact* needed to diversify the market by targeting medium-size companies. Furthermore, it should stop serving small companies because the clientele could not afford *Impact's* regular prices and the work was not profitable.
- **Receiving System Feedback:** Even when the customers were pleased with quality, the final orders were sent late; 73 percent of the projects arrived in the client's hands after the agreed deadline.
- **Processing System:** The organizational structure did not facilitate smooth functioning of *Impact's* processes. Lia designed a simplified structure – more like a matrix – that would help *Impact* operate as a process, where the output from each department met the input needs of other departments.
- **Processing System Feedback:** *Impact* invested, on average, 30 percent more production dollars than estimated in the original sales quotes. *Impact* was losing money.
- **Resources:** The turnover of graphic designers was 150 percent a year.

After analyzing *Impact's* TPS, Lia formed concrete and effective change strategies. Instead of feeling helpless, she was empowered: she knew exactly what to do and how to measure success. Figure 4-4 illustrates a total performance system analysis of *Impact*.

Figure 4-4. TPS of Impact

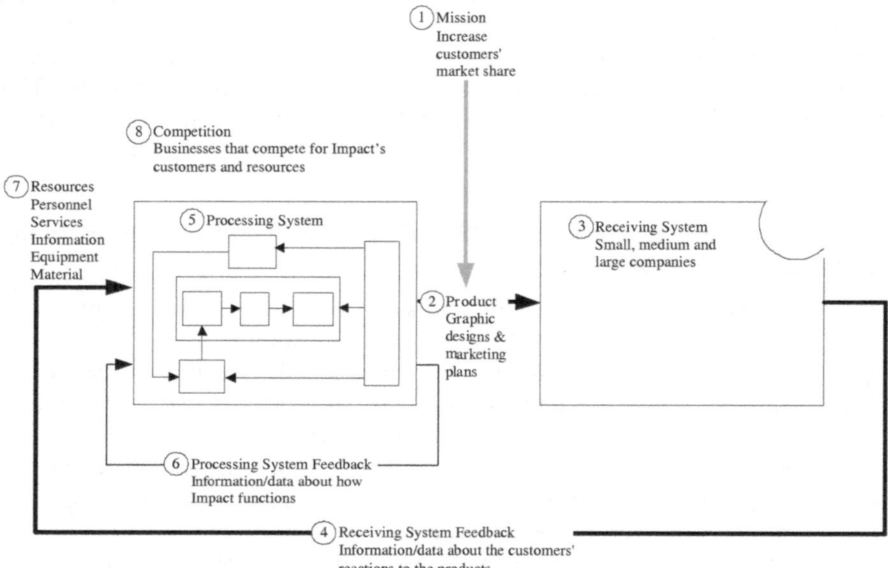

Attempting to change an organization – without knowing the true nature of its internal and external problems – generates anxiety and threatens its survival.

Strategic Plan

TPS is an invaluable tool for strategic planning, ensuring competitive advantage and profitability. The same questions used to analyze an organization today are applicable in planning its future direction of development.

> *Concept 4-17. Strategic Plan – specifying the organization's activities that ensure future competitive advantage and profitability.*

Following *Impact's* TPS analysis, Lia met with members of her leadership team and engaged in a strategic planning session. Table 4-1 summarizes the three-year strategic plan Lia and her team developed.

Conclusions

The analysis of the organization as a TPS shows another aspect of the constant and orderly component of the paradox of change, rooted in environmental selection. It is necessary to understand the environmental selection dynamics – from the receiving system and the macrosystem – operating upon the organization we are analyzing to address change effectively. The receiving system – the customers – impose demands on the organizations' aggregate products, which shape the way the organization is organized to meet such demands. That is, the local companies

Table 4-1. Outline of Impact's Strategic Plan

	Present	Within Three Years	Change Strategy
Mission	To increase the market share of products and services in customer organizations through marketing and advertising	Every person in the organization understands the mission and works toward it	-Incorporate the mission in training programs and regular materials of the organization -Use the mission to lead ongoing problem solving and organizational improvements
Products	Print advertising and marketing plans	Incorporate market research services	Develop market research services and offer them to current and potential customers
Receiving System	Percentage of total sales: 95% large and 5% small companies	Percentage of total sales: 70% medium, 30% large, and no small companies	Incorporate medium-size companies, eliminate small companies, and reduce the percentage of total sales from large companies
Receiving System Feedback	There are no systematic data	Data-based proof of customer satisfaction	Develop and implement an effective measurement system for receiving system feedback
Processing System	Complex and inefficient processes	Simple and efficient processes	Streamline processes
Processing System Feedback	There are no systematic data	Data-based proof of process efficiency	Develop and effective measurement system
Resources	50% turnover of graphic designers	90% retention of graphic designers	Develop and implement competitive salary and benefit programs
Competition	Prices higher than the competition	Offer competitive prices	Develop and implement pricing system so *Impact* is competitive

needing to advertise and market their aggregate products impose demands on the graphic designs and marketing plans of *Impact*.

Likewise, customers' practices are selected by the macrosystem demands of their own organizations' aggregate products. The advertising industry consists of the metacontingency that contains a business like *Impact* and its customers. In the previous chapter, the point was made that the analysis of the organization ought to start by the macrosystem that contains it. In this chapter, the emphasis was on analyzing the parameters of the organization metacontingency using the TPS. Figure 4-5 shows the first two components of the model.

Figure 4-5. Levels 1-2 of the Behavioral Systems Engineering Model

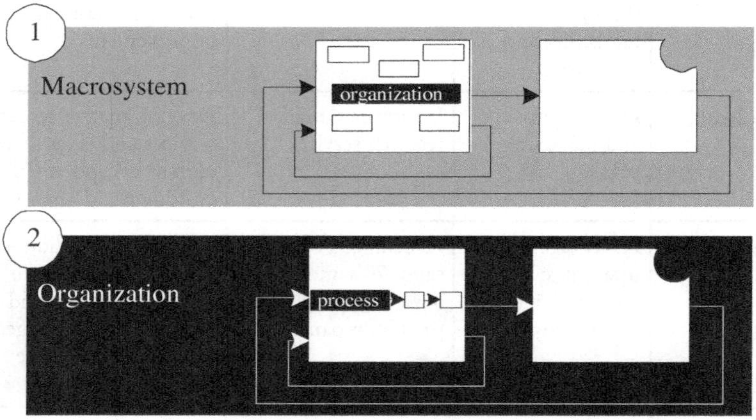

1
Macrosystem
organization
2
Organization
process

Analyzing an organization as a TPS provides an objective perspective because each component of the analysis is based on data, not just simple speculation. It also provides an opportunity for organizations to look at the company from the customer's point of view. The results of measurement are the starting point in organizational change; they should be the basis to set performance standards for each component of the TPS and to evaluate interventions.

The TPS analysis starts by distinguishing the mission and the organization's products and services. The following questions are then addressed: Who receives the products? What information/data verifies the receivers are satisfied with the products? What process generates the products? What information/data testifies that the process is working well? What processes are indispensable to transform the resources into products? Who competes for the resources and/or receiving systems? Ultimately, TPS provides a framework for strategic planning, where the overall activities of the organization are designed to meet the mission.

Review

- Perform a TPS analysis of an organization you are familiar with, following the diagram presented in Figure 4-6.

Figure 4-6. Total Performance System Framework

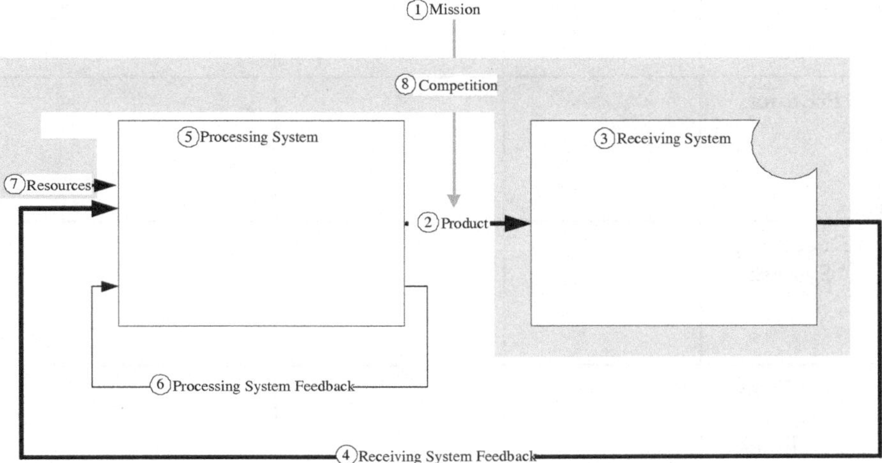

- Define and identify at least one measure (including type, unit, and standard) for each one of the TPS components: mission, products, receiving system, receiving system feedback, process, processing system feedback, resources and competition.

Based on the analysis of the TPS, outline your strategic plan for the development of your organization using Table 4-2.

Table 4-2. Strategic Planning Framework

	Present	Within Three Years	Change Strategy
Mission			
Products			
Receiving System			
Receiving System Feedback			
Processing System			
Processing System Feedback			
Resources			
Competition			

Chapter 5
Process

CHAPTER 5
PROCESS

Be not afraid of growing slowly, be afraid only of standing still.

Chinese proverb

Lost

When Daniel graduated sum cum laude from the master's program of public health, it was a dream come true. *It was all worth it,* he repeated over and over to himself as he walked toward the podium to receive his diploma.

Daniel's master's thesis was a success; as always, he earned an "A". One of the faculty members participating in his oral defense offered Daniel a job as a sales representative for *Salud Inc.*, a company for which the faculty member was a senior vice president. *Salud* distributes pharmaceutical products from the most established drug manufacturing companies in the country.

On his first day at work, the general manager's administrative assistant, Rose, led Daniel to an office where five employees were engaged in casual conversation, laughing loudly. When the group realized Daniel's presence, they silenced. *This is Daniel Salas, our new sales representative,* Rose said.

How long are you going to last? One of the men said. While Daniel struggled to recover from such an unwelcoming statement, John, who was going to be in charge of Daniel's training, said, *What are you doing here Daniel? Why would someone who graduated with honors come to work for a company like Salud? Why don't you go and work at Integration, the most successful company in the country. Here, we don't even know if we will have a job next month.* The others laughed.

Not knowing what to say, Daniel flashed an embarrassed smile and followed Rose to his new desk, where company literature awaited. He turned the various pages, pretending he was reading, but all Daniel could think about was looking for another job. He imagined his faculty advisor saying, *It's hard to believe that you did so well in school and so bad in the real world.* And then he imagined John, laughing while he sarcastically said, *I told you that you were "too good" for this lousy company.*

After two hours of "reading," Daniel armed himself with courage and went across the hall to John's office. *I need to have a general understanding of Salud: What is the mission? What are the goals for this year? What is the relationship between the sales department and the rest of the organization? What…*

John interrupted. In a mocking tone, he said, *Cooool down, brother! Don't be a pain! The only things that you need to know about are the products you have to sell.* John handed Daniel the same brochure he had on his desk. Then, pointing at the library shelves in his office, John said: *In that library, you will find the therapeutic manuals. Don't waste time; you have a lot to read.* Daniel glanced at the library filled with dust-covered, four-inch binders.

After a few days, Daniel realized that *Salud* was a disorganized mess. His confidence was gone, he was afraid, and he was lost. *Salud* was too chaotic and he had no idea where he stood in the organization. *How do I understand this organization? Can I even find my job in the organizational chart? Are all of the others as lost as I am?*

Finding Yourself in the Organization

It is common to question the relevance of one's job in the overall functioning of an organization. Most people do their jobs and maintain a narrow scope, never looking beyond the task at hand. They do not take the time to analyze the impact of the organization's mission on their jobs and departments. John could not help Daniel understand the organization because his scope of understanding was limited to his own department. He was oblivious to the interrelationships within the organization.

The method presented in this book helps to get the "big picture" of the organization and understand how each role relates to the overall success. Chapter 3 addressed how to define the mission of the organization based on the analysis of the macrosystem that contains it. The macrosystem of *Salud* – the health industry – consists of a multitude of interlocking behavioral contingencies that result in the treatment of illnesses and maintenance of health (aggregate products).

John told Daniel that the objective of *Salud* was to sell prescription drugs. But selling was quite different from preventing and curing illness. John suffered from organizational myopia – confusing the product of the organization with the mission. The mission was not to sell but to prevent and cure illnesses in order to contribute to the short- and long-term physical and psychological health of the population in a cost-effective way. *Salud* was not working toward achieving its true mission if the products were ineffective or harmful.

Chapter 4 described how to analyze an organization as a TPS. Some key elements of the TPS of *Salud* are the aggregate product and receiving systems – or customers. The final aggregate product was sales, which were measured in terms of units sold by product type. The customers were doctors, hospitals, labs, and pharmacies. However, doctors were the principal market. *Salud* divided its master list of doctors into categories – A, B, and C – according to the number of prescriptions they generated. For example, an "A" doctor generally had more customers and generated a higher level of prescriptions. This is the type of doctor *Salud* was most interested in.

The demand from customers shapes the characteristics of the aggregate products and therefore, their causal interlocking behavioral contingencies. In *Salud's* metacontingency, the unit demand of pharmaceutical products (aggregate products) might change its selling, purchasing, and shipment processes: as expected, based on the principle of environmental selection.

The emphasis of this Chapter is on analyzing the processing system of an organization; that is, what it takes to transform an organization's resources into its overall aggregate products. A process consists of a series of actions and its aggregate products directed to a particular purpose.

Concept 5-1. Process – series of actions and their aggregate products directed to a particular purpose.

Organizational processes are complex and chaotic, as described in Chapter 1. They involve a multitude of activities and products of many individuals affecting each other. Because of such complexity, it is important to understand processes from both general and detailed perspectives.

It is helpful to start with a general understanding of the processing system, otherwise we might get lost in details. This chapter provides a general perspective of how to think of an organization's processing system as a process, which involves the analysis of the relationship between internal metacontingencies (or departments). Chapter 6 will provide a detailed perspective of the processing system, which involves the analysis of the actions and products of each individual.

At this point, I should distinguish two terms: function and department. Function is the purpose of the action or a group of actions. Department refers to a section of the organization, generally separated by different administrative lines. Sometimes the function and the department are the same. For instance, a sales department's main function is to sell. So the selling function and the sales department are in the same place. But this is not always the case; for instance, a marketing department could be executing the sales function rather than the marketing function of analyzing potential and existing markets.

Concept 5-2. Function – purpose of one action or group of actions that generates an aggregate product.

Concept 5-3. Department – section of one organization generally separated by different administrative lines that generates a main aggregate product.

Studying the organization requires the analysis of its containing metacontingencies, those that describe the interactions between its main processes and departments. This analysis would help employees like Daniel and John to appreciate their role in the organization. Understanding the organization as a process involves three steps: performing a structural analysis, performing a department-function analysis, and contrasting the IS and the OUGHT TO BE of the organization's structure and department functions.

Structural Analysis

Start by taking the company's 38-page organizational structure and reducing it to one page. In order to simplify the structure, focus on the principal departments and exclude the details. Begin the process with this thought: *If we only had one page to illustrate how the organization is working, how would I show it?* Shade the areas that were directly related to sales success. Figure 5-1 illustrates the organization of *Salud.* Shaded are departments that directly affected Daniel's job.

Figure 5-1. Structural Analysis of Salud Inc.[1]

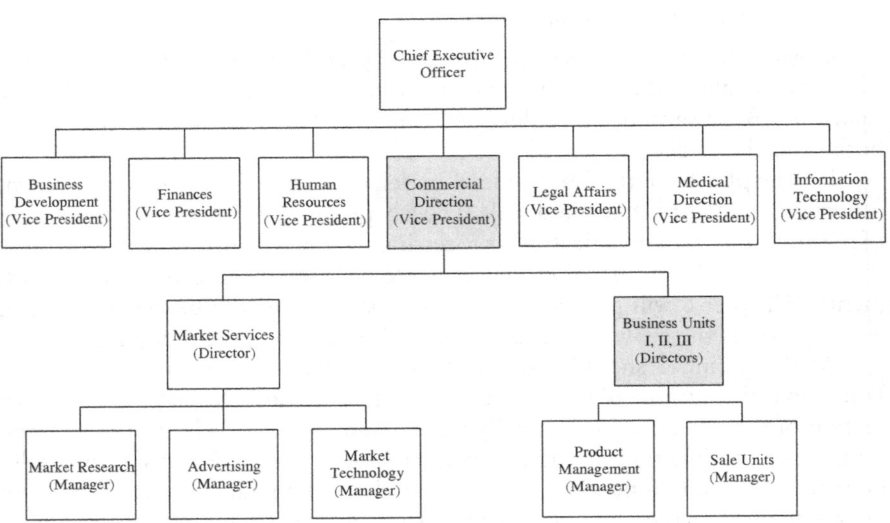

The structural analysis of *Salud* allows us to understand how the departments related administratively; in other words, to understand who reported to whom. For example, the chief executive officer (CEO) directed seven departments:

- Business Development – generates new business, such as drug patent acquisitions
- Finances – manages all business accounting and bookkeeping
- Human Resources – recruits and places personnel
- Commercial Direction – develops and implements market plans
- Legal Affairs – ensures compliance with regulatory prerequisites and legal product registration
- Medical Direction – prepares clinical studies
- Information Technology – oversees hardware management and

[1] *Figure 5-1 represents the administrative reporting of Salud Inc., which is a distributor of pharmaceutical products: not a manufacturer.*

technology development

The first reporting levels to the CEO were vice presidents, second directors and third managers. The Commercial Services vice president directed the Market Services department and the Business Units. The Market Services department managed three other departments: Market Research, which conducted research in potential and exiting markets; Advertising, which promoted the pharmaceuticals in *Salud's* portfolio; and Market Technology, which identified the methodology and strategies for researching the market.

Business Units I, II and III managed the Product Management department, which analyzed sales and margins for each specific product across the country and developed customized sales plans for each drug. Business Units I, II and III also managed the Sale Units, which sold pharmaceuticals in specific geographical locations across the country.

Daniel was a sales representative for the company. Each of the business units specialized in different types of pharmaceutical products. For instance, Daniel worked in Business Unit I, which sold products for the treatment of central nervous system disorders. The units were divided into regions, which corresponded to geographic locations. Business Unit II sold products for the treatment of sexual conditions. The remaining pharmaceuticals were sold in Business Unit III. Each business unit had an equivalent number of people in its sales force. Figure 5-2 shows the reporting structure of Business Unit I. In parenthesis is the number of managers and salespeople for each division.

Structural analysis refers to the visualization of the administrative line of reporting between departments and the levels of management. The reporting line is critical to understanding how the organization works: who evaluates whom and where loyalties might be. This knowledge is essential – but by no means sufficient – to succeed at organizational change.

> *Concept 5-4. Structural Analysis – study of the administrative reporting lines.*

Department-Function Analysis[2]

In addition to understanding how an organization is structured, it is useful to understand how its departments function. Department-function analysis includes creating a model of effective interactions between departments so that organizations can accomplish their goals. A department can be conceived as a metacontingency, involving a set of interlocking behavioral contingencies that generates aggregate products in demand by other departments. A department-function analysis requires specifying the function of each department in the organization; distinguishing core

[2] *Rummler and Brache (1995) presented the concept of cross-functional analysis in their book "Improving Performance: How to manage the white space of the organizational chart."*

Figure 5-2. Business Unit I[3]

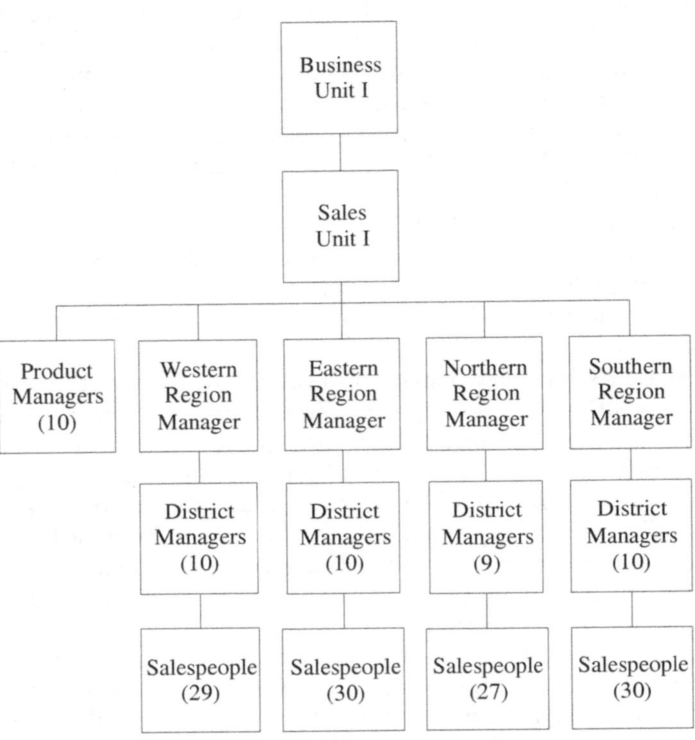

departments from supporting and integrating departments; and illustrating the relationship between departments.

> *Concept 5-5. Department-Function Analysis – study of the main functions or responsibilities of the departments, the interactions between departments and measures of success.*

Specification of the Department Functions

Employees rarely know what the function of each department is and, as Daniel showed when he asked John earlier, asking colleagues might be a waste of time. Therefore, create a frame of reference and conduct an investigation to see whether your speculation matches reality. Identify components of each department metacontingency, the aggregate product, the primary function or responsibility that

[3] *Figure 5-2 represents the administrative reporting of Business Unit I.*

summarizes the nature of its interlocking behavioral contingencies, and measures of success. Table 5-1 shows examples of function specification and measures.

Fill out the information in Table 5-1, based on hypothesis of how the organization ought to effectively work. To adjust and validate your supposition, collect data and discreetly observe employees from each department: especially those with considerable experience, like Sharon, who had worked for 20 years in a variety of jobs. You should answer the following questions: What is the major function of each department in the organization? How does each department contribute to *Salud's*, goals? How do departments interrelate?

The general assumption, in most companies, is that there are a few key employees who "know it all" – the company's past, present, and potential future. Daniel found out that this was not the case at *Salud*. The majority of the employees he interacted with were not interested in, nor did they have the time for, doing a systematic functional and measurement analysis of their respective departments. No one "knew it all."

Obtaining a general and objective understanding of any company requires effort and research. It involves interviews, data gathering, and observation. Incidentally, be cautious of basing your analysis on interviews exclusively. What people say they do and what people actually do are often different. Data gathering and direct observation are indispensable for a good understanding of the organization. Those who intend to improve an organization must create a frame of reference regarding how the organization works (the IS) and how it OUGHT to work.

Differentiate Between Core, Support and Integrating Departments[4]

When we do a department-function analysis, it is useful to identify three types of departments: core, support, and integrating. The core departments are the motor of an organization, the departments directly responsible for its income. These departments are driven by the external customer demands. Sales and Production are core departments in manufacturing businesses; the Sales department generates customer orders and the Production department executes the sales orders. Sales and Service are core departments in service companies. Purchasing and Sales are core departments in retail companies.

> *Concept 5-6. Core Departments – the motor of an organization, departments directly responsible for business income.*

Support departments provide specific products and services to other departments. These departments should be driven mainly by the demands of the core departments. For instance, Maintenance supports Production in manufacturing businesses by ensuring the working order of the equipment. Advertising supports

[4] *See M. E. Malott (1999) for a similar analysis.*

Table 5-1. Responsibilities, Aggregate Products, and Measures for Each function/Department of Salud Inc.

Department	Aggregate Product	Main Responsibility	Measures
Business Development	Gets new customers for the company	Identifies new customers	-New opportunities: number -Analysis of competition: dollars and percentage of sales and margins -Market share: percentage of company's product sales in the market; market ranking -Sales potential: dollars and percentage
		Incorporates products licensed to the business' portfolio	New products acquisition: number
Human Resources	Capable human resources	Provides needed employees Employee's professional development	-Vacancies: number -Employees' evaluation results -Position in the organizational hierarchy -Turnover: percentage
		Implements benefit packages	Employees' perception: survey results
Medical Direction	Medical studies	Coordinates the development of clinical studies according to the strategic plan	Lead time of clinical studies registry: time and duration
Legal Affairs	Legal compliance	Assures that the business fulfills the country's regulatory requirements in the generation, manufacturing, and distribution of products	Violations: number and cost in dollars
		Registers new pharmaceutical products	-Registered products: number -Registry lead time: number of weeks, months, years
Market Research	Marketing plan	Develops short- and long-term strategic plans for market penetration	-Sales: actual and estimated dollar sales -Client perception: survey results -Cost: percentage of sales expenses as a function of dollars sold -Market share: percentage of company's product sales in the market; market ranking
		Ensures implementation of marketing pan across company	-Feedback: tabulation of reports

Table 5-1. Continued.

Department	Aggregate Product	Main Responsibility	Measures
Product Management	Sales by product	Ensures implememtation of marketing plan for each specific goal, so that sales and margin objectives are met	-Sales: dollars and percentage -Margins: dollars and percentage
Business Units	Sales by units	Implements marketing plan for each corresponding region and therapeutic area	-Sales: current and projected dollars -Clients' perception: survey results -Margins: dollars and percentage -Cost: percentage of sales expenses as function of dollars sold -Market share: percentage of company's product sales in the market; market ranking -Employees' perception: survey results

Sales in service-oriented companies through promotions to potential markets. Property supports Operations in retail companies by buying properties for new stores.

Concept 5-7. Support Departments – provide specific products and services to other departments.

In most organizations, Finance, Human Resources, and Information Technology function as bridges – integrating all of the other departments. These departments should be driven by the demand of all the departments in the organization. Finance integrates departments because it receives or provides data on the financial health of the entire organization. Information Technology provides the technological infrastructure for the coordination of departmental data. Human Resource departments provide skilled and knowledgeable personnel to various departments.

Concept 5-8. Integrating Departments – receive and provide information across all the departments of the organization.

Representation of the Interaction Between Departments

Creating a one-page, department-function analysis – similar to the earlier structural analysis – is helpful. The graphic representation showing the relationship between the departmental functions, helps us to appreciate the interaction between

Figure 5-3. Department-Function Analysis of Salud Inc.

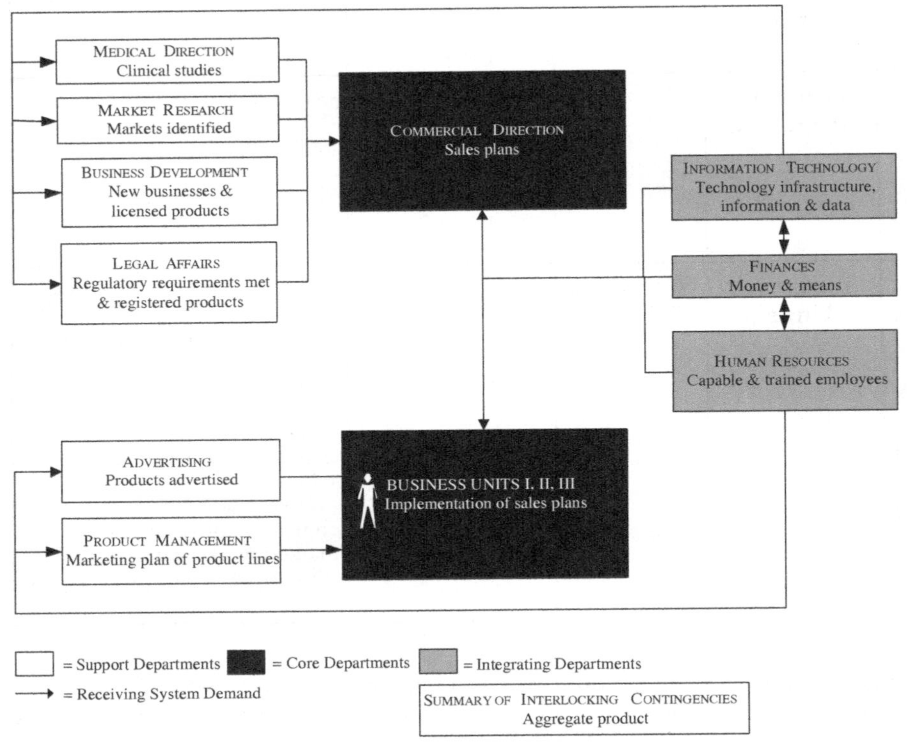

process metacontingencies existing in the organization, so the organization's processing system can be understood as a process where the outputs of some departments serve as input to others. Figure 5-3 shows a department-function analysis of *Salud*. In the Figure, department names summarize sets of interlocking behavioral contingencies; their results are the aggregate products and the arrows indicate the source of receiving system demand.

Core departments at *Salud* included Commercial Direction and the Business Units, which planned and executed sales. In the department-function analysis, Daniel's job is within the Business Units. His job, as a salesperson, was included under "implementation of sales plans." This is where detailed direction on how to approach the current and potential markets was provided. His job was to implement the sales plan, generated by the Commercial Direction department, in his corresponding geographical area and to meet sales and profit goals.

The Medical Direction, Market Research, Business Development and Regulatory Affairs departments supported sales-plan development. The Advertising and Product Management departments supported sales-plan implementation. Staff members from Information Systems, Finances and Human Resources provided integrated information, budget feedback and human resources to all of *Salud's*, departments, including their own.

Each organization is different. Departments with the same names can serve dissimilar functions. For instance, one Marketing department might focus on researching the various markets while another concentrates its efforts on advertising.

The most important aspects of the department-function analysis are to identify the main product (aggregate product generated by sets of interlocking behavioral contingencies) and the inputs needed by each department (source of receiving system demand) so that the organization works efficiently and effectively. This analysis is important because it shows how departments interact and align in pursuit of the organization's overall mission. In order to do such an analysis, it might be helpful to use the framework presented in Table 5-2.

Contrast the IS and the OUGHT TO BE of the Organization Structure and Department Functions

The third step in analyzing an organization as a process is to contrast the IS and the OUGHT TO BE of the organization's structure and departmental functions. Make a structural analysis based on the reality of the organization. Create a department-function analysis by establishing a hypothesis of how the departments should interact. Later, investigate your hypothesis to see if it corresponded to reality.

Salud presented the chaos typical of most organizations: from manufacturing to service, communication, and retail. Core departments did not work cooperatively, support departments did not assist the core departments, and integrating departments did not work to coordinate and streamline interdepartmental flow. Department personnel lost sight of the organization's mission and created their own missions, generating considerable redundancies in business functions.

The organizational structure could be simplified. The Market Services department did not have an essential function and the Market Research department was redundant to the Business Development department (both could be combined into one).

Core departments did not have the support they needed to function effectively. Staff members had to do the work expected from other departments in order to fulfill their main responsibilities. They ended up overloaded with responsibility and became ineffective and inefficient. The Sale Units were too overloaded with work because other departments did not serve the required supporting or integrating functions. For instance, the Regional Managers were responsible for selecting and training their own salespeople; they did not believe that the Human Resource department understood the Business Units needs. So they assumed the responsibility of recruitment and hiring their own salespeople. Another example was the failure to receive help from the Information Technology department. One of its salespeople, who loved computer technology, developed and maintained a computer application to provide the salespeople accurate information about the data. But the

Table 5-2. OUGHT TO BE Analysis of Departments

	Department Name	Aggregate Products	Resources Needed
Core Departments	Commercial Direction	Sales plans	-Clinical studies -Markets identified -New businesses and licensed products -Regulatory requirements met and registered products -Technology infrastructure, information and data -Money and means -Capable and trained employees -Sales plan implemented
	Business Units	Sales plans implemented	(See Figure 5-3 to continue filling in this column)
Integrating Departments	Information Technology	Technology infrastructure, information and data	
	Finances	Money and means	
	Human Resources	Capable and trained employees	
Support Departments	Medical Direction	Clinical studies	
	Market Research	Markets identified	
	Business Development	New businesses and licensed products	
	Legal Affairs	Regulatory requirements met and registered products	
	Advertising	Products advertised	
	Product Management	Marketing plan of product lines	

system he created was not integrated into any other applications. As a result, additional rekeying from one application to another was necessary.

The Business Units had many failed attempts requesting services from the Information Systems department. Information Systems had other priorities, and it never met the technology application needs of the sales force. Yet another example of the company's dysfunction was the lack of support from the Finance department. The salespeople invested several hours a week producing sales and cost reports because the Finance department did not understand its role: to provide financial information to the Business Units on an ongoing basis.

The two core departments, Commercial Direction and the Business Units, did not function cooperatively. In spite of the immense amount of work that Commercial Planning did to develop the marketing plans, the Business Units failed to implement them. The Business Units did not understand the plans and there were no incentives to implement them. On top of this, the Support departments were no help. As a result, the sales people had to do all of the above-mentioned functions – which left them little time to sell the products. Sales were the main product of *Salud*; without sales the business would eventually fail.

The discrepancy between the IS and the OUGHT TO BE should not be discouraging. On the contrary, the discrepancies are opportunities for improvement to achieve the organization's mission. The first step is to create a plan to start smoothing the rough edges between the company's departments. This will help employees like Daniel not to feel lost and gain direction and enthusiasm to contribute to the success of the organization.

Conclusions

Organizations are disorganized and chaotic. They often develop internal structures that do not make sense or get in the way of their overall success. However, the process through which they get to be disorganized and ineffective is orderly – it is based on the principle of environmental selection. This inherent contradiction makes change paradoxical.

This chapter brought the principle of environmental selection to the processing system of an organization. Like macrosystems and organizations change, based on their receiving system demands, so does each department within an organization. Such consistency in the evolution of systems, no matter how complex the system might be, brings back the constant and orderly aspect of the paradox of organizational change.

The processing system of an organization should be studied from general and detailed perspectives. This chapter presented the general perspective, which consists of analyzing the interaction of the main components of an organization – their department metacontingencies – whereas the aggregate products of some departments serve as main resources to other departments. Such analysis is the basis for the third component of the Behavioral Systems Engineering Change Model presented in this book. (See Figure 5-4.)

Understanding an organization as a process requires three steps: creating a structural analysis, designing a department-function analysis, and contrasting the IS and the OUGHT TO BE of the organization's structure and department functions.

The structural analysis shows the administrative reporting line. It provides a picture of who has the potential to control decision making and consequences for performance.

Figure 5-4. Levels 1-3 of the Behavioral Systems Engineering Model

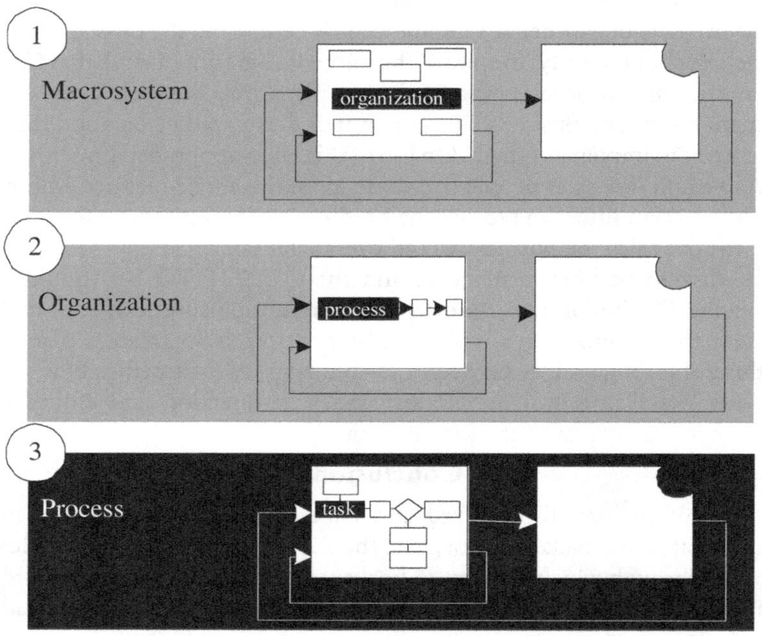

The department-function analysis shows the interactions between the metacontingencies involved in the organization – products of each department serve as resources for other departments. The analysis identifies the main functions or summaries of interlocking sets of behavioral contingencies, the aggregate products, and the receiving system demands that take place inside of the organization.

Comparing the IS to the OUGHT TO BE helps to identify and prioritize areas of improvement within an organization. Once those areas are identified, the analysis of the process should continue at a much more detailed level – presented in the next chapter.

Review

In an organization that you are familiar with:

- Present a one-page summary of the administrative structure (organizational chart).
- Prepare a department-function analysis and include the following:

  1. Specification of the responsibilities and measures for each function.
  2. Identification of the core, support, and integrating departments.

3. Create a one-page graphic representation.

- Explain the ways in which the department-function analysis describes the following:

  1. Summary of interlocking behavioral contingencies.
  2. Aggregate products.
  3. Receiving system demand.

- Compare the IS and the OUGHT TO be of the organization in terms of organizational structure and the department-function analysis. List potential areas for improvement.

Chapter 6
Task

CHAPTER 6
TASK

The difficult we do at once; the impossible takes a bit longer.

Anonymous Chinese proverb

Shoes on Sale[1]

Tom enjoyed reading the Sunday paper while sipping on a cup of coffee. As the shoe buyer for *VEN Inc.*, he always looked at the advertising circulars first. Reading an ad placed by his company, Tom almost dropped his cup of coffee. The sale price on his store's most popular athletic shoes, the Z-95, was listed at $60. The retail price was $75.

His annual bonus was based, in part, on the profit and sales from products he purchased. He worked hard to obtain a good price for the Z-95 because he was certain they would attract new clients to the store. The competitors were selling the same shoes for $80. *When will the printing errors end?* he furiously asked himself.

Tom tossed the circular on the floor. It was the first time the shoes were featured in the store's Sunday ad – an ad that took up more than half of the circular's first page and would appear in each of the store's markets. Tom estimated the losses that would result from the printing error: $15 for each pair of shoes; 500 pairs of shoes sold, on average, in each store; and 300 stores in the chain. The estimated loss was $7,500 per store with a grand total of $2,250,000!

Tom called Eva, the advertising department manager. *Did you read the paper?* he asked, in a distinctly rigid tone. *The Z-95 is practically being given away*. Eva had no idea what Tom was talking about, and the conversation ended as abruptly as it had started.

A retailer of clothing, shoes, and accessories for children, infants and adults, *VEN* opened in 1957. Founder Carl Pratt took a single, small store and grew it into a national chain with 300 locations: and a payroll of 20,000 people.

At 9 a.m. on Monday, Tom received notice of a meeting that would take place at 2 p.m. with representatives from the Purchasing and Advertising departments. Carl had requested the meeting to discuss the quality of the weekly circular.

In a calm – yet firm – voice, Carl began the meeting by recapping recent events. *In the last six months, we have made 18 significant mistakes in our weekly circular. To date, the estimated cost of those errors has reached $4 million.*

[1] *An earlier version of the story "Shoes on Sale" was published by M. E. Malott (2001a). Also see Garlock, 2001.*

Representatives from the Advertising department blamed the Purchasing department for providing incorrect information and last-minute changes. Purchasing department staff accused the Advertising department of printing the wrong price. *And what is the correct price?* demanded Eva. *All of you in the Purchasing department change the information you give us whenever you feel like it!*

Tom interrupted her. *You wouldn't see a donkey if it were standing right under your nose!* The discussion continued to escalate until Carl finally said, *That's enough!*

This was a daily problem. The interdepartmental processes were a complete mess. There was no effective communication and responsibilities were unclear. Was it possible to continue operating amid such internal chaos and still effectively compete in the market? The answer was NO. The competition was gaining on them and, in some markets, *VEN* was losing its competitive advantage and sales.

Task Analysis

The situation at *VEN* is not unique. Whenever there is crisis, people point fingers at each other instead of systems. It is easier to blame a scapegoat, particularly when the reasons behind the problem are unknown, than it is to take the time to study the sources of the problem.

Employees and managers are the victims of poorly-designed processes. Rather than blaming one another, it would be more effective to examine – in detail – the tasks that make up the organizational processes so that conflicts and inefficiencies can be identified. An objective and detailed task analysis is like taking an X-ray of the organization.

It takes time and dedication to study the tasks within processes. Skill and experience are needed because one can easily get lost in the details and miss the big picture. To avoid losing perspective, the study of tasks within processes should be done in a systematic fashion. This involves creating a general outline of the tasks within a process, analyzing what people do and produce, identifying the information-systems technology infrastructure, and determining the impact of task optimization.

General Tasks and Aggregate Products (Summary Map)

A process is a series of tasks – from a few to a hundred or even thousands – performed to accomplish a specific purpose. Therefore, before we begin a process analysis, it is helpful to create a frame of reference: a general outline. The outline consists of a graphic representation of the context in which the tasks take place. It is like having a view of the process from 20,000 feet above. The outline can appear graphically in an executive summary of the process. An executive summary consists of the following: identification, scope, subprocesses, units, general tasks, aggregate products, participants, uniqueness, and duration. Figure 6-1 shows the executive summary of the process that generates *VEN's* weekly circular.

Figure 6-1. Executive Summary of the Process that Generates VEN's Weekly Circular

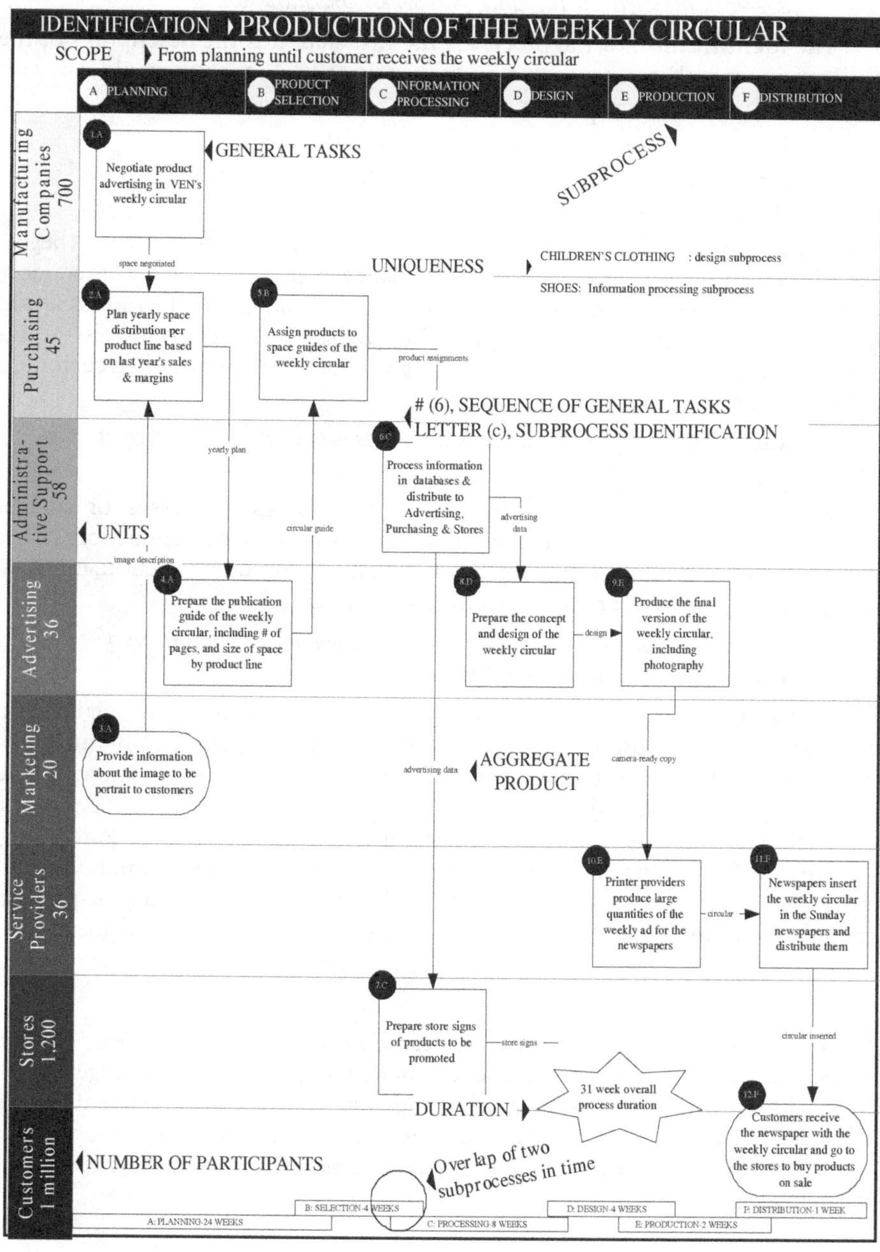

Concept 6-1. Process Executive Summary – graphic outline of the process. Includes identification, scope, subprocesses, units, general tasks, aggregate products, participants, uniqueness, and duration.

The **identification** of the process is the first step, it is the description of the metacontingency that we are analyzing. In the case of *VEN*, analysis would start with the weekly circular's production process.

Concept 6-2. Identification – a description of the process metacontingency being analyzed and where it fits into the overall functioning of the organization.

The **scope** refers to the limits of the process or metacontingency: where it begins and where it ends. The scope is arbitrary because every process is part of other, more complex, processes. The scope must be defined to avoid getting lost in irrelevant issues and not completing the analysis. The circular's production process begins when buyers plan which promotional products to include and ends when customers receive it with their Sunday newspapers.

Concept 6-3. Scope – the limits of the process metacontingency, where it begins and where it ends.

The main components of the overall process, **subprocesses** or smaller metacontingencies are listed in the order of occurrence. The production of the circular includes the following subprocesses: planning, product selection, information processing, design, production, and distribution.

Concept 6-4. Subprocesses – the main component metacontingencies of a larger process, listed in the order of occurrence.

The **units** involved in the process may be departments within the organization being analyzed – in addition to departments or groups of people from outside of the organization, such as suppliers, vendors, and customers. Without knowing who the participants are and what they do, it is impossible to understand the process.

Production of the *VEN's* weekly circular includes staff from Purchasing, Advertising, Administrative Support, and Marketing: as well as representatives from the 300 stores. The process also involves units outside of *VEN*, such as product manufacturers and service providers (including print shops and newspapers).

Concept 6-5. Units – departments or groups of individuals that participate in the process.

The participants are the people that carry out tasks within a process; in other words, those that participate in the set of interlocking behavioral contingencies. It is often amazing to discover the number of people affected by an apparently small process. The production process of the weekly circular involves 1,380 people from *VEN*, 700 manufacturing companies and approximately one million customers (receiving system).

Concept 6-6. Participants – individuals that play a role in the process and whose behavior are part of the interlocking behavioral contingencies being analyzed.

A **general task** consists of a group of activities carried out by different individuals and their aggregate product. In other words, a general task is a smaller metacontingency than that of a subprocess; a subprocess is a smaller metacontingency than that of a process; a process is a smaller metacontingency than that of an organization. As we have seen in the previous chapter, the aggregate product is the evidence remaining after the activity takes place. An individual behavioral product is the evidence left by the task of one individual. An **aggregate product** is the evidence left by the composition of many smaller products generated by individuals.

The difference between an individual behavioral product and an aggregate product is illustrated in an automobile assembly line. The product of each participant in the line consists of a car part with one more component added; the aggregate product is the finished automobile. At some point, each individual's product in the process ought to be identified. However, it is helpful that aggregate products are determined first in order to have an overall picture of the process.

Negotiating with vendors is an example of a general task in the process of producing the weekly circular. (Task 1.A in Figure 6-1.) Vendors pay or discount their selling price to *VEN* in exchange for advertising. This particular general task involves the actions and products of individuals working in the manufacturing companies that produce products sold by *VEN*. These manufacturers must analyze sales trends, customers' usage and market share. People from the Product Development department must meet with the Marketing and Sales department staff to discuss the pros and cons of advertising. Meanwhile, the Production department forecasts schedule capabilities to meet higher product demands resulting from special promotions. The aggregate product of all these specific tasks included in the general task 1.A, is space allocation for advertising vendor products in the weekly circular.

In Figure 6-1, general tasks are identified with a number, which indicates the sequence of that task in the process, and a letter, which refers to the subprocess being analyzed. For instance, the general task 1.A refers to the first general task involved in the process of producing the circular – which belongs to the planning subprocess. A summary map helps to identify the aggregate products of general tasks performed by multiple individuals. In other words, it allows us to understand the relationships of the metacontingencies involved in a process. A more detailed map helps to identify aggregate products of tasks performed by a single individual.

Concept 6-7. General Task – a summary of a metacontingency that forms part of a process; that is, a group of interlocking behavioral contingencies carried out by different individuals, the resulting aggregate product, and the source of receiving system demand.

Uniqueness refers to the variation of single subprocesses. It is common to discover that certain subprocesses are not implemented consistently. By identifying the variations (or uniqueness) within a process, we can appreciate some of its complexity. For instance, even though the production process of the weekly circular was fairly standard among the product-line buyers, certain tasks designed to promote shoes and children's clothing were unique. When it came to promoting shoes, the buyer basically carried out all the tasks typically assigned to administrative assistants, making the process of information processing a unique variation from other product lines. When it came to promoting children's clothing, the design subprocess was more elaborate, making the promotion of children's clothing unique.

Concept 6-8. Uniqueness – variations of single processes.

Duration indicates the time it takes to complete a process. It is helpful to determine how long each subprocess takes before attempting to calculate duration. The production time for each circular is 31 weeks, with planning – the subprocess with the greatest duration – taking up 24 of those weeks. Each department performed a number of tasks to produce the circular. For instance, the buyer alone had to review information from the previous year, select the products that had generated the most profit, review the sale price, review the report on the competitor's price, review the images in the electronic library, and handwrite a summary of the information in a list that would eventually go to the Advertising department. It is important to specify duration because streamlining processes usually involves reducing time expenditures.

Specific Tasks and Individual Products (Detailed Map)

In order to improve a process, it is important to understand the specific tasks and products generated by each participant. A detailed understanding of a process involves gathering information about what people do and produce. It also involves diagramming the relationship between the participants' tasks in a detailed map to visualize disconnects, redundancies and inefficiencies.

Information About What People Do and Produce

A **specific task** refers to one individual's action or set of actions and their aggregate product. There are two differences between a general task and a specific task. First, a general task includes many specific tasks performed by multiple performers from different units (metacontingency); a specific task is one or more actions performed by a single person. Second, the product of a general task is the aggregate result from several performers' products; the aggregate product of a specific task is that of only one performer. A general task is a metacontingency; however, a detailed task is not. The product-generating action or actions in a detailed task are done by one individual and not by the interaction of multiple individuals.

An example of a specific task is the generation of a report by one individual. The task produces one product – the report – but it requires several actions of that individual, such as locating past reports, reading e-mails, making calls, entering data into a computer, and printing.

Concept 6-9. Specific Task – an individual's action or set of actions and the resulting behavioral product.

The task-analysis guide is a tool for gathering the details of specific tasks in a process to facilitate understanding of what people do and produce. (See Figure 6-2.) Each task is thoroughly analyzed:

Who executes it? The person that carries out the task.

What does it consist of? Description of the task itself.

How long does it last? The approximate time it takes to complete the task.

What does it produce? Remaining proof after the task is completed.

What are the indispensable resources? The necessary resources to carry out the task.

Who receives the product? The person or group of people that receives the product. The person that receives the product from Task A is the person who executes Task B.

Figure 6-2. Task Analysis Guide

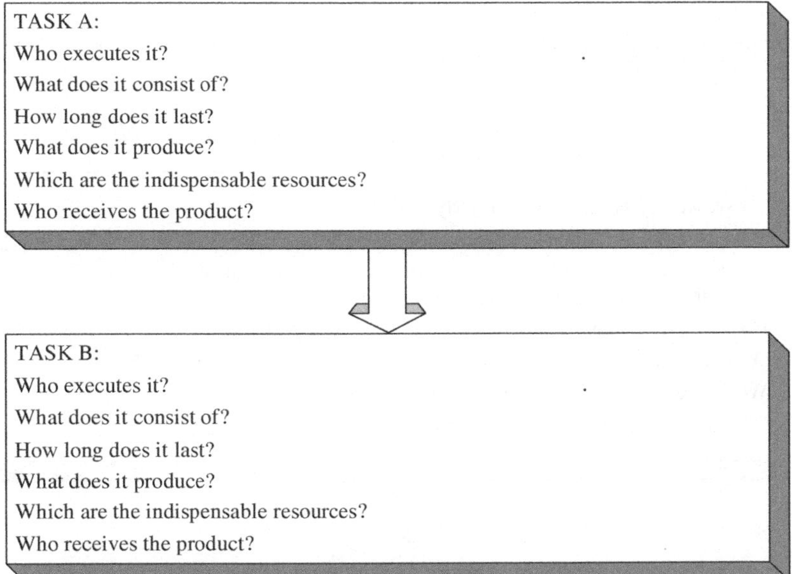
TASK A:
Who executes it?
What does it consist of?
How long does it last?
What does it produce?
Which are the indispensable resources?
Who receives the product?
TASK B:
Who executes it?
What does it consist of?
How long does it last?
What does it produce?
Which are the indispensable resources?
Who receives the product?

Concept 6-10. Task Analysis Guide – a tool for analyzing specific tasks within a process. It provides answers to the following questions: Who executes it? What does it consist of? How long does it last? What does it produce? What are the indispensable resources? Who receives the products?

Figure 6-3 shows how questions in the task analysis guide are integrated into a systems framework, where each task is described as a total performance system (TPS). Notice that the Task A product is a Task B resource and a Task A receiver is a Task B performer.

Figure 6-3. Task Analysis as a TPS

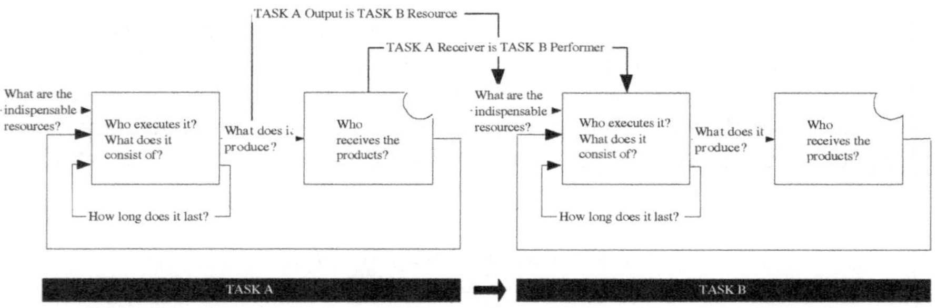
TASK A Output is TASK B Resource
TASK A Receiver is TASK B Performer
What are the indispensable resources?
Who executes it? What does it consist of?
What does it produce?
Who receives the products?
How long does it last?
What are the indispensable resources?
Who executes it? What does it consist of?
What does it produce?
Who receives the products?
How long does it last?
TASK A
TASK B

Figure 6-4 shows a task analysis of two tasks carried out within the data processing subprocesses of *VEN's* weekly circular.

Figure 6-4. Example of the Use of a Task Analysis Guide

TASK A: Key Product List # 1 in System B

Who executes it? Administrative assistant

What does it consist of? Keys information from Product List # 1 in System B, which transfers to the Advertising department

How long does it last? An average of fifteen minutes per list

What does it produce? Information from Product List # 1 in System B

Which are the indispensable resources? Product List # 1

Who receives the product? Advertising editor

TASK B: Key text printed from System B into System C

Who executes it? Advertising editor

What does it consist of? Keys text printed from System B into System C, which produces the weekly circular that goes to the printer

How long does it last? An average of twenty minutes per product

What does it produce? Circular text in System C

Which are the indispensable resources? Printed text from System B

Who receives the product? Designer 1

Information included in the task analysis guide should be gathered by interviewing and observing people performing the tasks. Sometimes it is more convenient to interview a group rather than individuals, especially when the participants play relatively small roles in the process and do not understand what the rest of the people do within that process. Complementing interviews with direct observation allows the gatherer to contrast verbal reports with what actually occurs – particularly helpful given the frequent discrepancies between what people say and what they do.

To avoid digression and speculation, it is helpful to focus on the end product generated by each task. For this reason, it is important to gather a sample of each task's product. In addition to this collection of products, it is helpful to know the type of information the participants use. This will be invaluable when designing the information-systems technology that supports process redesign.

To emphasize again – as done in the previous chapter: In order to understand a process, objective data needs to be gathered, direct observations performed, and actual products analyzed. Relying on verbal reports exclusively will give an inaccurate picture of the process.

Relationships Between Specific Tasks and Products

Once information is gathered about specific tasks and products within a process, the relationship between the participants' actions and their products should be studied. A detailed process map[2] is used, which consists of a graphic description of what goes on in the process. It contains all the subprocesses, units and uniqueness presented in Figure 6-1 – the executive summary of the process; but it includes specific tasks, rather than general.

> *Concept 6-11. Detailed Process Map – graphic representation of the relationship between specific tasks and products among individuals and units involved in a process.*

Figure 6-5 shows an example of how to include each specific task within a detailed process map. The buyer must determine which products to advertise in the weekly circular.

Figure 6-6 shows a detailed process map of a general task: task 6.C of the executive summary presented in Figure 6-1. The general task 6.C was part of the information processing subprocess. It consisted of processing information in the existing databases and distributing the results to the Advertising and Purchasing departments (as well as the stores).

[2] *See Rummler & Brache (1995) for other versions of cross-functional maps.*

Figure 6-5. Representation of a Specific Task within a Detailed Map

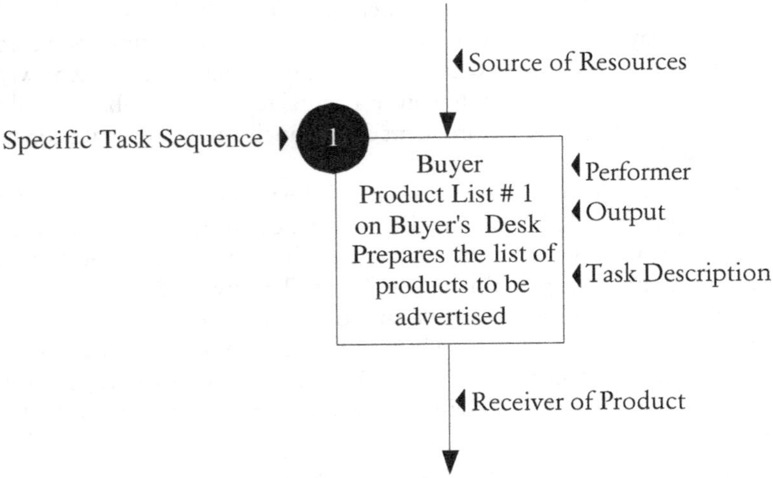

Source of Resources

Specific Task Sequence 1

Buyer
Product List # 1
on Buyer's Desk
Prepares the list of
products to be
advertised

Performer
Output
Task Description

Receiver of Product

The personnel of the Administrative Support department are mainly responsible for processing information. The general task 6.C, however, involves 42 specific tasks and 15 participants interacting between the Purchasing and Advertising departments, in addition to the stores. All tasks shaded in the detailed process map would not be necessary if the list of promotional products was precise and complete the first time the buyer generated it.

The following was learned from this graphic representation of the detailed process map:

1. The general task of processing/distributing information, pertaining to the promotional products, involved 42 specific tasks and 15 people from four different units: the Purchasing, Advertising, and Administrative Support departments – and the stores.
2. The 42 specific tasks are part of the information-processing subprocess and account for only one general task in the production of the weekly circular (Task 6.C from Figure 6-1).
3. The analysis shows that the process is ineffective and redundant. The shaded tasks are not necessary. The information that passed from one place to another is incomplete or incorrect. The buyer and the buyer's assistant provide partial or inaccurate information, creating problems for the rest of the participants: including the stores and the Advertising and Purchasing departments.
4. There is a fair amount of micro-management: Four people – the buyer, the buyer's assistant, the advertising editor, and the advertising manager from the stores – monitor what the administrative assistant

does. Too much double-checking takes the responsibility for providing accurate information away from the administrative assistant, ignores the responsibility of the buyer and buyer's assistant to provide the correct information in the first place, and generates unnecessary work for everyone.

5. There appears to be an unhealthy separation of duties between jobs. For instance, only the administrative assistant keyboards information into certain databases and distribute it from one place to another, even though it might be more practical and cost effective for the whole process if the buyer or buyer's assistant perform some of those tasks. For instance, a buyer writes the information on a form and gives it to the administrative assistant to enter in the database; and this pattern is repeated multiple times as information is corrected or changed. So, rather than one person having to redo the tasks, each change requires the actions of at least two people.

In summary, let's review the steps necessary to streamline a process so that redundant tasks are eliminated and some tasks are added/modified to generate the expected products.

1. Define the aggregate products that contribute to an organization's competitiveness and long-term survival.
2. Create a summary map that provides the "big picture" of the process, to avoid getting lost in the details later. The map consists of an analysis of the metacontingencies involved in the process. Specify the scope, the main subprocesses (or less complex metacontingencies), the units or departments participating in the process, the general tasks, the aggregate products, the participants, the unique variations of the process, and the duration.
3. Gather data on what people do and produce using the Task Analysis Guide.
4. Diagram the relationship between the tasks and products generated by each participant in a detailed process map.
5. Highlight areas for improvement. Study the detailed tasks in the map and look for redundancies tasks that produce the same or similar products by different individuals (this will help in deciding which tasks to eliminate).
6. Identify needed tasks that should be modified because the product that they generate does not meet the expected criteria of quality, volume, or cost. Afterwards, highlight those tasks and specify the required modifications.
7. Identify gaps (missing products) in the process and determine the tasks that most effectively and efficiently could generate those products.

Figure 6-6. Detailed Map of the Information Processing Subprocess

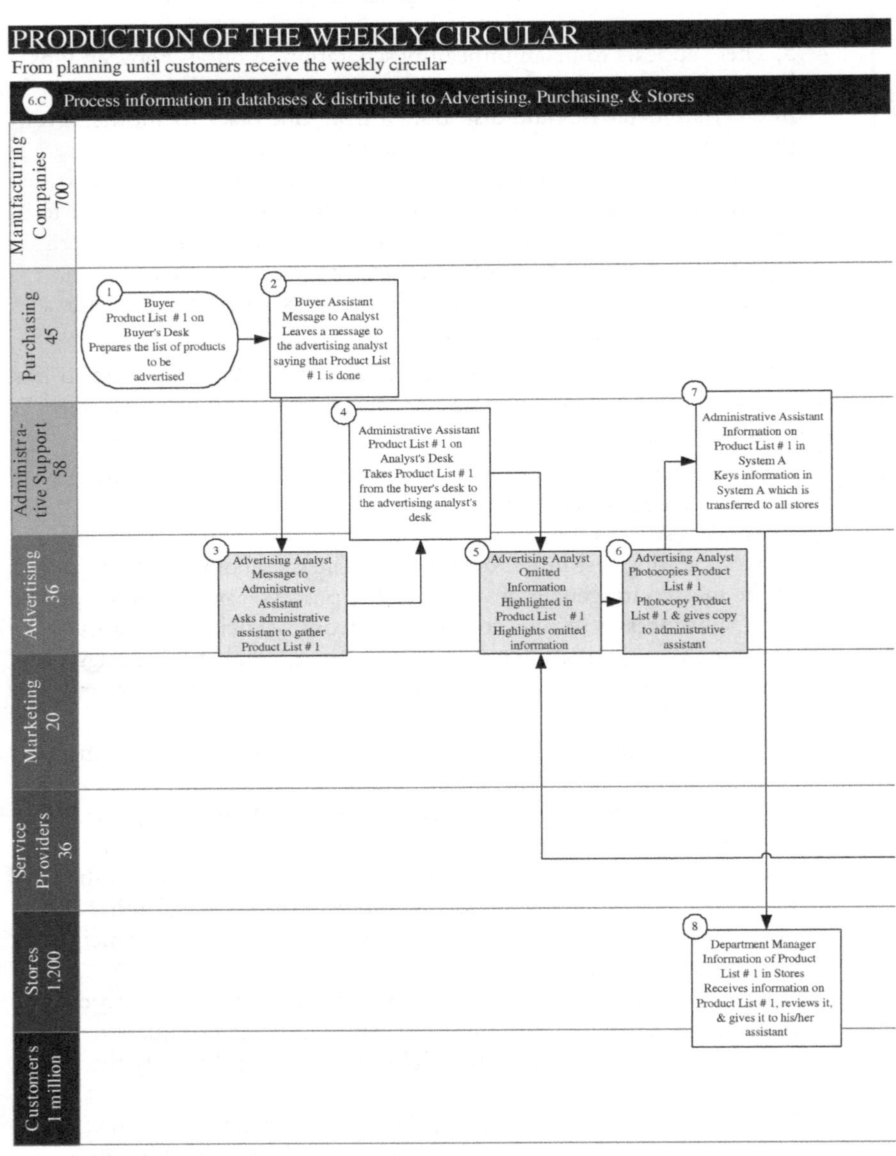

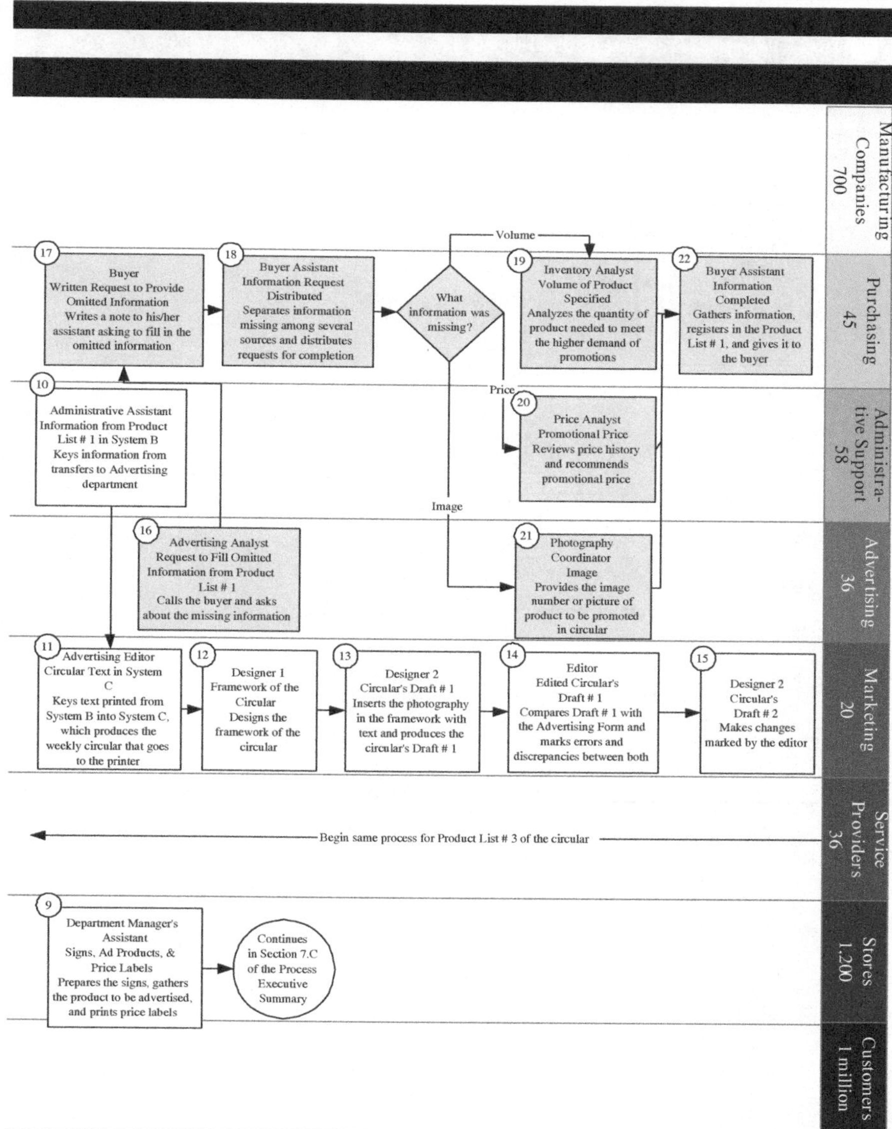

Manufacturing Companies 700
Purchasing 45
Administrative Support 58
Advertising 36
Marketing 20
Service Providers 36
Stores 1,200
Customers 1 million
17 Buyer Written Request to Provide Omitted Information Writes a note to his/her assistant asking to fill in the omitted information
18 Buyer Assistant Information Request Distributed Separates information missing among several sources and distributes requests for completion
What information was missing?
Volume
Price
Image
19 Inventory Analyst Volume of Product Specified Analyzes the quantity of product needed to meet the higher demand of promotions
22 Buyer Assistant Information Completed Gathers information, registers in the Product List # 1, and gives it to the buyer
10 Administrative Assistant Information from Product List # 1 in System B Keys information from transfers to Advertising department
20 Price Analyst Promotional Price Reviews price history and recommends promotional price
16 Advertising Analyst Request to Fill Omitted Information from Product List # 1 Calls the buyer and asks about the missing information
21 Photography Coordinator Image Provides the image number or picture of product to be promoted in circular
11 Advertising Editor Circular Text in System C Keys text printed from System B into System C, which produces the weekly circular that goes to the printer
12 Designer 1 Framework of the Circular Designs the framework of the circular
13 Designer 2 Circular's Draft # 1 Inserts the photography in the framework with text and produces the circular's Draft # 1
14 Editor Edited Circular's Draft # 1 Compares Draft # 1 with the Advertising Form and marks errors and discrepancies between both
15 Designer 2 Circular's Draft # 2 Makes changes marked by the editor
Begin same process for Product List # 3 of the circular
9 Department Manager's Assistant Signs, Ad Products, & Price Labels Prepares the signs, gathers the product to be advertised, and prints price labels
Continues in Section 7.C of the Process Executive Summary

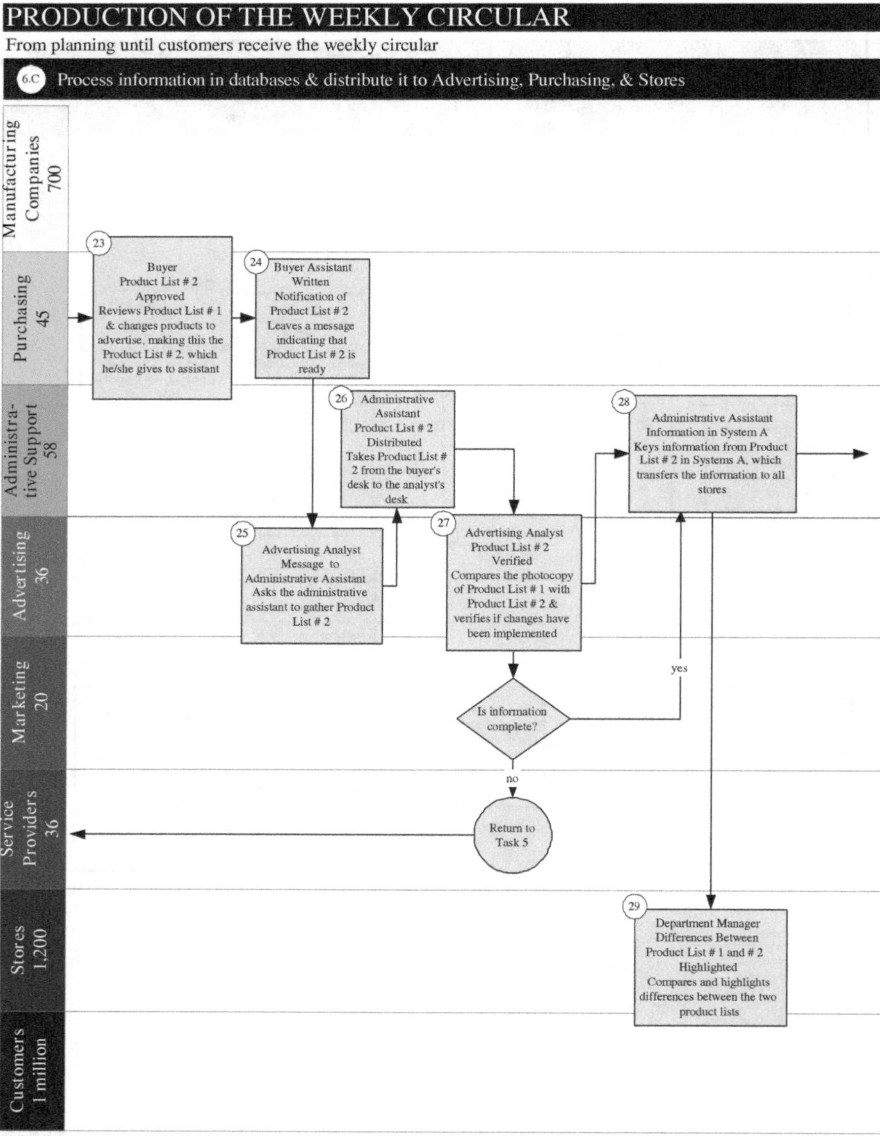
PRODUCTION OF THE WEEKLY CIRCULAR
From planning until customers receive the weekly circular
6.C Process information in databases & distribute it to Advertising, Purchasing, & Stores
Manufacturing Companies 700
Purchasing 45
Administrative Support 58
Advertising 36
Marketing 20
Service Providers 36
Stores 1,200
Customers 1 million
23 Buyer Product List # 2 Approved Reviews Product List # 1 & changes products to advertise, making this the Product List # 2, which he/she gives to assistant
24 Buyer Assistant Written Notification of Product List # 2 Leaves a message indicating that Product List # 2 is ready
25 Advertising Analyst Message to Administrative Assistant Asks the administrative assistant to gather Product List # 2
26 Administrative Assistant Product List # 2 Distributed Takes Product List # 2 from the buyer's desk to the analyst's desk
27 Advertising Analyst Product List # 2 Verified Compares the photocopy of Product List # 1 with Product List # 2 & verifies if changes have been implemented
Is information complete?
yes
no
Return to Task 5
28 Administrative Assistant Information in System A Keys information from Product List # 2 in Systems A, which transfers the information to all stores
29 Department Manager Differences Between Product List # 1 and # 2 Highlighted Compares and highlights differences between the two product lists

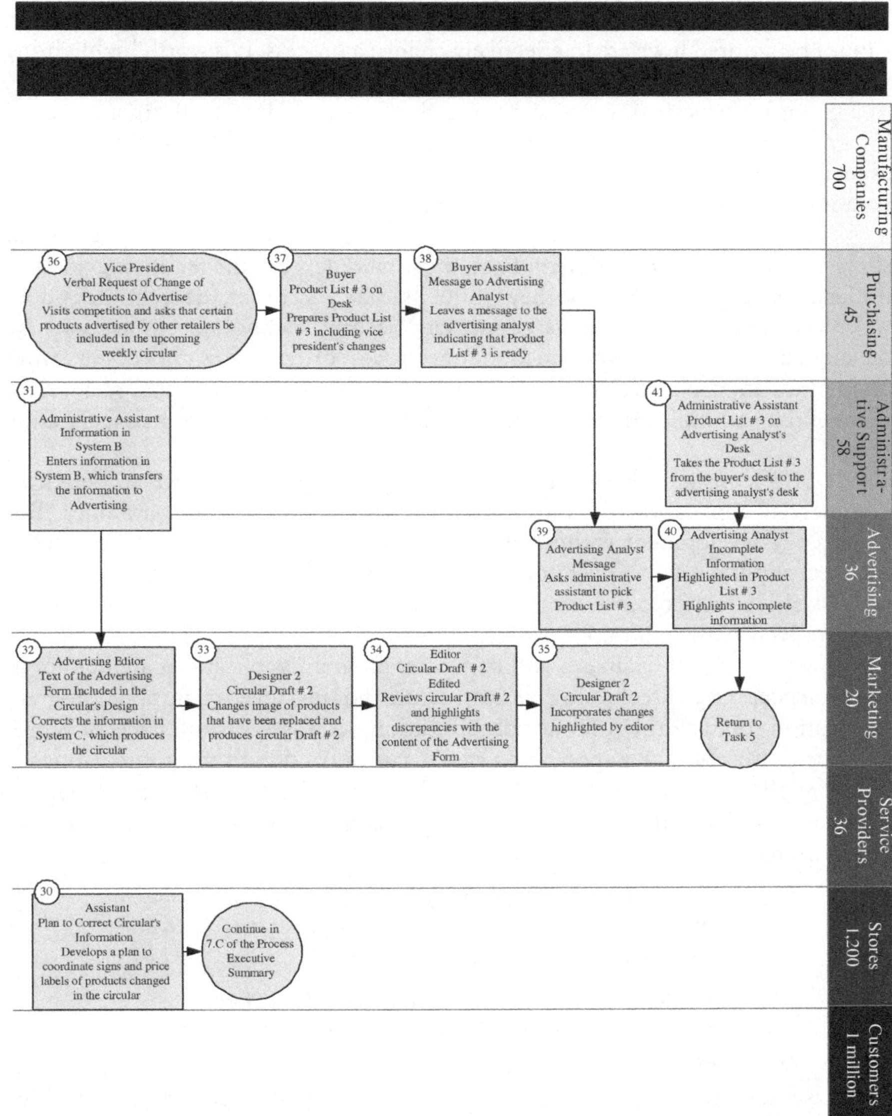
Manufacturing Companies 700
Purchasing 45
Administrative Support 58
Advertising 36
Marketing 20
Service Providers 36
Stores 1,200
Customers 1 million
36 Vice President Verbal Request of Change of Products to Advertise Visits competition and asks that certain products advertised by other retailers be included in the upcoming weekly circular
37 Buyer Product List # 3 on Desk Prepares Product List # 3 including vice president's changes
38 Buyer Assistant Message to Advertising Analyst Leaves a message to the advertising analyst indicating that Product List # 3 is ready
31 Administrative Assistant Information in System B Enters information in System B, which transfers the information to Advertising
41 Administrative Assistant Product List # 3 on Advertising Analyst's Desk Takes the Product List # 3 from the buyer's desk to the advertising analyst's desk
39 Advertising Analyst Message Asks administrative assistant to pick Product List # 3
40 Advertising Analyst Incomplete Information Highlighted in Product List # 3 Highlights incomplete information
32 Advertising Editor Text of the Advertising Form Included in the Circular's Design Corrects the information in System C, which produces the circular
33 Designer 2 Circular Draft # 2 Changes image of products that have been replaced and produces circular Draft # 2
34 Editor Circular Draft # 2 Edited Reviews circular Draft # 2 and highlights discrepancies with the content of the Advertising Form
35 Designer 2 Circular Draft 2 Incorporates changes highlighted by editor
Return to Task 5
30 Assistant Plan to Correct Circular's Information Develops a plan to coordinate signs and price labels of products changed in the circular
Continue in 7.C of the Process Executive Summary

Information-Technology Infrastructure

As shown in Chapter 2, a processing system involves much more than behavior and interlocking behavioral contingencies. It also involves the interaction of the behavior with the resources in the system. The understanding of that interaction cannot be ignored if we are to effectively change a process. It is worth highlighting the interaction between behavior and the information available in the system.

Complex processes, especially those that involve a lot of information, need integrated technology to function efficiently. It is not unusual for an organization, especially a large one, to process millions of data records a day. Undoubtedly, the data infrastructure makes a difference in people's actions.

Technology often fails to facilitate processes because of two significant shortcomings in its development. First, those who develop the technology do not understand the process because they are not its users. As a result, the technology does not meet the needs of the users/performers. Second, technology applications are developed in silos; the development of one process often creates unnecessary work and redundancy in other processes. These two limitations in technology development end up complicating employees' process-related tasks rather than facilitating them.

It is a constant dilemma, for most organizations, whether to purchase commercial applications – and customize them – or develop new ones. But technology development, without understanding what people do within the process, can be costly and useless. Therefore, the ideal scenario is one where process changes actually drive technology – not the other way around – process designers work cooperatively with technology experts.

The concepts of databases and computer program applications are helpful in the understanding of technology infrastructure. For instance, a computer program application could be any commercial application, such as Microsoft Excel or Word. Of course, any computer application can be customized to fit the particular needs of the application can be customized to fit particular needs of an organization. Databases are depositories of data, which are manipulated with computer program applications.

> *Concept 6-12. Computer Program Application – list of instructions in a programming language that tells a computer to perform a certain task and allows the user to manipulate information.*
>
> *Concept 6-13. Database – systematically arranged collection of computer data, structured so that it can be automatically retrieved or manipulated.*

It is important that every performer has the data and information needed for process optimization. Whether or not performers have access to the critical data – and are able to manipulate the information with technology – is an essential issue in process redesign. Process designers should have a minimal understanding of the data, know where the information is stored and possess the ability to manipulate it. Table 6-1 shows a way to analyze information technology.

Table 6-1. Information-Technology Analysis

Fields	Databases					
	Item	Advertising	Image	Layout	Display	Pricing
Item Number	X A, B, C	X				X
Item Code	X					
Item Description	X					
Customer ID Number						
Retail Price						X
Purchasing Price						X
Sales Price						X
Image Code Number			X			
Image Description			X			
Image Date			X			
Page Layout				X		
Items Advertised				X		
Advertised Text				X		
Advertising Start Date		X				
Advertising End Date		X				
Shelf Location					X	

In Table 6-1, each row lists an information field relevant to the advertising process at *VEN*. The top row identifies several databases; the "X" identifies databases where a specific field is located; and the letters in italics, in the top left quadrant, refers to various applications that can manipulate a specific data field from a database. For instance, the item-number field is located in the item, advertising, and pricing databases.

It is also helpful to map how information travels within a technology infrastructure, using the information from Table 6-1. The map in Figure 6-7 shows the technology infrastructure used in all of the advertising processes, including the production of *VEN's*, weekly circular. The information system technological infrastructure includes eight databases in the advertising process, six of which consist of applications exclusively for advertising and two of which interact with other corporate processes (such as the pricing system). The databases, most of which are not compatible, are not interrelated. Consequently, performers in the process must manually extract data from a database, manipulate the information, and enter it in a different database using different applications. Such complications make the process inefficient and prone to errors.

Figure 6-7. Map of the Existing Information-Technology Infrastructure at VEN Inc.

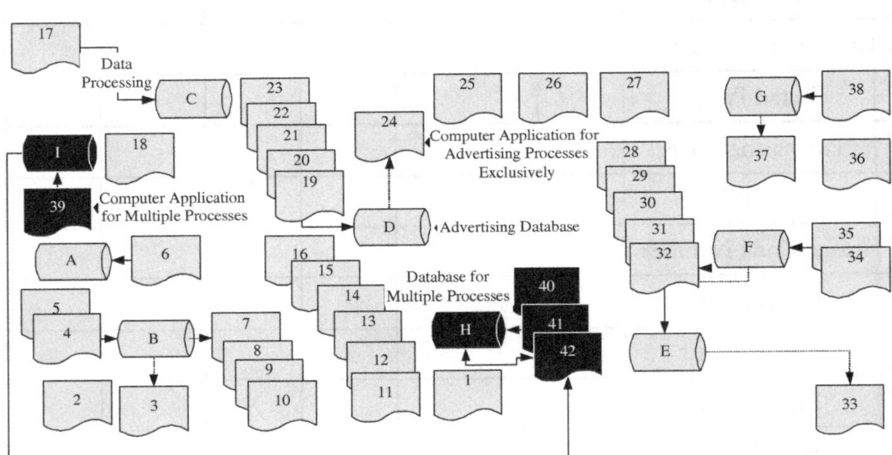

A technology map, unlike a detailed process map, does not include actions of individuals. It only refers to how information gets from one point to another. The analysis of the technology infrastructure answers some critical questions in process design, such as: Where is the information located? How can the data be accessed? Can performers manipulate the data? Do the performers have the information needed to do the job?

Understanding how technology impacts a person's job assists in development and increases the likelihood it will produce efficient processes. It also assists in identifying interfaces between departments that a process map may not highlight.

Impact of Task Optimization

The task analysis concludes by determining which specific tasks should remain, which could be eliminated, and which should be modified. This step is done after the detailed map is analyzed. In order for *VEN* to produce its weekly circular, there are some critical tasks that should happen within various subprocesses:

1. The buyer provides a list of promotional products and information

such as price and product description.
2. The advertising coordinator creates an outline of the circular, based on information provided by the buyer.
3. The designer develops the page(s) using product information provided by the buyer.
4. The administrative assistant sends the final version of the circular to the printing shop.
5. The circular is printed.
6. An employee from the print shop delivers the circular to the newspaper.
7. Newspaper employees insert the circular in the Sunday edition.
8. The newspaper distributor delivers the papers – with the weekly circular tucked inside – to potential and current customers.

After studying the specific tasks in the detailed process map, and sorting the dispensable from the indispensable, is obvious that streamlining production of *VEN's* weekly circular is possible. Simply by eliminating redundancies, many specific tasks can be omitted.

But before attempting to change the process, impact measures of process improvement must be determined. For instance, by examining the potential impact of simplifying the production of the weekly circular using volume, quality, quantity, and cost measures.

Volume. One of the six subprocesses, Information Processing, consists of 42 specific tasks. If the remaining five subprocesses required that many, the whole production process would include more than 250 specific tasks. If all of the redundant specific tasks were reduced (refer to the shaded areas in Figure 6-6), then 71 percent of these specific tasks could be eliminated from the circular's weekly production process. The number of steps is one of the volume measures used in this process. Another relevant measure is the number of circulars produced. It is possible that, by altering the process, it may be profitable to increase or decrease the number of ads published.

Quality. A quality process does not produce errors. There are two types of errors – print and process errors. *VEN's* print errors appeared as the result of its process errors. Staff members had made 18 significant errors in a six-month period: a loss of $4 million in revenue.

Sometimes these process errors were detected and corrected before the circular was sent to the printer: a costly step because of the number of people involved in the correction process. If an error was not detected in the pre-press stage, it became a print error.

The process errors consisted of discrepancies between the input and product information processed in a specific task. For example, an error would occur when the price of the product provided by the buyer did not coincide with the price that the administrative assistant entered into the database.

Duration. The entire production process took 31 weeks. This slow pace created a problem: The price of the products advertised was vulnerable to competitor's price changes. Initially, Tom decided to sell the Z-95 athletic shoes for $85; however, the competitors surprised him by advertising a sale price of $80. Two days before sending the final version to the print shop, Tom changed the price. He decided that an aggressive price would motivate new customers to purchase the shoes at *VEN* stores. The Advertising department's copy editor was baffled, as Tom had already changed the price five times. On one of the ad-copy drafts, Tom himself had mistakenly promoted the Z-95 for $60 – the price printed on the circular. Nobody caught the error in the process itself: neither Tom, his assistant, the designer nor the copy editor. Shortening the duration of the process might eliminate the need for price changes.

Cost. *VEN* currently devotes 160 hours each month to advertising its shoes in the circular. Between the Publishing and the Purchasing departments, 40 hours a week (or one full-time employee equivalent) are invested in preparing the shoe ads. Women's clothing requires even more hours because it has more ads. Combined, the three product lines require 487 hours each month: the equivalent to more than three full-time employees.

The Publishing and Purchasing departments invest 5,844 working hours each year (487 hours per month **x** 12 months) to promote accessories, shoes, and women's clothing in the weekly circular. If the average cost per hour is $30 (including benefits), monthly costs are $14,610 (487 hours per month **x** $30 per hour). The annual cost to produce the promotional ads for accessories, shoes, and women's clothing is $175,320 ($14,610 per month **x** 12 months). If the company's remaining six product lines are taken into account, the annual labor cost for producing the circular is approximately $1,051,120 per year.

In addition to the labor cost is the price of fixing detected errors after the circular is printed. The right price correction needs to be transmitted to the stores so each of the 300 locations can alter its pricing system. Correcting the price prevents discrepancies between an item's tagged version and the one scanned at the cash register. Generally, the price correction is not a problem if the actual price is lower than the circular's advertised price; however, if the error is the other way around, and the advertised product scans higher at the register, customers become unhappy.

An analysis of the impact of process optimization is needed to determine if it is worth changing the process. In the case of *VEN,* it was. The production process of its advertising circular had significant potential for reduction of tasks, duration, and cost. This would improve the quality of information handling in the processing and printing of the weekly circular.

Conclusions

Behavioral systems analysis, as we have studied so far, goes from general to specific metacontingencies: the study of the macrosystem, the organization, the main processes in the organization, subprocess, and general tasks. Such analysis is a necessary component of the method presented in this book to change organizations. We can't change organizations effectively unless we understand their components and dynamics.

The method presented thus far brings about the orderly part of the paradox of organizational change. Organizational processes can be so complex that they look chaotic and unpredictable. However, the method of analysis suggests that there is a systematic way through which processes evolve.

Aggregated products in all four organizational levels evolve based on environmental selection. The macrosystem's aggregate products are determined by the demands of a larger macrosystem; an organization's overall aggregate product is determined by the demands of its customers; a department or process's aggregate product is determined by the demands of other departments or processes; and a general task's aggregate product is determined by demands of other general tasks in a process. In spite of the fact that systems at all levels are dynamic and chaotic, the way they evolve is constant and orderly – as the analysis of behavioral systems shows. Here, it is the paradoxical nature of change.

The transition from metacontingency analysis to behavior of a single individual lies in the specific task. The specific task involves an action or actions of one single individual and a product. There are no interlocking behavioral contingencies at the level of a detailed task.

The transition from systems analysis to individual behavior allows us to see that, among the thousands of tasks that make up an organization, there are some tasks more critical than others for an organization's long-term survival. The fourth component in the model for change refers to the detailed analysis of the organization viewed as a system. It consists of detailing the tasks that make up the processes. (See Figure 6-8.)

In this chapter, we studied a systematic approach for task analysis within the organizational processes. This strategy consists of (1) creating a summary of the process; (2) analyzing the information systems technological infrastructure; (3) detailing specific tasks and products; and (4) determining the impact of task optimization through measures of performance.

1. The process executive summary outlines the general tasks in the process – the least complex metacontingency that we have studied. The executive summary has the following components: identification, scope, subprocesses, units, general tasks, aggregate products, participants, uniqueness, and duration.
2. The analysis of specific tasks and products is carried out using two different tools: a task analysis guide and a detailed process map. The task analysis guide allows gathering of information. It includes answers to the following questions: Who executes it? What does the task consist of? What does it produce? How long does it take? Which are the indispensable resources? Who receives the product? The detailed process map graphically represents the relationship between the specific

Figure 6-8. Levels 1-4 of the Behavioral Systems Engineering Model

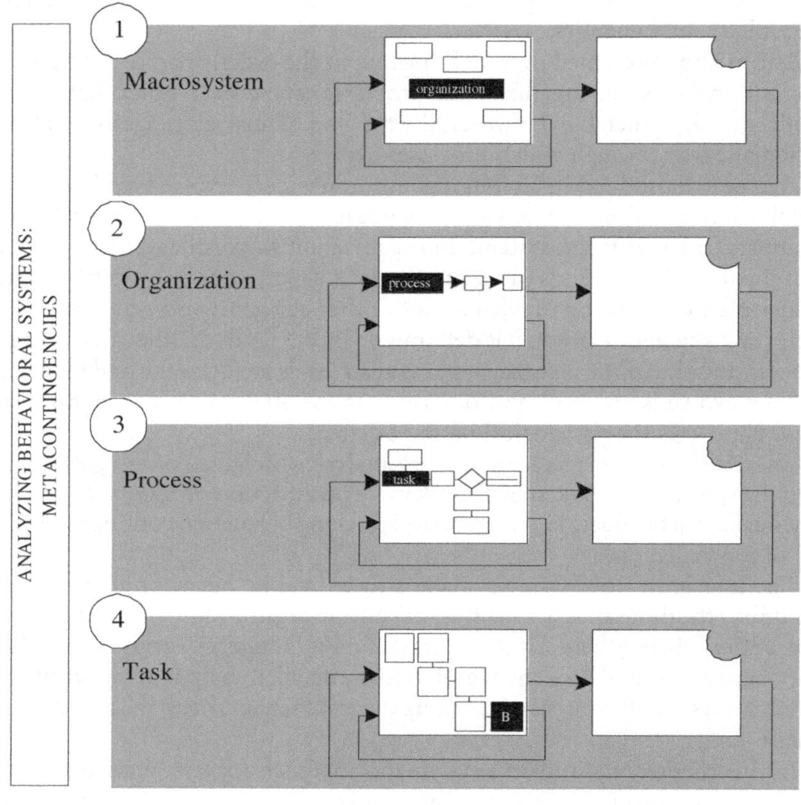

tasks and products among participants.
3. The analysis of the information-technology infrastructure consists of identifying the databases, operational systems, and applications with which the participants interact. It is common for the existing technology to complicate the processes. The information technology is a critical resource of a processing system that cannot be ignored when analyzing interlocking behavioral contingencies.
4. The detailed task analysis concludes by determining the impact of process optimization based on measures of the current process.

Review

Identify a process in your organization and perform a detailed analysis of what people do within that process. Follow these steps:

- Prepare an executive summary for that process. Specify process identification, scope, subprocesses, units, general tasks, aggregate products, participants, uniqueness, and duration.

- Analyze the information systems technology used in the process.
- Use a task analysis guide to gather information about what people do and produce.
- Create a detailed process map to diagram the relationship between the participants' tasks and their products in the process.
- Indicate the method and units of measure that you would use to determine the potential impact of task optimization in the process.

Chapter 7
Behavior

PART I

CHAPTER 7
BEHAVIOR: PART I

Man is what he does!

André Malraux (1901–1976)[1]

Hell on Earth[2]

I was in Northern Thailand, giving a lecture on the behavioral analysis of traffic safety, when – at the end of my presentation – a man approached me: *Dr. Maria Malott, I am Dr. Chang Sang. I work for the State Hospital and I urge you to visit us and give a talk to our doctors, nurses, and staff about improving traffic safety in the community.*

Tomorrow is my last day in town and I have made other plans, I replied.

Dr. Sang insisted. *Dr. Malott, traffic accidents are a very serious problem in our country, even worse in our state. We have tried everything but it has been of no avail. We need to learn how to handle this problem from a behavioral systems perspective.*[3]

Dr. Sang was so persistent that he convinced me to give a talk the next day. What neither of us knew at the time, however, was that I would be the one who would learn the most from this experience.

As we approached the hospital the following morning, I noticed a large group of people waiting outside. Directly in front of the main gate were roughly two hundred adults and children in a roofless, open patio. They had brought with them silverware and bags filled with clothes and other belongings. It seemed as if they had literally moved in.

What is this? I asked, shaking my head in disbelief. *They are the relatives of our hospital's patients*, Dr. Sang said. *They have nowhere else to stay so they remain outside to look after their hospitalized relatives during visiting hours.*

The hospital's reception area had horrifying pictures of traffic accidents posted on walls. Adjacent to the pictures were written statements such as, *Wear helmets. Do not drink and drive. Drunk driving is a crime.*

[1] *André Malraux (1901-1976) was a French novelist, archeologist, art theorist, political activist, and public official.*

[2] *Traffic accidents are a serious global problem: 1,171,000 people die and 10 million people suffer physical injuries in traffic accidents each year.*

[3] *Traffic accidents are a serious problem in Thailand. Leonard Evans (1991) reported that in 1987 there were 17 vehicles for every 1,000 inhabitants, and 5 deaths per 1,000 vehicles in Thailand. On the other hand, in 1989 there were 778 vehicles for every 1,000 inhabitants and 24 deaths for every 1,000 vehicles in the United States.*

Dr. Sang watched silently as I read the messages and looked at the pictures. *For at least 10 years, we have been importing a large number of inexpensive motorcycles,* he said. *The motorcycles are the most financially affordable means of transportation today, although motorcycle accidents are often fatal or result in severe brain damage.*

After a pause, he continued. *If we could make people wear helmets, we could save so many lives! We have tried everything we can think of with no success. People don't wear helmets because they are uncomfortable, especially with our region's unbearable heat. Besides, half of all traffic accidents involve alcohol intoxication.*

Dr. Sang took me to the women's ward first. There, we saw patients of all ages suffering from the loss of amputated limbs, blindness, and other tribulations. It was the same story when we walked through the men's ward.

Once I was convinced that I had seen enough misery, Dr. Sang said, *Allow me to show you one last room: the emergency room. These are the patients that will die within the next 48 hours.*

I could not believe my eyes. Men, women, and children lying on separate beds in a single room … a man with two recently amputated limbs … another with an open wound in his skull. There were no curtains, no sheets, and no covers. There was only anguish and despair. It was like hell on earth.

I recalled the "right of personal freedom" arguments I had heard so many times when lecturing about traffic accidents. *We ought to have the freedom to choose the speed with which we drive; we ought to be able to choose whether or not to use seatbelts. After all, these are our lives.* However, right in front of my eyes – in an emergency room in Northern Thailand – was the evidence why no one should have the freedom to cause physical harm to others. Poor traffic safety was not just a problem for the perpetrators but the community, its families, and individuals.

On our way to the auditorium, where I was scheduled to speak, I heard a bell and a voice in Thai coming through the loudspeakers. Dr. Sang informed me that they were announcing my lecture.

Approximately 90 people entered the small auditorium and sat down. I asked for a glass of water and took a deep breath. At that moment, I decided to leave my notes aside and change my talk. This was the first time that I wished to speak with the help of an interpreter, so I could think of what to say next while the interpreter translated.

How many of you have a relative or close friend who has been involved in a serious traffic accident? I asked. Approximately 70 people raised their hand. *How many of you think that it is relatively easy to put on a helmet?* All raised their hands. *How many of you know that we would save many lives if we wore helmets?* All raised their hands.

Traffic accidents are the number one cause of death in Thailand, I continued. *But what I saw in this hospital today speaks louder than any statistic because it showed me human suffering. I don't have to tell you how tragic this problem is, you are the ones that live it day after day.*

Putting on a helmet is a relatively simple behavior. Why, then, is it so uncommon for people to wear helmet's? Why is it so difficult for people to follow simple behavioral rules?

Functional Assessment (Part I)

The audience knew that if people wore helmets, many lives could be saved[4]. They witnessed every day the tragic consequences of a nation not adopting preventative measures.[5] Likewise, the general community was aware that helmet use would prevent trauma and death. They knew it from the ongoing campaigns on radio, television, newspapers, and roadside billboards. They knew it from their own loss of family members due to preventable traffic accidents. Yet, knowing was not enough.

We often assume that people do not do what they are supposed to do because they lack the knowledge. So we overwhelm them with memos, informational meetings, and training programs that have no impact. If knowledge was sufficient to change what people do, behavioral change would be easy.

When information-sharing efforts do not work, we assume that people lack motivation and willingness; therefore, we accuse them of being lazy or having no initiative. In other words, we blame them –victims of a poorly designed system. But as we have seen in previous chapters, blaming takes us nowhere – other than detracting attention from other improvement alternatives.

So why is it that the people in Dr. Sang's community fail to wear helmets if they know that compliance could save their lives? If the failure to wear helmets was not due to lack of knowledge or lack of desire, what was the cause? A functional assessment provides answers to these questions. It helps observers understand why desired behavior does not happen at all: or why undesired behavior happens so often[6].

Functional assessment is based on the law of effect, on the assumption that behavior is determined by the environment and not by individuals' internal attributes. We will be more successful affecting what people do if we know what maintains their current behavior. That is why functional assessment is a pre-requisite for behavioral change. A functional assessment consists of providing answers to the following questions:

1. What behavior is under analysis?
2. How often does it occur?
3. Whose behavior is under analysis?
4. What is the consequence?

[4] *For impact of the helmet-use law, "Bicycle Helmet Use in British Columbia ... " 2000, April.*

[5] *For information on the use of helmets and their impact on traffic safety, refer to Chenier & Evans (1987); Thompson, Rivara, & Thompson (1996).*

[6] *For a behavioral analysis of safety, refer to Krause, 1997; McSween, 1995; Sulzer-Azaroff, 1998.*

5. Which are the antecedent stimuli?
6. Does the contingency directly control behavior?
7. What type of contingency is it?

Concept 7-1. Functional Assessment – a study of the environmental relations that maintain behavior.

In this chapter, we will review questions one through six. In the following chapter, we will study question seven as well as the relationship between tasks and behavior.

What Behavior Is Under Analysis?

Behavior is an action of an organism. For example, putting on a helmet is a behavior. To define behavior clearly, it is helpful to distinguish action from a condition that lacks movement. Researchers use the "dead man test"[7] – if a dead man can do it, it is not a behavior. The lack of action is not behavior: a dead man can have a helmet on. Behavior indicates activity such as writing, walking, talking, and putting on a helmet.

Concept 7-2. Dead Man Test – if a dead man can do it, it is not a behavior.

Concept 7-3. Behavior – an organism's action.

It is important to specify which behavior is under analysis. Although that sounds easy, it is sometimes a challenge. Identifying examples and non-examples of the chosen action is helpful when defining a target behavior. For instance, the behavior of interest to Dr. Sang was putting on a helmet before getting on a motorcycle. A non-example was putting on a hat.

How Often Does It Occur?

The only way to know if we are effectively changing what people do is by measuring behavior before and after our intervention. The most typically used behavioral measures are frequency and rate of responding. Frequency consists of number of responses and rate consists of number of responses per unit of time. For instance, we might want to measure the number of traffic violations received (frequency) or the number of late arrivals to work per week (rate). We might also be interested in measuring other aspects of behaviors, such as force, latency, and duration.

Whose Behavior Is Under Analysis?

We ought to know who is performing the behavior under analysis. For instance, we can study the behavior of motorcycle drivers and passengers putting on a helmet.

[7] *Ogden Lindsley invented this concept in 1965, referenced in Malott, Malott & Troyan, 2000.*

Or we could study other behaviors, such as alcohol consumption or speeding of motorcycle drivers. We would not study behavior of individuals who are not relevant to the problem we are analyzing.

What Is the Consequence?

The consequence of behavior consists of a stimulus, event, object, or condition that is a result of the behavior and affects its future occurrences. In other words, there is a causal relationship between the response and that stimulus, event, object, or condition. A causal relationship is what is known as a contingent relationship. I will use the term "after" and consequence interchangeably in the rest of the text.

> *Concept 7-4. After Condition – the consequence of behavior; in other words, a stimulus, event, object, or condition that is presented contingent on behavior.*

Our future actions are determined by what happened to us when we acted the same way in the past. Such is the underlying assumption of the law of effect, which states that the consequences of behavior determine its future likelihood. Some consequences increase the future likelihood of the response and others decrease it. Those stimulus, events, objects, or conditions that increase the future likelihood of a response are known as reinforcers; those elements that decrease the future likelihood of the response are known as aversive consequences.

> *Concept 7-5. Reinforcer – a stimulus, event, object, or condition that when presented immediately after the behavior, increases its future likelihood.*

> *Concept 7-6. Aversive Consequence – a stimulus, event, object, or condition that, when presented immediately after the behavior, decreases its future likelihood.*

For example, it is uncomfortable to wear a helmet in hot regions. Excessive heat is often an aversive stimulus, causing the likelihood of helmet use to decrease. On the other hand, pressing down on the accelerator is a behavior that generates a breeze. In extreme hot weather, the breeze often acts as a reinforcing stimulus, causing the future probability of speeding to increase.

The reinforcing or aversive value of stimuli is established based on the individual's history with those stimuli; therefore, their value is relative. For instance, it is possible that speeding is a reinforcing stimulus for some people and an aversive stimulus for others, based on their unique past experiences.

Although the reinforcing value of a stimulus is relative, there are a few stimuli with "one size fits all" reinforcing properties because they are paired with positive events or other incentives. Those stimuli are called generalized conditioned reinforcers. For example, attention tends to serve as a generalized conditioned reinforcer for most people's behaviors because attention is usually paired with comfort and caring. Money also tends to serve as a generalized conditioned reinforcer because it is often paired with the acquisition of a variety of other reinforcers[8].

Concept 7-7. Generalized Conditioned Reinforcer – a stimulus, event, or object that has acquired reinforcing properties for most individuals through pairing with other reinforcers (e.g., attention and money).

It is important to avoid the mistake of assuming that an organism responds in order to obtain a consequence. This is a teleological assumption – attributing the causes of present behavior to future events. Future events do not control present behaviors, past events do.

Concept 7-8. Teleology – the cause for an action is in the future.

What Are the Antecedent Stimuli?

Behavior is not only affected by consequences but also by antecedent stimuli. The term "antecedent" is used as a generic term to refer to something that exists or happens before the behavior. Antecedent stimuli can serve different functions. It is worth differentiating between the following functions: the before condition, the discriminative stimulus, and the establishing operation.

Concept 7-9. Antecedent Condition – a stimulus, event, object, or condition that precedes the response.

The "Before" Condition

The before condition is one type of antecedent condition (other two types described in this section are establishing operation and discriminative stimuli). To identify a consequence and its effect on behavior, it is helpful to contrast the "after" condition (or consequence) to the "before" condition. Everything that happened prior to the behavior is considered the "before" condition. The "after" condition is always relative to the before condition. For example, if/when a motorcyclist puts a helmet on in North Thailand, there is heat (before) and substantially more heat (after) if he or she leaves it on. In the case of speeding behavior, the preceding condition to speeding (behavior) is breeze (before) and the subsequent condition is increased breeze (after).

Concept 7-10. Before Condition – a condition that exists before the behavior occurs. The contrast between the before and the after conditions helps to define the behavioral contingency.

The behavioral contingency is a basic unit of analysis that describes a causal relationship between a behavior and its consequences. Such a relationship takes place under a specific antecedent condition.

[8] *For an analysis of pay systems to improve an organization's performance, see Abernathy, 1996; Case, 1995; Lincoln, 1951, 1961; Stack, 1992.*

Concept 7-11. Behavioral Contingency – a casual relationship between the behavior and its consequences, given specific antecedent conditions.

The contingency can be represented by a description of the behavior and the "before" and "after" conditions. Figure 7-1 shows a behavioral contingency diagram and Figure 7-2 shows an example of a behavioral contingency.

Figure 7-1. Behavioral Contingency Diagram

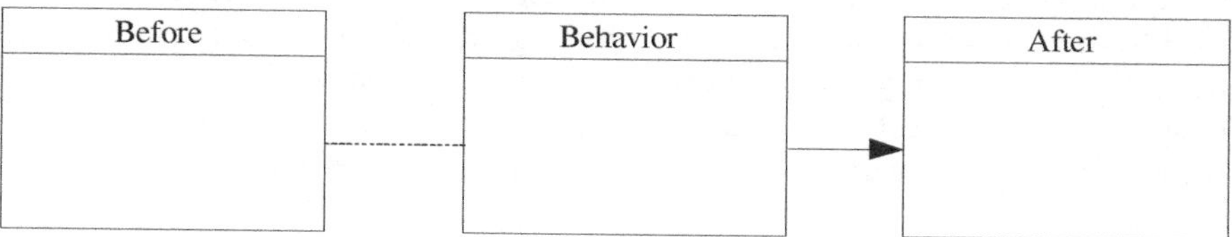

Figure 7-2. Example of a Behavioral Contingency

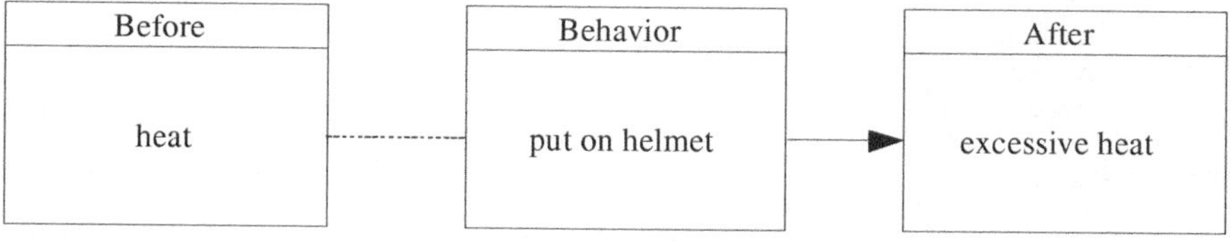

The "before" condition typically does not evoke behavior. That is why the connection between the behavior and "before" condition is a dotted line rather than an arrow (which indicates a causal relationship).

Establishing Operation

An establishing operation consists of an *environmental event, operation, or stimulus condition that affects an organism by momentarily altering (a) the reinforcing effectiveness of other events and (b) the frequency of occurrence of the type of behavior that had been consequated by those events.* (Michael, 1993, pp. 58[9].) In other words, the establishing operation increases the value of a consequence in such a way that the frequency of the behavior is altered (either decreases or increases).

[9] *Michael mentions that Keller and Shoenfeld first used the "establishing operation" definition in 1950.*

Concept 7-12. Establishing Operation – environmental event, operation, or stimulus condition that affects an organism by momentarily altering (a) the reinforcing effectiveness of other events and (b) the frequency of occurrence of the type of behavior that had been consequated by those events.[10]

For instance, adding too much salt to food is an establishing operation for drinking water because it increases the value of water and affects consumption (temporarily increases drinking water). Satiating a person with too much food is an establishing operation that alters the reinforcing value of food and therefore affects our eating (temporarily decreases eating). Excess sun exposure increases the value of sun block and affects the likelihood of putting on sun block. Figure 7-3 shows the relationship between the establishing operation and behavior.

Figure 7-3. Establishing Operation and the Behavioral Contingency[11]

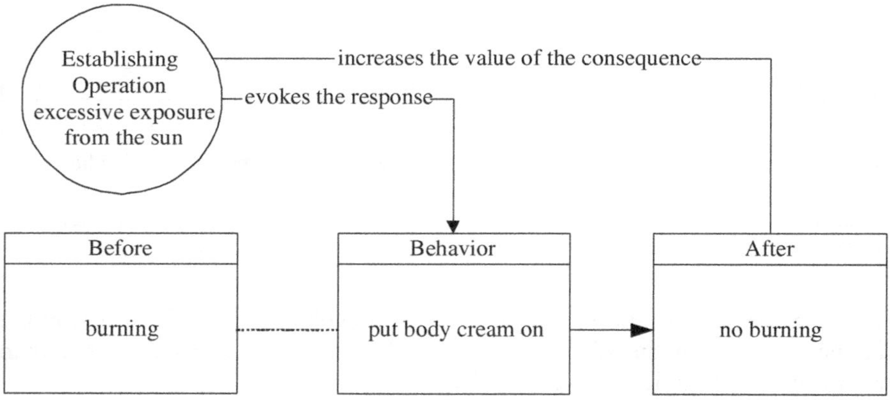

Discriminative Stimulus

A stimulus, object, or event could also serve as a discriminative stimulus. A stimulus in the presence of which a contingency is in effect is called a discriminative stimulus (S^D). A stimulus in the presence of which the contingency is not in effect is called an S^Δ. (The symbol $^\Delta$ is pronounced delta.)

[10] *Michael (1993).*

[11] *The connector between establishing operation and consequence does not have an arrow because the arrow is only used if the stimulus "evokes" the response.*

Concept 7-13. Discriminative Stimulus (S^D) – a stimulus in the presence of which a contingency is in effect.

Concept 7-14. S^Δ – a stimulus in the presence of which the contingency is not in effect.

For instance: If the stoplight is red (discriminative stimulus), and I continue to drive (behavior), it is highly possible that I will receive a traffic ticket (consequence) for running a red light. Only in the presence of the red light will my driving behavior produce a traffic ticket. However, in the presence of a green light (S^Δ), when I continue driving (behavior) there will not be a traffic ticket because there is no consequence for driving through a green light. So the green light acts as an S^Δ. Not all contingencies involve discriminative stimuli. Figure 7-4 shows the difference between S^D and S^Δ.

Figure 7-4. Example of S^D and S^Δ

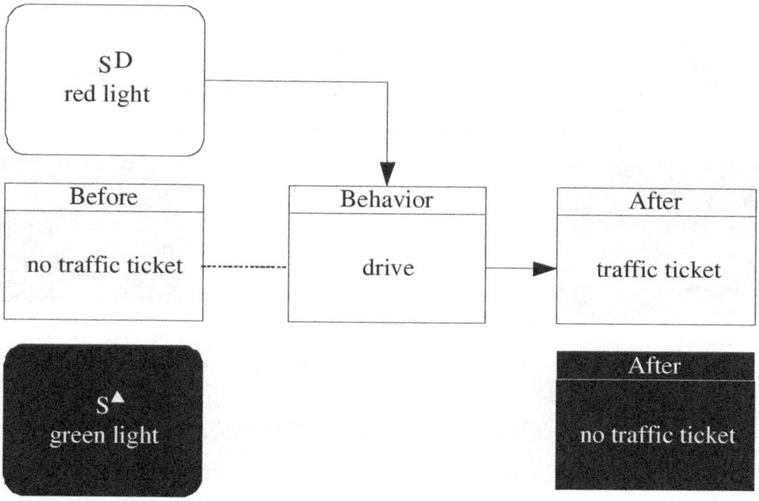

The same stimulus or object could have different functions. For instance: A light could act as a consequence[12], as an S^D, as an S^Δ, or as an establishing operation. Therefore, it is important that we distinguish various stimulus functions on behavior. Figure 7-5 shows a summary of various antecedent stimulus functions.

Figure 7-5. Summary of Stimulus Functions

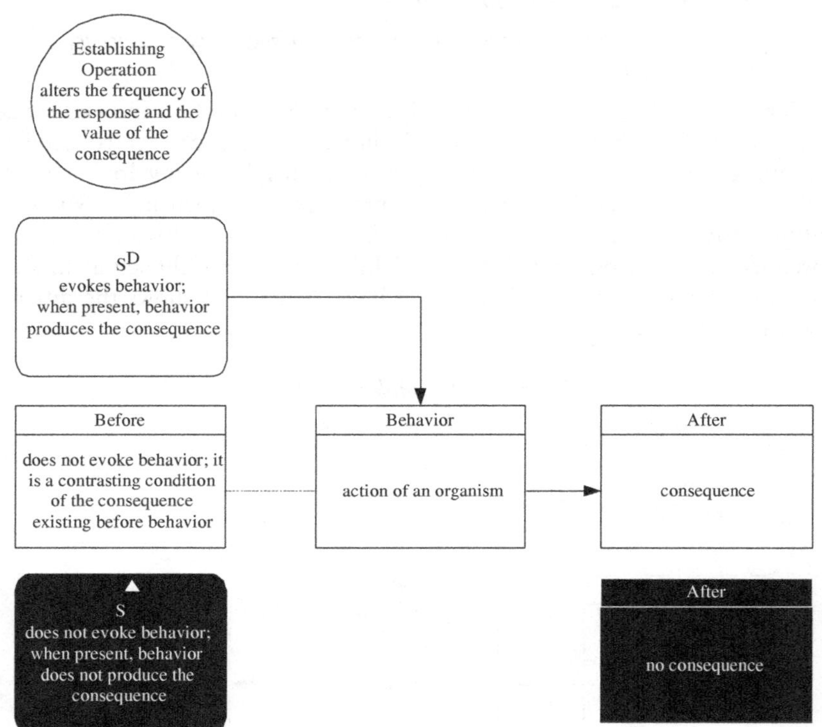

Does the Contingency Directly Control Behavior?

A direct-acting contingency is one that directly affects a behavior's frequency without the need of other processes. A direct-acting contingency affects the behavior when the consequence involved is immediate, probable, and sizable. Figure 7-6 shows a graphic representation of a direct-acting contingency.

> *Concept 7-15. Direct-Acting Contingency – contingency that involves a consequence that is immediate, probable, and sizeable that directly increases or decreases the future likelihood of the behavior that precedes it.*

[12] *For a light to serve as a consequence it must have acquired conditioning properties through specific behavioral procedures.*

Figure 7-6. Direct-Acting Contingency

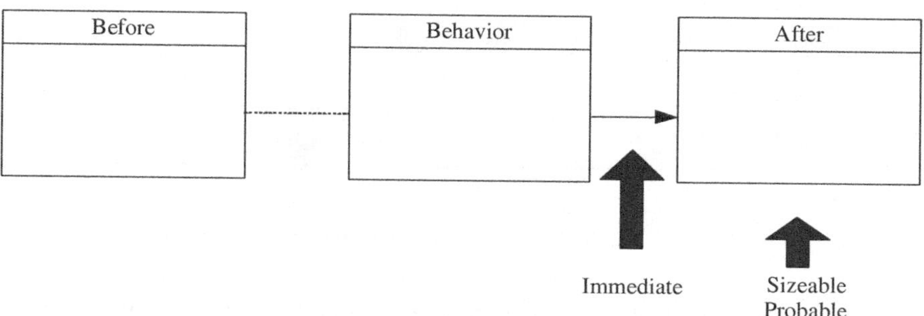

The following is an example of a direct-acting contingency: When the stove is hot (before), and I touch it (behavior), I burn myself (after). Burning is an immediate, probable, and sizable consequence that will effectively reduce the likelihood that I will touch a hot stove in the future.

In order to determine whether a contingency is direct-acting and what control it exerts on behavior, it helps to understand three points: (a) the dimensions of the consequence, (b) the difference between direct-acting and indirect-acting contingencies, and (c) the role of behavioral rules.

Dimensions of Consequences[13]

Let's review, in more detail, the dimensions of the consequences involved in contingencies. The dimensions are temporality, probability, and size.

> *Concept 7-16. Dimensions of a Consequence – temporality, probability, and size.*

Temporality

Temporality refers to the duration of time between the behavior and the consequence. In order to be effective, the consequence must immediately follow the behavior. For practical purposes, consider any delay between the response and the consequence greater than 60 seconds a delayed consequence. Figure 7-7 is a graphic representation of a contingency involving a delayed consequence.

> *Concept 7-17. Contingency with Delayed Consequences – the consequence is presented more than 60 seconds after the behavior.*

[13] *R. W. Malott, 1988, 1992; R. W. Malott & M. E. Malott, 1987,1990; Malott, Malott, & Trojan, 2000; Malott, Malott, & Shimamune, 1992a, 1992b.*

Figure 7-7. Contingency Involving a Delayed Consequence

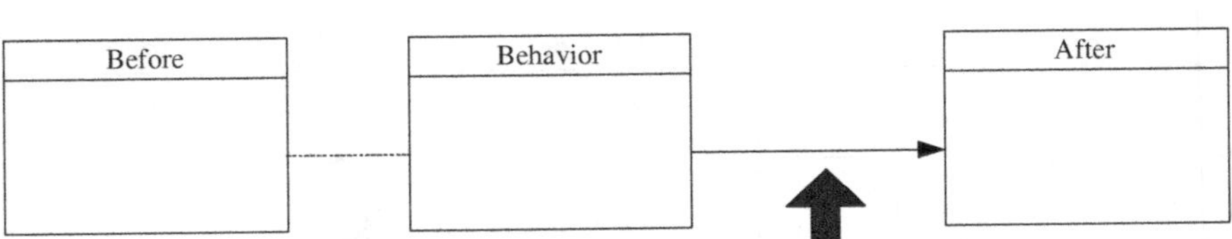

To illustrate the distinction between delayed and immediate consequences, consider the following example: When I place a coin in a vending machine, and press the selection of a snack (behavior), I receive the snack. Before, there is no snack. After pressing the selection, there is (after). As a result, I will more likely use the same vending machine in the future because the consequence of pressing the snack selection is immediate, probable, and sizeable.

The following is an example of a contingency involving a delayed consequence. It is cold (before). I turn on the thermostat (behavior) and the temperature increases a few minutes later (after). Even though I will turn the thermostat on the next time I am cold, there are other processes (discussed later in this chapter) responsible for increasing the future likelihood of behavior when the consequence involved is delayed.

Probability

Probability refers to the certainty with which a consequence is contingent on behavior. The situation described by Dr. Sang, in regards to the infrequent use of motorcycle helmets, involves a contingency with an improbable consequence.

> *Concept 7-18. Contingencies with Improbable Consequences – the behavior's consequence may or may not occur.*

There is a rare probability of physical harm (before) when a person gets on a motorcycle. Wearing a helmet (behavior) reduces the probability of serious physical harm in the event of an accident (after). However, the consequence of the reduction of physical harm is improbable because the probability of an accident is rare. Therefore, the decrease in the probability of preventing physical harm – through the use of a helmet – is so low that this contingency is not effective in increasing the likelihood of putting on a helmet. Figure 7-8 shows a basic diagram of a contingency involving an improbable consequence.

Figure 7-8. Contingency with an Improbable Consequence

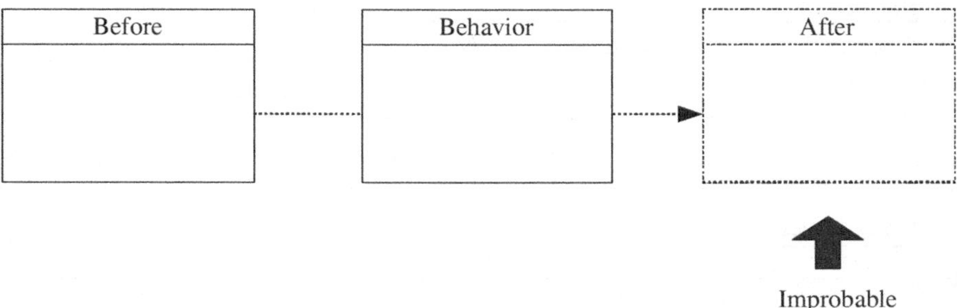

Contingencies involving improbable consequences exist in industrial and non-industrial safety situations. Common examples include putting on a safety helmet in construction areas, wearing steel-toed shoes in a fabricating plant, and buckling a seatbelt when driving or riding in a car. When a person carries out these safe behaviors, the probability of reducing physical harm is low because physical harm is rare in these scenarios. Therefore, contingencies involving improbable consequences do not effectively influence behavior.

Size

The size refers to whether or not the consequence is significant. This type of contingency involves a consequence so insignificant that it does not affect the future likelihood of the behavior; however, the cumulative effect of repeated occurrences of the behavior may have a significant result over the organism.

> *Concept 7-19. Contingency with Small Consequences – the consequence of behavior is so small that only the cumulative effect of repeated incidents of that behavior have a significant effect.*

Smoking cigarettes is an example of a behavior involving a contingency with a small but cumulative effect. First, there is the absence of smoke (before). Inhaling a single puff (behavior) produces an almost unnoticeable physical harm (after). One cigarette puff does not really matter; it is not harmful. It is the cumulative effect of cigarette smoking, over a long period of time, which produces serious illnesses. Figure 7-9 illustrates a graphic representation of a contingency that involves a small consequence with cumulative effect.

Figure 7-9. Contingency with a Small Consequence and a Cumulative Effect

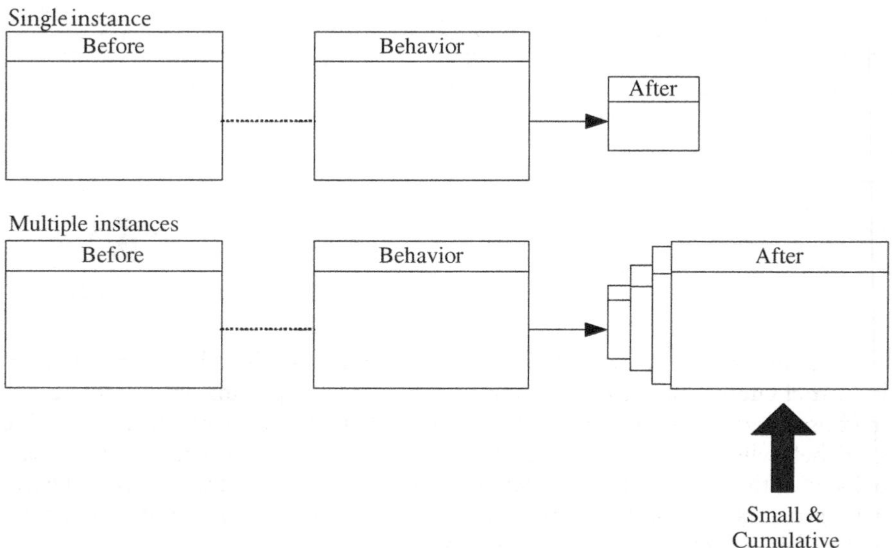

Even in the case of people aware of the relationship between smoking and cancer, the natural result of smoking does not cause them to quit smoking because the consequence of each instance of smoking is too small.

Another relevant example is the contingency involved in dieting. Eating one high-fat meal does not increase a person's weight. However, the cumulative effect of multiple occurrences of high calorie and fat consumption is increased weight. The long-term cumulative effect of consuming excessive amounts of calories is not enough to influence consumption of meals high in calories and fat.

Difference Between Direct-Acting and Indirect-Acting Contingencies

Direct-acting contingencies involve immediate, probable, and sizeable consequences that directly increase or decrease the future likelihood of the response. Verbal behavior (language) is not necessary for direct-acting contingencies to have an effect over the behavior. For instance, after touching a hot stove and being burned your pet will probably not touch that hot stove again – nor will an adult or a child.

Contingencies involving delayed consequences, though probable and sizeable, are called indirect-acting contingencies. The contingency is indirect-acting because it does control the future likelihood of the behavior, as we will see later on in this chapter. The control of an indirect-acting contingency on behavior is the result of other processes and not a direct result of the consequence's effect.

Concept 7-20. Indirect-Acting Contingencies – contingencies that involve delayed, though probable and sizeable, consequences. They control behavior through additional processes other than the contingency itself.

For instance: The behavior of turning the heater on produces a delayed consequence, but it often influences the behavior because the change in temperature is highly probable and sizeable. Such is the case of pain relief medication. Consuming strong medication to alleviate a headache will increase in the future, even though its effect is not immediate, because it is probable and sizeable. Both of these examples involve indirect-acting contingencies.

Ineffective contingencies are those that involve a consequence so small or improbable that the consequence has no effect on future occurrences of behavior.

Concept 7-21. Ineffective Contingencies – do not control behavior because they involve a consequence that is too small or improbable.

The relationship between buckling a seatbelt and traffic accidents establishes an ineffective contingency because the likelihood of getting into a traffic accident is relatively rare. The relationship between smoking one cigarette and cancer establishes an ineffective contingency because the effect of one cigarette on an individual's health is so small. Contingencies involving improbable or insignificant consequences cause most self-control problems. Table 7-1 classifies the effect of the contingencies based on the dimensions of the consequences.

Table 7-1. Contingency Effect Based on the Dimensions of the Consequences

		Dimension of the Consequence		
Effect on Behavior		**Temporality**	**Probability**	**Size**
Effective	Direct-acting	Immediate	High	Significant
	Indirect-acting	Delayed	High	Significant
Ineffective		NA	Low	Insignificant

Role of Behavioral Rules

Indirect-acting contingencies that have improbable or small consequences do not control behavior; however, those with delayed but probable and sizable consequences do. For an indirect-acting contingency to be effective another phenomenon comes into play: behavioral rules. A rule is a verbal description of a contingency. The following verbal description provides an example: *If the stove is hot, and you touch it, you will get burned.* The rule describes the conditions in which the behavior occurs, the behavior, and its consequences.

Concept 7-22. Rule – verbal description of a contingency.

It is difficult for people to establish a connection between smoking and physical harm without an explicit description of the relationship using behavioral rules. For example: *If you smoke consistently, over a period of years, you might develop lung cancer.*

In most daily work situations, rule specification is necessary because the work-related contingencies are often indirect-acting. Therefore, it would be unproductive to wait for the individual to develop a rule based on his or her direct experiences with the contingencies.

Behavioral rules are easy to follow when they describe effective contingencies (direct and indirect-acting contingencies). They are difficult to follow when they describe ineffective contingencies. For example: *Consume only 2,200 calories per day to avoid weight gain.* This is a difficult rule to follow because it describes an ineffective contingency. Consuming 100 extra calories does not have a significant effect on a person's weight. However, the cumulative effect of many exceptions to this rule will result in weight gain.

It would be naive to expect the people of North Thailand to wear helmets simply because we recite the following behavioral rule to them: *Wear a helmet when riding on a motorcycle to avoid physical harm in the case of an accident.* This is a hard rule to follow because it involves an ineffective contingency. It is improbable that an accident or physical harm will occur. Furthermore, there is a direct-acting contingency in effect that decreases the probability of wearing a helmet. The helmet causes an immediate, probable, and significant increase in heat. This heat is uncomfortable, which effectively decreases helmet use. So there is no reason why we should expect the people in Dr. Sang's town to wear helmets without additional contingency support: as we will see in future chapters.

The study of contingencies and rules that operate on behavior allows us to understand the relationship between the behavior and its consequences. For instance, it is possible to appreciate why the people in Northern Thailand don't wear helmets. Using helmets increases heat and discomfort when driving a motorcycle. The existing contingencies are not enough to support a high frequency of helmet use. If we understand this relationship, we can invest energy in designing contingencies that will help generate the desired behavior. This would be more productive than blaming people whose behaviors lack the support of effective contingencies.

Conclusions

In this chapter, we began studying the simple aspect of the paradox of organizational change – that is, its fundamental unit of analysis. Although organizations are complex because they are formed by many behaviors and multitudes of variables affecting each other, there is one main element upon which complexity is created: the behavioral contingency.

We also reviewed, as part of this chapter, some of the necessary elements of the analysis of existing behavior, which will be concluded in the next chapter. The analysis of existing behavioral contingencies that support current behavior is an essential component of reengineering an organization.

Rather than attributing the cause of behavior to people's internal motivation, the focus should be on studying the relationship between a behavior and its consequences. This type of study is called functional assessment – an analysis of the variables that control behavior. In this chapter, we analyzed the first six components of functional assessment:

1. What behavior is being analyzed? Behavior is defined as an action and the "dead man test" helps to define behavior: If a dead man can do it, it is not a behavior.
2. How often does it occur? This consists of finding out if the desired behavior is happening infrequently or not at all – and the frequency of the undesired behavior.
3. Whose behavior is under analysis? This refers to the specific individual or group of individuals whose behavior is under analysis.
4. What is the consequence? A consequence of behavior can be reinforcing or aversive. The value of the consequence depends on each individual's learning history.
5. What are the antecedent stimuli? Antecedent stimuli are those that affect the behavior and occur before the response. Three different antecedent stimulus functions were described: the "before" condition, the establishing operation, and the discriminative stimulus.
6. Does the contingency directly control the behavior? Direct-acting contingencies involve immediate, probable, and sizeable consequences. These contingencies are called direct-acting because the consequence directly affects the future likelihood of a response. Indirect-acting contingencies involve delayed but probable and sizeable consequences: they are effective in controlling behavior. Ineffective contingencies involve consequences that are too improbable or too small to have any effect on behavior.

The remaining component of functional assessment – type of contingency – is presented in the next chapter.

Review

Define the following terms:

- Law of effect
- Behavioral contingency
- Direct-acting contingency
- Indirect-acting contingency
- Behavioral rule

Provide an original example of each one of the following indirect-acting contingencies – contingencies involving a consequence that is:

- Delayed
- Improbable
- Small with a cumulative effect.

Chapter 8
Behavior

PART II

CHAPTER 8
BEHAVIOR: PART II

Actions speak louder than words.

Anonymous

Chopin Concert

At her death, Leonora Arazola had donated a good part of her estate to Saint Guadalupe's University to build the Frederic Chopin Theatre. Construction took two-and-a-half years and the wait created great expectations of the theatre's inauguration. Leonora studied music at Saint Guadalupe's University when she was young and became a renowned pianist. She toured around the world for years, playing the piano with the Lombardo Symphonic Orchestra. Leonora loved the romantics from the XVIII century, such as List, Berlioz, and Mendelssohn. But nobody came close to her favorite: Frederic Chopin. She mastered his entire work – including the two concerts, twenty-seven etudes and a variety of waltzes, mazurkas, and Polynesians.

The auditorium was filled to capacity the night of the inauguration. Leonora's family sat with the university elite: the president, provost, deans, and high administrators. Special seats were reserved for professors and students from the school of music. The rest of the theatre was overflowing with staff, other students, and relatives.

University President Anthony Ferraro began the evening's festivities by speaking about Leonora's life and her contributions to music and the university. Then he spoke about Leonora's passion for Chopin and the stories she shared about the great composer with her students, stories Ferraro himself had heard more than once: how little Frederic was so sensitive that his eyes would fill with tears whenever he listened to piano music ... how he had given his first concert at the age of eight ... how the competent Joseph Elsner, director of the Warsaw conservatory, had helped Chopin reach success as a composer and pianist at the age of 19 ... how he had moved to Paris when the revolution began in Warsaw ... how fragile his health was ... and his death at the age of 39.

That night, the concert included a respectable group of pianists. But the opening piece had been reserved for Pam, Leonora's 19-year-old granddaughter. She had grown up playing Leonora's favorite Chopin piece: the Nocturne in C sharp minor, Op. Posth, which lasted three minutes and 59 seconds. Pam had played that piece for Leonora in the last days of her grandmother's life to bring her peace. And that was the nocturne that would open the concert, the only piece that Pam would play that night.

Pam walked to the center of the stage, took a deep breath and allowed her fingers to fly over the piano. With each keystroke, one could feel her body and soul fill the theater with passion and sweetness. As Pam played Chopin's nocturne, the audience felt the emotion and appreciated the beauty. It was as if time had come to a stand still for 150 years; her music revived the same emotion in the audience that Chopin generated a century and a half ago and that Leonora evoked before her death.

Functional Assessment (Part II)

Why did Pam develop the behavioral repertoire of playing the piano with so much passion? Why do some people develop such complex behavioral repertoire, such as Leonora and Chopin, and others do not?

There are several common factors between Pam, Leonora, and Frederic Chopin himself: even if their skill level, technique, and creativity varied. All three invested in many hours of practice. The other common factor was that a close relative appreciated music and had some level of skill as a pianist and influenced their repertoire's development. Such had been the role of Leonora and Chopin's parents, as well as the role Leonora played in her granddaughter's life. Their close relatives provided behavioral contingencies that effectively increased the frequency of practicing the piano as well as the appreciation for music.

In the previous chapter, various aspects of functional assessment were explained: What behavior is being analyzed? How often does it occur? Whose behavior is under analysis? What is the consequence of behavior? Which are the antecedent stimuli? Does the contingency directly control the behavior?

This chapter begins with the last component of functional assessment: What type of contingency is it? In order to illustrate the types of contingencies, fictional situations will be reviewed that may have affected the development of Pam's repertoire.

Behavioral repertoires result from an incalculable number and type of behavioral contingencies. It is impossible to determine the specific behavioral contingencies that founded a sophisticated repertoire such as the one Pam developed. A behavioral history is too complex to grasp in retrospect. The behavioral repertoire's complexity is even greater when we consider that, in any given moment, a person is exposed to several behavioral contingencies at once. However, given the lack of scientific evidence, we can deduce the predominant behavioral contingencies that shape a behavioral repertoire. Even if the deduction is speculative, it provides an appreciation of how environment may play a role in shaping behavior.

What Is the Type of Contingency?

To identify the type of contingency operating on behavior, it must be established whether the consequence is reinforcing or aversive for the individual who emits the response. As detailed in the previous chapter, events or stimuli are not inherently reinforcers or aversives: their value depends on the individual's history. For instance, looking down from the top of a cliff may be a reinforcer for some and aversive for others. However, some stimuli are neutral because they do not influence behavior.

Concept 8-1. Neutral Stimuli – do not have any influence on behavior.

Second, it must be known if the relationship between the behavior and the consequence is one of presentation or removal. The combination of the consequence value and its relationship to behavior describes the four basic behavioral contingencies: (1) presentation of a reinforcing stimulus, known as reinforcement; (2) removal of a reinforcing stimulus, known as penalty; (3) presentation of an aversive stimulus, known as punishment; and (4) removal of an aversive stimulus, known as escape. Two of the contingencies tend to increase the future likelihood of a behavior, *reinforcement* and *escape.* The other two tend to decrease the future likelihood of a behavior, *punishment* and *penalty.* Table 8-1 summarizes the distinction between the four basic behavioral contingencies.

Table 8-1. Distinction Between the Basic Behavioral Contingencies

	Relationship to Behavior	
Consequence Value	Presentation	Removal
Reinforcer	Reinforcement (Increase frequency)	Penalty (Decrease frequency)
Aversive	Punishment (Decrease frequency	Escape (Increase frequency)

In addition to the basic contingencies, there are two avoidance contingences that prevent either the presentation of an aversive condition or the removal of a reinforcer (more on this later in the chapter).

Basic Contingencies

Reinforcement

Presenting a reinforcer immediately after the behavior increases the future likelihood of that behavior. This contingency is known as reinforcement.

Concept 8-2. Reinforcement – stimulus, event, object, or condition that when presented immediately after the behavior increases its future likelihood.

Figure 8-1 shows an example of a reinforcement contingency: Before playing the piano, Pam feels no emotion (before). Playing the piano (behavior) generates emotion (after). The change between the "before" and "after" conditions resulted in the presentation of emotion.

Figure 8-1. Two Examples of Reinforcement Contingencies

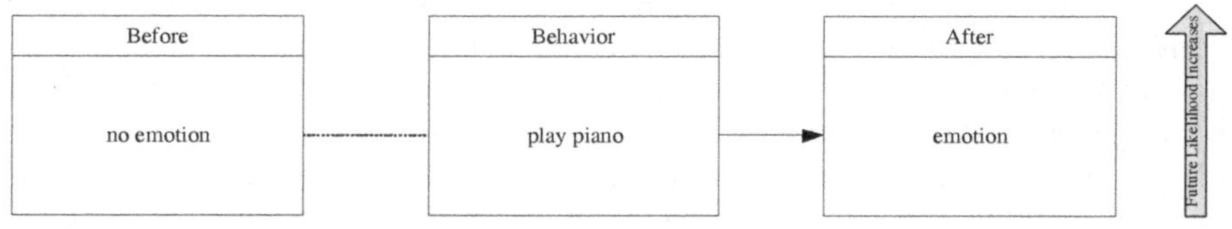

Escape

When the behavior causes the removal of an aversive stimulus, event, or situation, the future likelihood of that response increases. This contingency is known as escape.

> *Concept 8-3. Escape – aversive stimulus, event, or condition that when removed immediately after a behavior increases the future likelihood of that behavior.*

Figure 8-2 shows an example of an escape contingency. Assume that Pam often feels stressed and playing the piano calms her. Before playing the piano, Pam experiences anxiety (before). Playing the piano (behavior) reduces that anxiety (after) by producing a feeling of liberation from the aversive tension.

Figure 8-2. Example of an Escape Contingency

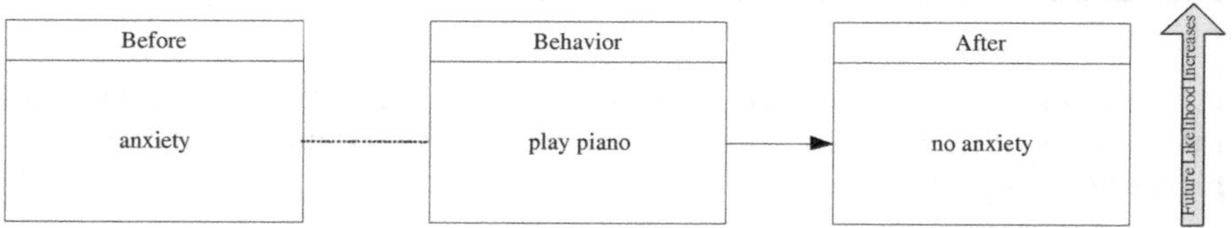

Punishment

When an aversive stimulus, event, or condition is contingent on behavior, the future likelihood of that behavior decreases. This contingency is known as punishment.

Concept 8-4. Punishment – aversive stimulus, event, or condition that when presented immediately after a behavior decreases the future likelihood of that behavior.

For instance, if playing the piano (behavior) is usually followed by Leonora's criticism, the absence of criticism before playing (before) and the presence of criticism after playing (after) results in a decreased probability that Pam will play the piano in front of Leonora in the future. Figure 8-3 shows an example of a punishment contingency for piano playing.

Figure 8-3. Example of a Punishment Contingency

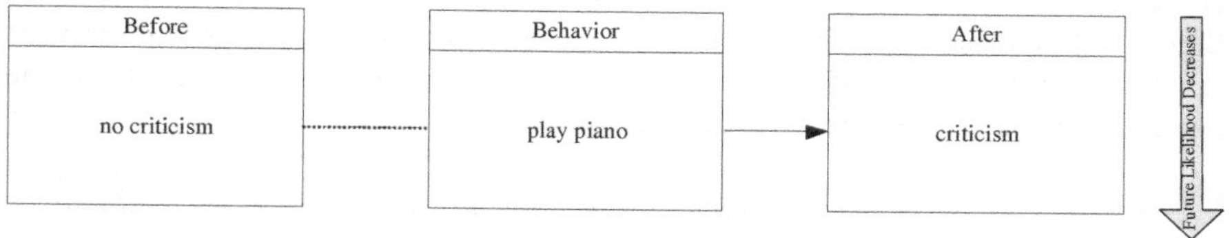

Penalty

When the behavior causes the loss of a reinforcing event or condition, the future likelihood of that behavior decreases. This contingency is known as penalty.

Concept 8-5. Penalty – stimulus, event or condition that when removed immediately after a behavior decreases the future likelihood of that behavior.

For instance, the frequency with which Pam plays the piano will decrease if the audience leaves while she plays. Before playing, Pam has an audience (before). When she plays the piano (response), she loses her audience (after). Figure 8-4 shows a diagram of a penalty contingency.

Figure 8-4. Example of a Penalty Contingency

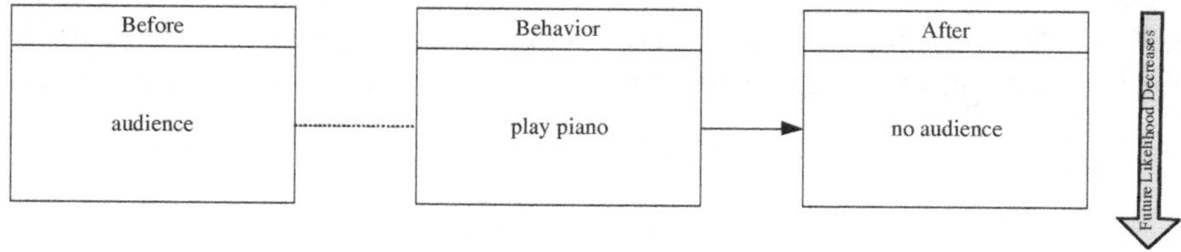

Avoidance Contingencies

An avoidance contingency is one that either prevents the presentation of an aversive stimulus or prevents the removal of a reinforcer. Both types of avoidance contingencies cause an increase in the future probability of the response.

> *Concept 8.6. Avoidance Contingency – the behavior prevents the presentation of an aversive stimulus or the removal of a reinforcer.*

Avoidance of the Presentation of an Aversive Condition

Because Pam's piano playing might have been punished by the constant criticism of Leonora in the past, Pam could do something that prevents Leonora's criticism; for instance, asking Leonora not to attend her piano practice sessions. Before asking there will be criticism (before). Asking (behavior) will prevent criticism (after). Figure 8-5 shows a contingency diagram of the example of the avoidance of the presentation of an aversive condition.

Figure 8-5. Example of the Avoidance of the Presentation of an Aversive Condition

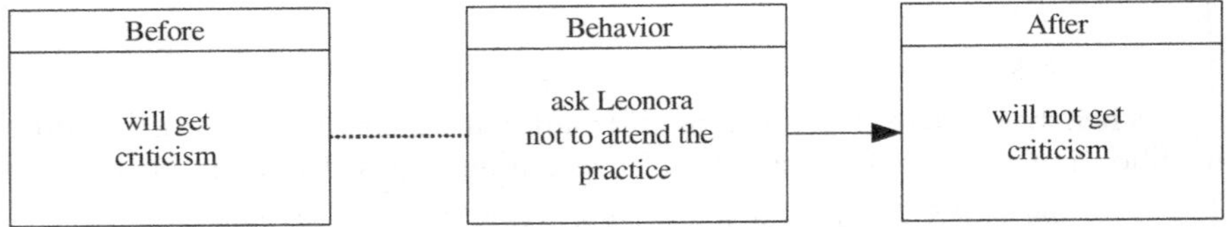

Avoidance of the Loss of a Reinforcer

There is nothing that Pam loves more than having an attentive audience during her practice sessions.[1] She gets annoyed when the telephone rings during the session because someone will leave the room and the audience will be distracted from her music. This happens almost every day. Pam can prevent losing the attention of the audience by disconnecting the phone before her practice. Initially, Pam lost the attention of the audience (before). By disconnecting the telephone (behavior) she will no longer lose the attention (after). This contingency consists of avoidance of the loss of a reinforcer. Figure 8-6 illustrates this type of avoidance contingency.

[1] *Of course, there are other reinforcers for playing the piano, in addition to having an audience. For instance, the sound of the music. In this example, however, I highlight the audience as a reinforcer to illustrate avoidance of the loss of a reinforcer.*

Figure 8-6. Example of Avoidance of the Loss of a Reinforcer

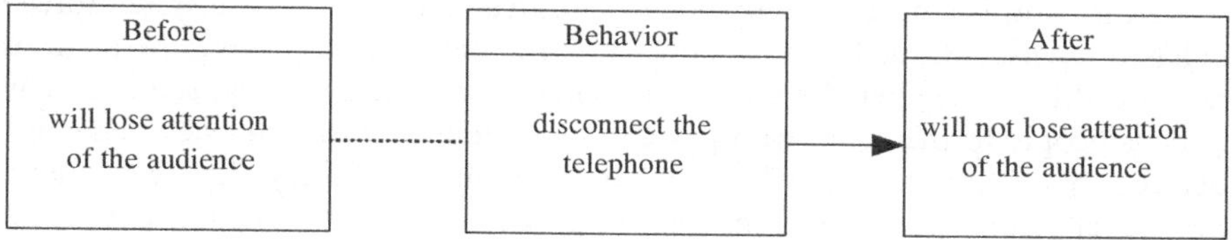

Avoidance of the loss of a reinforcer could involve a deadline. Deadlines set the occasion for avoidance of the loss of the opportunity for a reinforcer. For instance, assume that Pam loves to attend her piano lessons. But her music instructor is very uptight, and if Pam arrives one minute after 6 p.m. (the scheduled time) the instructor leaves and Pam loses out on her piano lesson. So Pam will avoid losing the opportunity for her piano lesson by arriving at 6 p.m. (behavior). In this case, 6 p.m. acts as a discriminative stimulus. Any time after 6 p.m. acts as an S^{Δ} because the condition after arriving is that she will lose the opportunity for a piano lesson. Figure 8-7 illustrates this avoidance contingency.

Figure 8-7. Avoidance of the Opportunity to Lose a Reinforcer

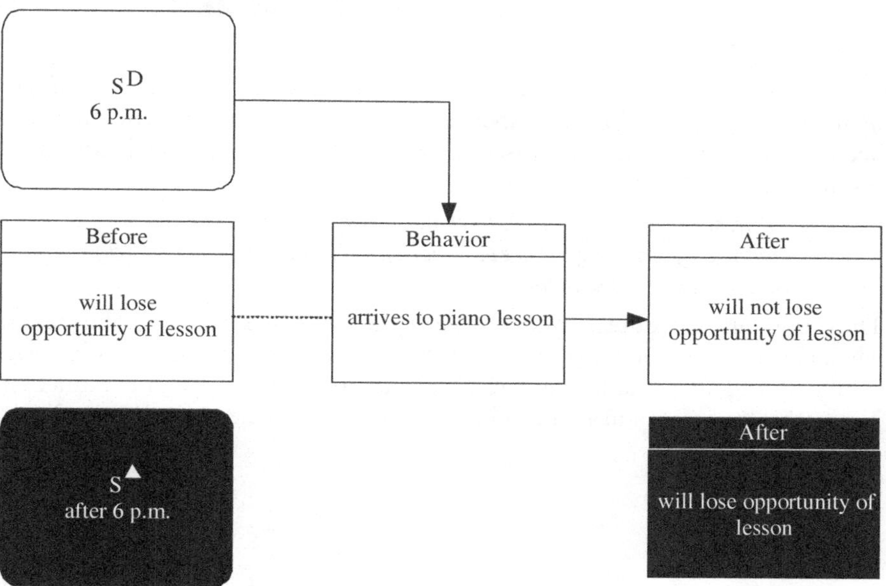

Extinction

Extinction is a procedure in which reinforcement of a previously reinforced behavior is discontinued. Let's suppose that the behavior of playing the piano is reinforced by the audience's attention. When Pam begins to play, she normally attracts people to the room who pay devoted attention to her music. Generally, before playing the piano, Pam does not have an audience (before). Playing the piano (response) results in the audience entering the room (after). In the extinction procedure, playing the piano no longer attracts an audience. Figure 8-8 illustrates the difference between reinforcement and extinction.

Figure 8-8. Comparison Between Reinforcement and Extinction

Before	Behavior	After	
no audience	play piano →	audience	**Reinforcement**
no audience	play piano →	no audience	**Extinction**

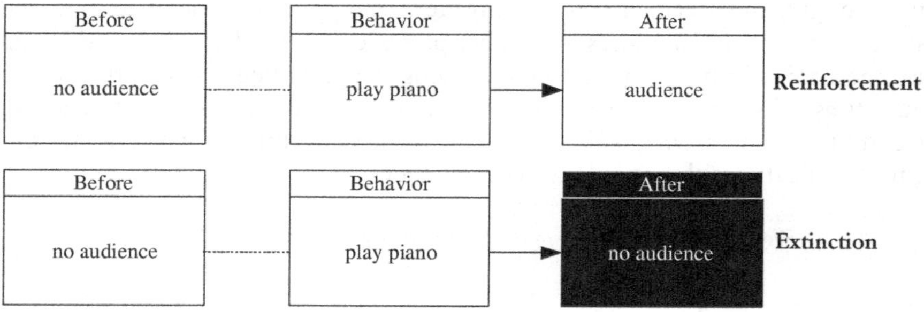

When the extinction procedure of a reinforcement contingency is implemented, the frequency of the response tends to increase temporarily and later decreases until the behavior ceases to occur. This phenomenon is known as resistance to extinction.

> *Concept 8-7. Resistance to Extinction – when the reinforcement contingency is not in effect, the behavior's frequency increases temporarily and then decreases until the behavior ceases to occur.*

The extinction procedure may likewise be applied to escape. This might be the case when playing music no longer eases anxiety (if, in the past, playing the piano was soothing). Figure 8-9 illustrates the differences between escape and extinction. Notice that the before and after conditions are the same in the extinction condition.

Figure 8-9. Comparison Between Escape and Extinction

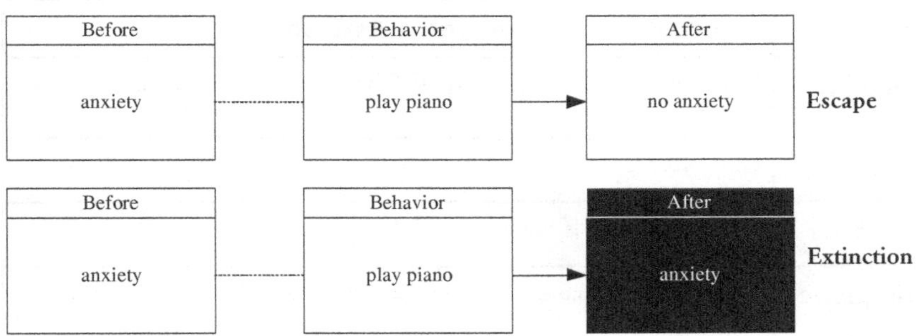

Concept 8-8. Extinction – procedure in which reinforcement of a previously reinforced behavior is discontinued. In the extinction procedure, the before and after conditions are the same.

How Do You Complete a Functional Assessment?

A functional assessment allows us to identify the contingencies that support a behavior before attempting to change it. It answers, in a systematic fashion, to questions such as: What function does the behavior play on the environment? What is the relationship between the behavior and its consequence? Why doesn't the appropriate behavior occur frequently or why does the inappropriate behavior occur too often?[2] Table 8-2 summarizes the questions of a functional assessment.

[2] *For texts about basic principles of behavior analysis, see Baldwin & Baldwin, 1998; Daniels, 1989, 1994, 2000; Malott & Whaley, 1976; Martin & Paer, 1996; Miller, 1997; Sulzer-Azaroff & Mayer, 1991.*

Table 8-2. Functional Assessment

	Functional Assessment
Behavior	What behavior is under analysis? Give an example and a non-example.
Frequency	How often does it occur?
Performer	Whose behavior is under analysis?
Consequence	Is the consequence a reinforcer, an aversive condition, or a neutral stimulus?
Antecedents	What are the antecedent stimuli?
	- Specify the before condition.
	- If there is an establishing operation, specify.
	- If there is a discriminative stimulus, specify.
Contingency	Does the contingency directly control behavior?
	Specify the dimensions of the consequence: immediate or delayed, probable or improbable, significant or too small.
	Specify if the contingency is direct-acting, indirect-acting, or ineffective.
	Specify if the relationship between the behavior and the consequence is presentation, removal, or avoidance
	What type of contingency is it? Choose one of the following:
	- Specify if the contingency is reinforcement, punishment, penalty, or escape.
	- Specify if the contingency is avoidance, either by the prevention of an aversive stimulus, or by the prevention of the removal (or the loss of an opportunity) of a reinforcer.
	- Specify if there is no contingency. Extinction.

As a matter of illustration, Table 8-3 shows an example of a functional assessment of Pam's piano-playing behavior.

Table 8-3. Example of a Functional Assessment.

	Example of a Functional Assessment
Behavior	What behavior is under analysis? Playing piano.
Frequency	How often does it occur? Everyday about 9 p.m.
Performer	Whose behavior is under analysis? Pam's.
Consequence	Which consequence is under study? Attentive audience.
Antecedents	Which are the antecedent stimuli? The before condition is no audience.
	SD: 9 p.m. is when people at home rest and look forward to her playing.
Contingency	Does the contingency directly control behavior? The contingency controls behavior indirectly because the attentive audience is a probable, sizeable, and delayed consequence. It takes several minutes for the audience to come to the living room when they first listen to the music.
	Specify the contingency: indirect-acting.
	Relationship between behavior and consequence: The audience (consequence) is presented after playing the piano (behavior).
	Type of contingency: a basic reinforcement contingency.

Other contingencies play a role in Pam's piano playing. Once Pam begins to play, the melody she generates directly reinforces her desire to continue playing during practice. A behavior is generally influenced by several contingencies at the same time. A functional assessment allows focusing on the contingencies that most likely influence the behavior under study.

From Task to Behavior

Systems analysis allows us to focus on an organization's critical aspects. This is important because a behavioral change takes time, effort, and resources. If we examine an organization in a random fashion, we may invest time in irrelevant aspects.

Chapters 3 to 6 described how to use behavioral systems analysis with metacontingencies. The analysis went from the general to the specific: macrosystem, organization, process, subprocess, and general tasks. Transition from interlocking behavioral contingencies to individual behavior is done through the analysis of the specific tasks. A task consists of a group of behaviors that generates a product. A task analysis – as seen in Chapter 6 – concludes with an indication of the tasks that must remain, the ones that may be eliminated, and the ones that should be modified to improve the processes.

Going from a detailed task analysis to a more specific behavior analysis requires two steps: the specification of behaviors within critical tasks and a functional assessment of the last behavior within analogs to stimulus-response chains.

Specification of Behaviors Within Critical Tasks

Chapter 6 (Task) centered on a story involving the publishing of a weekly advertising circular. The production of the weekly circular involved six subprocesses. One of them alone – information processing – involved more than 250 tasks carried out by 15 different people from several departments. The task analysis concluded with the identification of eight critical tasks: one of which was generating a list of promotional products. The list included the information necessary to publish an ad; for instance, the price of the item and date of the advertisement. The buyer carried out this task, which involved more than the behavior of writing the information on the weekly circular. The buyer had to review information from the previous year, select the products that had generated the most profit, review the sale price, review the report on the competitor's price, review the images in the electronic library, and handwrite a summary of the information in a list that would eventually go to the Advertising department.

The tasks that the buyer had to carry out, in order to create a list of necessary products, constituted a stimulus response chain in which the final behavior was writing out the information. The term stimulus-response chain generally refers to a sequence of discriminative stimuli and responses in which each response, except for the very last one in the chain, serves as a discriminative stimulus for the next response.

> *Concept 8-9. Stimulus-Response Chain – a sequence of discriminative stimuli and responses in which each response, except for the very last one in the chain, serves as a discriminative stimulus for the following response.*

As far as Pam's behavior of playing the piano, it is easy to understand the stimulus-response chain. Pressing one piano key serves as a discriminative stimulus for pressing the next key in a melody: the presence of the sound in one key, the next keystroke, will produce a component of a melody.

However, the behaviors involved in generating a list of promotional products are not contiguous like in playing a melody. It is possible that a buyer may be interrupted in the middle of filling out the information, pause, and continue it later: or begin to fill out the information and realize that part of it is incorrect. Generating the list might take several days.

Because of the lack of contiguity between responses, the behaviors involved in generating the promotional list represent an analog to stimulus-response chain. An analog is a process that is similar to another, but it is inherently different. The chain of responses necessary to produce a musical piece is similar to the chain of responses necessary to generate a list of promotional products. They are similar in that they both involve a series of behaviors that reach a final product: a melody or a list. However, they are different because the contingencies involved in generating the product are of a different nature. A stimulus-response chain, in the case of Pam's playing the piano, involves direct-acting contingencies only – with immediate, significant, and probable consequences and no need of rule statements to control behaviors in the chain. A stimulus-response chain, in the case of generating a list of promotional products, involves indirect-acting contingencies – with delayed consequences and the need for rule statements between instances of behavior in the chain to generate the final product.

> *Concept 8-10. Analog to Stimulus-Response Chain – sequence of stimuli and responses in which one response may serve as an antecedent stimulus for another response, with the exception of the last one. The sequence between the components of the chain is not continuous and it involves indirect and ineffective contingencies.*

Functional Assessment of the Last Behavior in the Chain

Each task in a detailed process map involves the behavior (or group of behaviors) of a single individual and the aggregate product. When we study behavior, we ought to go one more level of analysis down from the task. We ought to analyze the set of behaviors involved in each single task and determine the last behavior in that set, which results in the task's aggregate product.

A functional assessment of the last behavior in a stimulus-response chain is enough to establish the basis for behavioral change. If we are able to affect the last behavior, the rest of the behaviors in the chain will most likely be affected as well.

If very complex chains are chosen, it is possible that no results will materialize. A rule of thumb for establishing the chain of behaviors' level of specificity is selecting behaviors that have to be carried out within a few hours. If the chosen chain's components take weeks or months, the chain will be too general to prove effective in a behavioral change. In such a case, general tasks would be used – not behaviors in detailed tasks.

The functional assessment concludes with a summary of the critical performers, behaviors, the frequency with which the behaviors occur, and the description of existing contingencies that maintain the rate of those behaviors. Figure 8-10 shows an example of a functional assessment of the existing contingencies for critical behaviors in the production of the weekly circular in Chapter 6.

Figure 8-10. Functional Assessment Summary of Critical Behaviors in the Production of a Weekly Circular[3]

EXISTING CONTINGENCIES

WHOSE BEHAVIOR?	BEFORE?	BEHAVIOR?	AFTER?	HOW OFTEN?	WHAT CONTINGENCY?
Buyer	no effort	writes a list of products to advertise	effort	rarely	PUNISHMENT (direct-acting)
Advertising Coordinator	nothing happens	creates a sketch for the weekly circular on time	nothing happens	never	EXTINCTION (there is no contingency on timeliness)
Designer	no comments on quality	turns in a quality page	no comments on quality	20% of pages meet quality standards	EXTINCTION (there is no contingency on quality)
Administrative Assistant	will lose opportunity to publish	e-mails camera-ready copy to printers on time	will not lose opportunity to publish	100% compliance	AVOIDANCE (indirect-acting)
Production Coordinator	will lose opportunity to insert in Sunday's newspaper	prints circular on time	will not lose opportunity to insert in Sunday's newspaper	100% compliance	AVOIDANCE (indirect-acting)
Helper	will lose opportunity to insert in Sunday's newspaper	delivers circular to newspaper on time	will not lose opportunity to insert in Sunday's newspaper	100% compliance	AVOIDANCE (indirect-acting)
Newspaper Employee	will lose opportunity for newspaper delivery	stuffs circular in Sunday's newspaper on time	will not lose opportunity for newspaper delivery	100% compliance	AVOIDANCE (indirect-acting)
Distributor	will lose opportunity for customers	distributes newspaper on time	will not lose opportunity for customers	100% compliance	AVOIDANCE (indirect-acting)

Figure 8-10 shows a functional assessment summary of the last behavior in analogs to stimulus-response chains for eight critical tasks identified in Chapter 6. The analysis shows that the existing contingencies are ineffective in generating the desired behavior for the buyer (writing a list of products to advertise), the advertising coordinator (creating a sketch for the weekly circular on time), and the designer (turning in a quality page). The natural contingency for writing a list of products to advertise involves more effort from the buyer, and there are no contingencies in place for the advertising coordinator or for the designer's behavior.

[3] *In the case of the advertising coordinator, finishing a sketch does not produce any consequences. Therefore, there is no incentive for completing it on time.*

Notice that the existing contingencies for the critical behaviors of the remaining performers in the process consist of indirect-acting avoidance. At the end of the process, deadlines have to be implemented in order for the circular to be inserted in the Sunday edition of the newspaper. Deadlines establish opportunities to complete the next critical step in the process. For instance, if the administrative assistant does not e-mail the camera-ready copy on time, there will not be an opportunity to publish the circular; if the production coordinator does not print the circular on time, there won't be an opportunity to deliver it to the newspaper...

Deadlines are not effective, however, if they do not have a bearing in the delivery of the consequence. Such is the case for preparing the sketch on time. There are no consequences for the advertising coordinator to meet timeliness criteria. Because the deadline is not enforced, it does not make a difference.

Conclusions

With this chapter, the section regarding functional assessment of behavior is concluded. The behavior level is the fifth component in the model for change and the first component of engineering and sustaining change with behavioral contingencies. Figure 8-11 shows the first five components of the model for organizational change.

As presented all along in this book, the environment where change occurs – organizations and their processes – is complex and dynamic, making the evolution of organizations seem chaotic and unpredictable. This chapter addressed the most elemental component of change: the existing behavioral contingencies that sustain current performance. The behavior contingency illustrates simple, constant, and orderly aspects of the paradox of change. The constant aspect is based on the relationship between behavior and its consequences, which always affects future behavior. The orderly aspect comes from the ability to predict future behavior based on the understanding of the existing behavioral contingencies.

In this chapter, the last component of a functional assessment was studied: What type of contingency is it? There are three types of relationships between the behavior and the consequence: presentation, removal, and avoidance of either a reinforcer or an aversive stimulus. Those behavior-consequence relationships determine the four basic contingencies: reinforcement, punishment, penalty, and escape. It is also the classification for two types of avoidance contingencies. Extinction of previously reinforced behavior was also discussed.

Finally, we saw that the processes within an organization involve a multitude of tasks. It is important to focus on the critical tasks within a process in order to simplify the analysis and pinpoint the tasks that may be eliminated and the tasks that should be modified to increase the effectiveness of a process.

A behavioral analysis of all behaviors in a task may be complex and unnecessary. Going from a detailed task analysis to a more specific behavior analysis requires two steps: the specification of behaviors within critical tasks and a functional assessment of the last task within a chain of responses.

Figure 8-11. Levels 1-5 of the Behavioral Systems Engineering Model

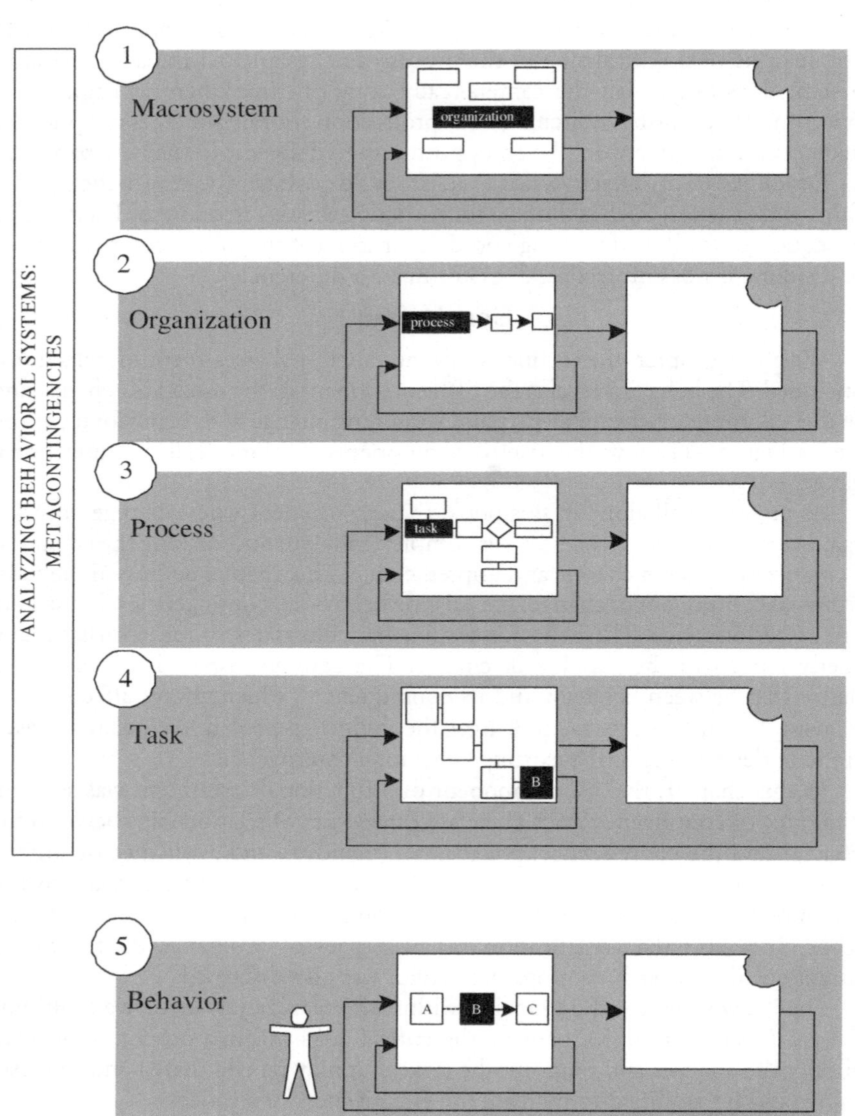

Review

1. How do you link a task analysis to a functional assessment of a behavior? Explain.
2. Identify an undesirable behavior in your workplace that happens on a regular basis. Perform a functional assessment using Table 8-4.

Table 8-4. Application of Functional Assessment

	Functional Assessment
Behavior	What behavior is under analysis? Give an example and a non-example.
Frequency	How often does it occur?
Performer	Whose behavior is under analysis?
Consequence	Is the consequence a reinforcer, an aversive condition, or a neutral stimulus?
Antecedents	What are the antecedent stimuli?
	- Specify the before condition.
	- If there is an establishing operation, specify.
	- If there is a discriminative stimulus, specify.
Contingency	Does the contingency directly control behavior?
	Specify the dimensions of the consequence: immediate or delayed, probable or improbable, significant or too small.
	Specify if the contingency is direct-acting, indirect-acting, or ineffective.
	Specify if the relationship between the behavior and the consequence is presentation, removal, or avoidance.
	What type of contingency is it? Choose one of the following:
	- Specify if the contingency is reinforcement, punishment, penalty, or escape.
	- Specify if the contingency is avoidance by the prevention of an aversive stimulus, or by the prevention of the removal (or the loss of an opportunity) of a reinforcer.
	- Specify if there is no contingency. Extinction.

Chapter 9
Management

CHAPTER 9
MANAGEMENT

The end may justify the means as long as there is something that justifies the end.

Attributed to Leon Trotsky (1879–1940)[1]

The Penalty[2]

In the United States alone:

- Traffic accidents are the number one cause of death for individuals between the ages of six and 33.
- Someone dies in a motor vehicle crash every 11 minutes.
- Nearly 42,000 people die each year in traffic accidents.
- More than four million traffic-accident survivors suffer significant physical damage.
- The annual cost of medical treatment for victims of traffic accidents is more than $71 billion, including more than $46 million in salaries.
- Using a seat belt would prevent approximately 55 percent of accident-related deaths and 65 percent of physical injuries.
- There are laws regarding seat belt use in 49 states and the District of Columbia.
- Approximately 39 percent of the population does not wear a seat belt.[3]

Since retiring as a division commander from the police force, ex-captain Jim Harmond worked in a government-funded agency helping communities across the United States increase seat belt usage. How? Through the implementation of Publicized Enforcement, an intervention program developed in Elmira, New York[4].

[1] *Trotsky, Leon (1879-1940), Russian Marxist, who organized the revolution that brought the Bolsheviks to power in 1917.*
[2] *Malott, M. E. (in press).*
[3] *To consult statistics about the number of traffic accidents, check Faigin, 1991; National Highway Safety Administration, 2000; Sleet, 1987.*
[4] *For references about the Elmira study, see Williams & Lund, 1986; Williams Preusser, & Lund, 1990; Williams, Wells, & Lund, 1987; Williams, Lund, Preusser, & Blomberg, 1986; Williams, Preusser, Blomberg, & Lund, 1987.*

Here is how it works: A time frame is established wherein a community's police officers actively increase the number of tickets they write to drivers *and* passengers not wearing seat belts. This time frame is announced publicly, through the media, prior to the event. Various organizations are invited to participate in the implementation, including the local police agency, area newspapers, the chamber of commerce, and the community's major businesses.

Although each intervention is adapted to the characteristics of the respective community, all have the same components[5] : education, baseline data collection, media campaign, increased enforcement, and post-intervention data collection[6] .

Education. The first step in the Publicized Enforcement process is to educate representatives from organizations involved with social, economic, and personal consequences of failure to use a seat belt – including members of the regional media and the police departments. Data on actual accidents are presented, including physical descriptions of those who wore seat belts versus those who did not. The data allow participants to appreciate the positive benefits of using seat belts. Participants are also informed about the program's mission to increase seat belt usage in other communities. Summary: The training sessions detail the need for intervention to prevent unnecessary deaths and physical injuries due to failure to buckle up.

Baseline Data Collection. The second component of the intervention involves collecting baseline data on seat belt use, which is measured as the percentage of the members of the community who use seat belts. Teams of volunteers from the representative organizations collect two weeks worth of data from locations with the heaviest traffic volume. Using a random sampling procedure, they record the number of cars audited along with the number of drivers and passengers wearing seat belts.

Media Campaign. The third step in the process is to educate the public through a media campaign, detailing the baseline measures of seat belt use in their area (usually showing a significant opportunity for improvement) and the success of Publicized Enforcement in other communities. Through newspapers and radio/ television programs, the public is informed about the annual number of deaths and

[5] *For other interventions conducted to increase safe behaviors of passengers and drivers, see, Berry & Geller, 1991; Geller & Lehman, 1991; Geller & Ludwig, 1990; Geller, Rudd, Kalsher, Streff, Lehman,1987; Hagenzieker, 1991; Jonah & Grant, 1985; Jonah, Dawson, & Smith, 1982; Ludwig & Geller, 1991; Lund, Stuster, & Fleming, 1989; Ragnarsson & Bjorgvinsson, 1991; Rothengatter, 1991.*

[6] *Publicized Enforcement consists of an intervention packet involving several behavioral procedures (i.e., education, media campaign, and increased enforcement). Further research would be needed to empirically demonstrate which of these three procedures is more effective in controlling behavior. However, based on the principles presented in this book, it could be anticipated that increased enforcement is the critical element of success.*

injuries from traffic accidents. In addition, the community is advised about the upcoming effort to increase police enforcement of seat belt use. An example of this type of advisory is as follows: *Between August 15th and 30th, area police officers will intensify their traffic-safety efforts. Drivers and passengers not wearing seat belts will be ticketed.*

Increased Enforcement. The fourth step requires the police department to increase its number of patrol units during the event, especially in heavy traffic zones. Sponsors believe writing a ticket to an unbelted individual is a contribution to the well-being of that person and the community. Police officers write their tickets during the intervention and are rewarded afterwards with praise by their peers and managers, based on the number of tickets issued.

Post-Intervention Data Collection. The final step of the intervention consists of measuring seat belt usage immediately following the period of increased enforcement, with the same procedures used during the baseline data collection. Figure 9-1 shows the seat belt use in 12 different cities in the United States before and after a Publicized Enforcement intervention. Figure 9-1 clearly indicates increased seat belt usage after each Publicized Enforcement intervention.

Figure 9-1. Effect of Publicized Enforcement Interventions in Cities Across the United States

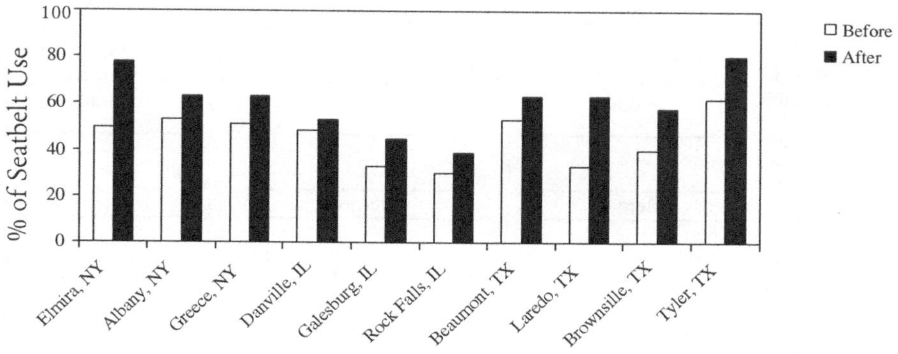

Performance Management

The success of Publicized Enforcement interventions is attributed to performance management – implementing effective contingencies when existing contingencies do not bring about the expected behavioral change. Effective contingencies require probable and sizable consequences.

Existing Contingencies

Existing contingencies are the conditions that maintain the behavior before attempting to change it. Consider the existing contingencies for seat belt use before the community-wide Publicized Enforcement intervention took place.

There are two existing contingencies in effect that could be considered. The first is ineffective and does not support seat belt use. Upon entering the car, there is an infinitesimally low probability of injury or death (before). Buckling the seat belt (behavior) causes an infinitesimally lower probability of injury or death (after). The probability of injury or death is very low before and after buckling up. Thus, the low probability involved in this existing contingency does not affect behavior[7].

The other existing contingency consists of an effective direct-acting punishment contingency, which decreases seat belt use. There is no discomfort (before) prior buckling the seat belt (behavior). Immediately afterwards, however, there is discomfort (after). This is an effective contingency in reducing seat belt use. Summary: One existing contingency is ineffective at increasing seat belt usage and the other is effective at decreasing it. Figure 9-2 shows the two existing contingencies operating in reference to buckling up.

Concept 9-1. Existing Contingency – a contingency that maintains behavior before a performance management intervention.

Figure 9-2. Ineffective and Effective Existing Contingencies of Seat Belt Use

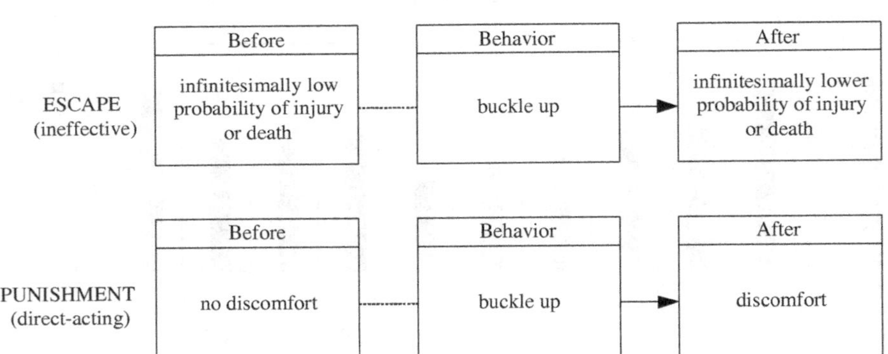

Performance Management Contingencies

When existing contingencies do not support the target behavior intended for change, performance management contingencies are implemented.

[7] *Some people have a strong history of rule following. Compliance with rules that involve ineffective contingencies might have been consistently reinforced and non-compliance might have been consistently punished. People with such behavioral repertoire might be able to follow rules that normally do not control behavior, such as buckling up when there is an insignificant reduction of the probability of an accident or death.*

Concept 9-2. Performance Management Contingency – an artificial contingency used as an intervention to alter a target behavior not supported by existing contingencies.

The Publicized Enforcement intervention involves an effective performance management contingency for seat belt use where existing contingencies fail. Between August 15th and August 30th, there is a higher probability of getting a ticket (before). Buckling up (behavior), however, eliminates the probability of being ticketed for a seat belt infraction (after).[8] This is an indirect-acting escape contingency because buckling up effectively eliminates the chances of getting a seat belt ticket. Figure 9-3 shows the performance management contingency implemented in the Publicized Enforcement intervention.

Figure 9-3. Management Contingency for Seat Belt Use in the Publicized Enforcement Intervention

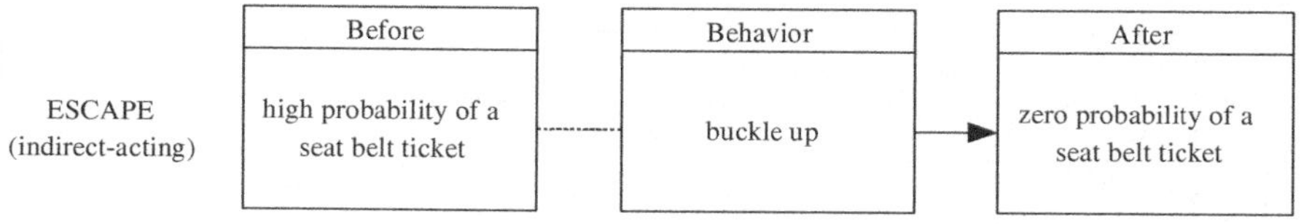

Performance management contingencies often involve deadlines. For instance, homework is due on a specific day or the opportunity for evaluation is lost. An employee has to arrive at 8 a.m. or the boss will issue a reprimand. Deadlines impose an opportunity to lose something (either a reward or removal of aversive conditions). Deadlines act as discriminative stimuli because the individual prevents losing a reward or receiving an aversive consequence by engaging in the expected behaviors[9]. The high probability of getting a ticket only exists between August 15th and August 30th. The probability of getting a seat belt-related ticket outside of this time frame is low. Deadlines bring about conditions that set up fear, worry, or other sorts of aversive conditions. For instance, students worry about failing the night before an exam, so studying (behavior) reduces the aversive feeling.

Engineering Interlocking Behavioral Contingencies

Two months after the Publicized Enforcement intervention, Jim Harmond returned to the community. He brought together the team that collected data for the

[8] *The announcement of the intervention also involves other information, such as frequency of accident and number of deaths due to failure of buckling up.*
[9] *See Malott, et al. (2000).*

first intervention and sent them out once again: this time to assess maintenance of increased seat belt usage after the intervention. The data revealed that seat belt usage had decreased significantly.

A second Publicized Enforcement intervention was then conducted. Results were similar to those generated by the first intervention: seat belt usage increased. Jim returned four months after the second intervention, gathered together the same team and collected more follow-up data. Again, results showed the percentage of seat belt usage had decreased.

Eight months after the second Publicized Enforcement intervention, the team measured again. Seat belt usage had decreased even further; it was almost reaching baseline levels. Figure 9-4 shows the percentage of seat belt usage after the two Publicized Enforcement interventions and follow-ups.

Figure 9-4. Follow-ups on the Percentage of Seat Belt Use After the Publicized Enforcement Intervention

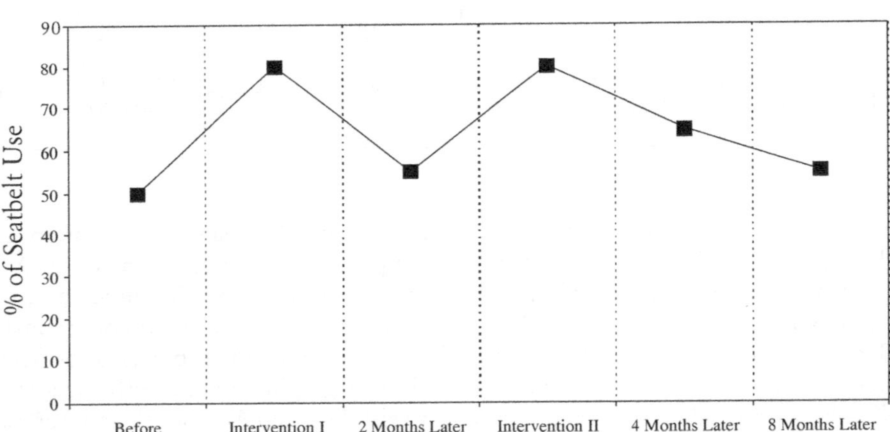

The post-event decrease in seat belt usage was repeated in each community that Publicized Enforcement interventions took place. Team members became frustrated. Why – after all of the training, information gathering, public media campaigns, and police officer recognition – were the results not maintained?

Jim realized that issuing tickets was critical to maintaining high rates of seat belt usage among drivers and passengers; and police officers were the ones responsible for penalizing those who failed to buckle up. The police officers were performance managers because they delivered the consequences of the Publicized Enforcement intervention.

> *Concept 9-3. Performance Manager – one who is in charge of delivering the consequences when implementing performance management contingencies.*

It is important to distinguish between performance managers and administrative managers. Administrative managers are those to whom we report administratively; they are the ones that evaluate our performance and determine our pay. Performance managers are those who ensure that the consequences of performance management interventions are delivered. The administrative managers are often in the best position to serve as performance managers, but this is not always the case. To effectively change behavior we need performance managers. Administrative managers who do not arrange for implementing performance management contingencies will not stimulate change effectively.

To understand why seat belt use decreased after both Publicized Enforcement interventions, it is important to understand what happens to the behavior of the performance managers (police officers) writing tickets. Figure 9-5 shows the percentage of tickets the police wrote two and four months after a Publicized Enforcement intervention in a different community.

Figure 9-5. Rate of Ticketing After Two and Four Months of Implementing the Publicized Enforcement Intervention

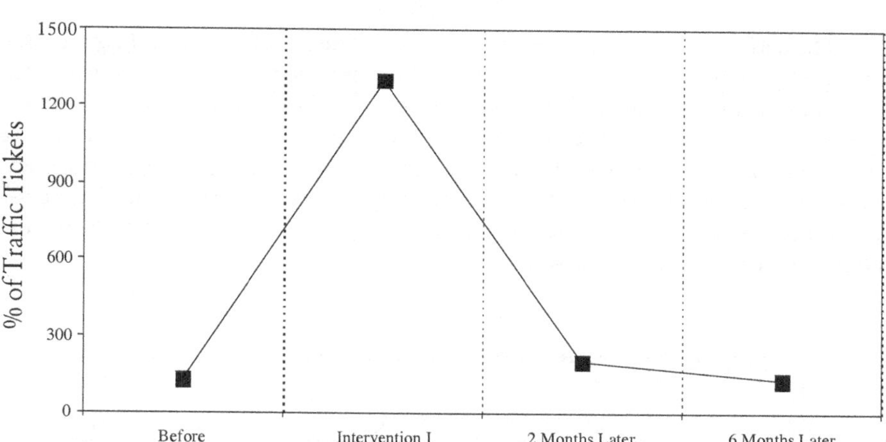

Ticketing frequency decreased in proportion to seat belt usage. People stopped buckling up because they were no longer penalized for noncompliance. Why would police officers stop writing tickets if they realized how important the traffic reprimands were to increasing the community's safety?

During the two weeks of Publicized Enforcement, the police agency monitored the number of tickets issued and recognized/rewarded the police officers who issued the highest number. When the two weeks of Publicized Enforcement ended, however, so did the recognition/reward element. There was no system in place to maintain a high rate of ticketing.

Take a look, now, at the existing and performance management contingencies operating here. There were no consequences for writing seat belt related tickets before the Publicized Enforcement intervention. Police officers considered non-compliance a minor offense and they were far more interested in major crimes. Issuing a seat belt ticket added work that did not result in professional recognition or advancement. The existing contingency consisted mainly of the increased effort resulting from writing the ticket; this was a direct-acting punishment contingency that effectively decreased the frequency of issuing tickets. Figure 9-6 shows a diagram of the existing contingency.

Figure 9-6. Existing Contingency for Police Officers Issuing Traffic Tickets

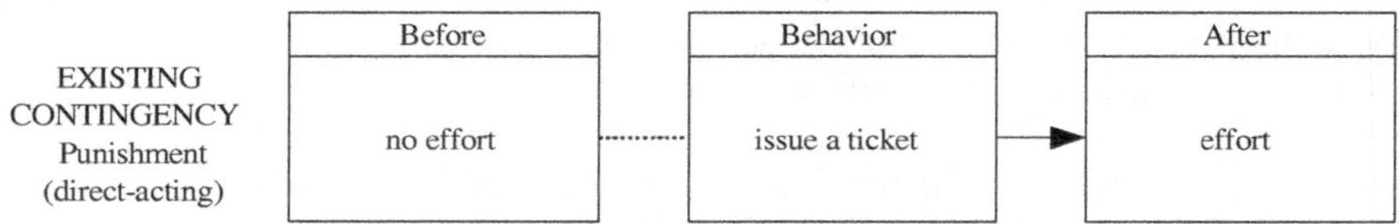

The performance management intervention added an effective contingency that operated during the two weeks of Publicized Enforcement. Prior to writing a ticket, there was the opportunity to lose positive feedback (before). A high rate of ticketing (behavior) resulted in not losing the positive feedback (after). The performance management contingency consisted of an indirect-acting avoidance contingency. Ticketing prevented the loss of the opportunity to receive recognition. Figure 9-7 shows the performance management contingency for the police officers during the Publicized Enforcement intervention.

Figure 9-7. Performance Management Contingency for Issuing Traffic Tickets

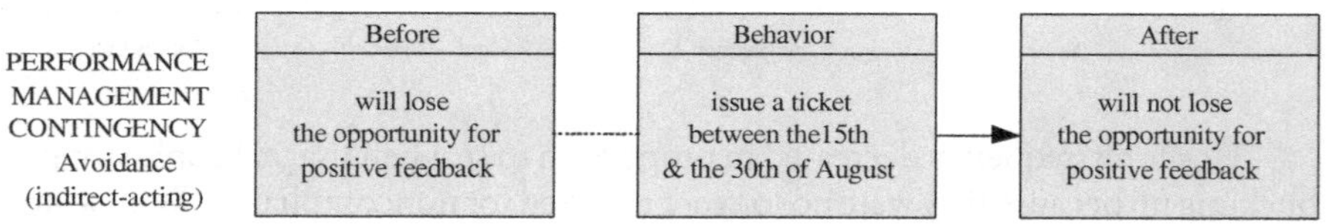

A contingency analysis should not stop with the behavior of the police officers. Figure 9-8 shows the levels of management and specific behaviors requiring performance management to support a high rate of seat belt usage.

Figure 9-8. Levels of Performance Management Needed to Support Publicized Enforcement Interventions[10]

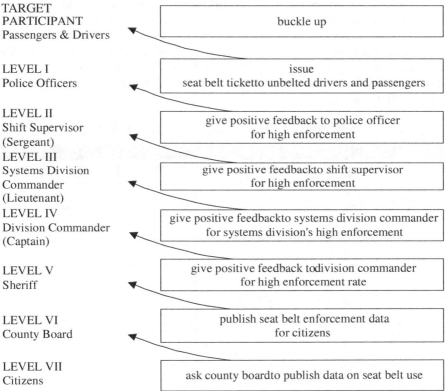

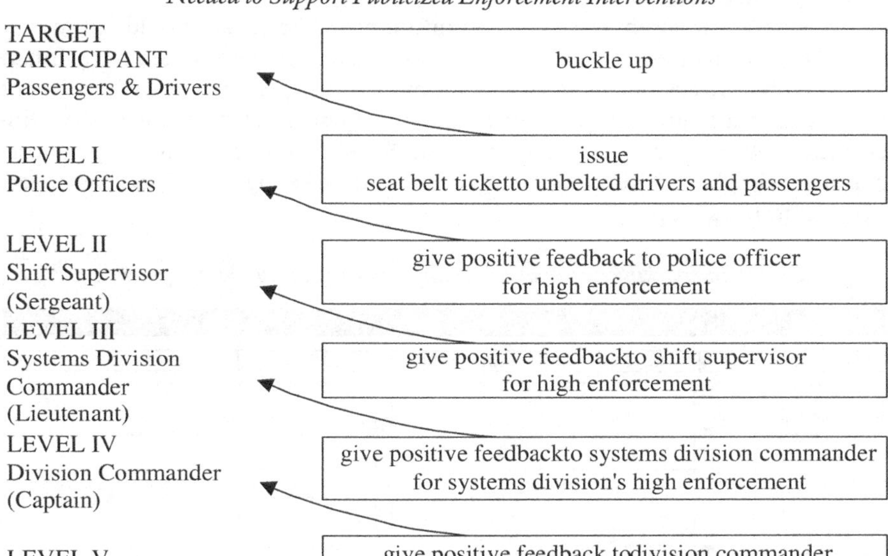

Concept 9-4. Management of the Manager – contingencies that maintain the behavior of the manager implementing consequences for the behavior change of others.

Concept 9-5. Interlocking Behavioral Contingencies at Various Levels of Management – design behavioral contingencies at all levels of management that ultimately support the targeted behavior change. The interlock consists of a manager delivering the consequences for the contingencies of those in the level below.

Private citizens and influential groups have the power to exert tremendous pressure on public administrators, particularly if the people exerting the pressure have suffered the devastating consequences of being in a car accident without wearing a seat belt – or know someone who has. Citizen groups in the United States

[10] *In some counties, the sheriff is elected by the citizens.*

have influenced legislative changes and increased enforcement of seat belt usage, speeding, and drunk driving.

A similar situation exists in organizations. Customers should ultimately support performance management interventions, otherwise it is hard to maintain them. How can customer demands become the last performance management contingency in change interventions? By designing interlocking behavioral contingencies at all levels of management. Figure 9-9 shows an analysis of behavioral contingencies that can support the intervention of ticketing drivers and passengers who fail to buckle up.

Figure 9-9. Interlocking Behavioral Contingencies at Various Management Levels

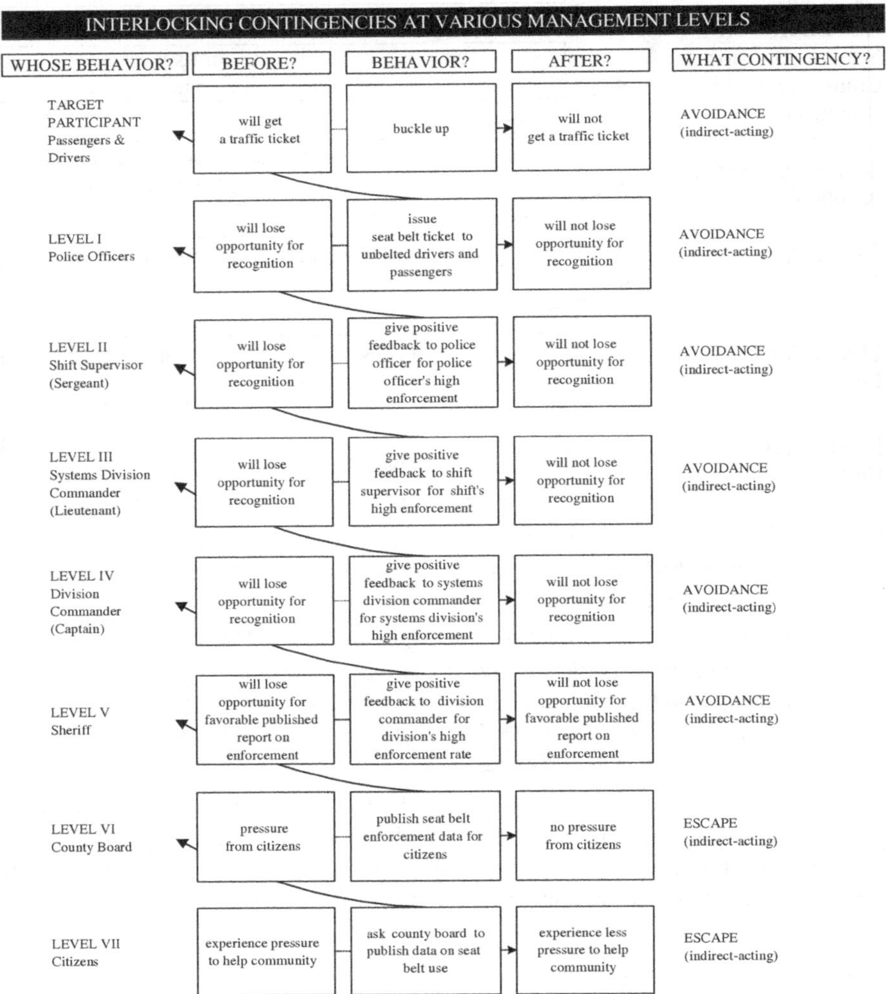

Figure 9-9[11] shows the contingency design necessary to successfully implement an intervention affecting the use of seat belts in the community. Notice that opportunities for positive feedback establish avoidance contingencies.

It is foolish to attempt organizational change by focusing all reform efforts on the last person in the hierarchy, the one who ultimately performs the processes. The police department wants officers to write more tickets for seat belt infractions; however, it does not alter the behaviors of those who rank above the officers. This is usually because those who make the decisions for change – upper management – exclude themselves from the change equation. Without changing the behavior of those in the middle- and upper-level hierarchy, interventions are not maintainable.

The more levels of administrative management in an organization the harder the change process. Why? Because it takes a tremendous amount of design work to create interlocking behavioral contingencies that are directly linked to the ultimate target behavior. A direct link might be an impossible task if the organization is too bureaucratic.

Developing Control Systems

In order to maintain multiple levels of behavior management contingencies, we need a control system. A control system is one that provides information to evaluate if contingencies are maintained and expected aggregate results are obtained. Typically, control systems involve integrated feedback systems.

> *Concept 9-6. Control Systems for Behavioral Engineering – provide information to evaluate the implementation of behavioral contingencies at multiple management levels and the accomplishment of expected aggregate results.*

In order to maintain a high frequency of traffic tickets, a system needs to be designed to provide data about the implementation of all interlocking behavioral contingencies involved in the intervention. It is essential to keep track of the percentage of passengers and drivers who buckle up; the frequency with which police officers issue tickets; the percentage of sergeants who provide positive feedback to police officers for high enforcement of seat belt use; the percentage of lieutenants who give positive feedback to sergeants for high enforcement of their shifts... and so on.

As you can imagine, it would take a tremendous amount of work to collect and process information about the implementation of multiple-level, interlocking behavioral contingencies. That is why, in order to develop effective interventions, contingencies and the technology infrastructure that allows process feedback (like presented in Chapter 6) need to be designed. Without effective technology, it would

[11] *Figure 9-9 specifies the interlocking contingencies at the same levels of management presented in Figure 9-8.*

be hard to maintain behavioral interventions due to the high response cost needed for ongoing evaluation.

Organizations often fail to develop effective control systems for their change interventions. At their best, they develop systems to collect data on the organizations' aggregate products, such as sales, market share, and inventory turns. Although such data are needed, they are not sufficient to sustain behavioral interventions. Data on implementation of performance management contingencies and their results are essential if organizations are to avoid "watering down" their change interventions.

Adjusting Interlocking Behavioral Contingencies

The engineering of behavioral contingencies is never ending. Just like the systems we are trying to change are constantly evolving, the fine-tuning of contingencies – at all levels of management – must continually change. Control systems provide information needed to fine tune behavioral contingencies.

By no means should the design and implementation of behavioral interventions be viewed as the end of a change process. The interventions ought to constantly change based on feedback and the organization's dynamics. After the implementation of the first set of interlocking behavioral contingencies, we might have to add, change, or get rid of some contingencies to adjust to other organizational changes – such as, alterations of the reporting structure, acquisition of technology, and modification of existing processes. Without ongoing adjustment, our interventions could soon become obsolete.

Conclusions

One aspect of the paradox of organizational change is that the environment where change takes place is dynamic, complex, and chaotic. Behavioral interventions ought to adjust to these properties. The other side of the paradox is that the process through which we adjust our interventions to such challenging organizational environments is constant because the consequences always affect future behavior: It is simple because the essential component lies in the behavioral contingency and it is systematic because it can follow an orderly method and have predictable results.

The sixth component in the model of organizational change is performance management. Figure 9-10 shows the six components of the model and the ongoing analysis and intervention adjustment.

Figure 9-10. Levels 1-6 of the Behavioral Systems Engineering Model

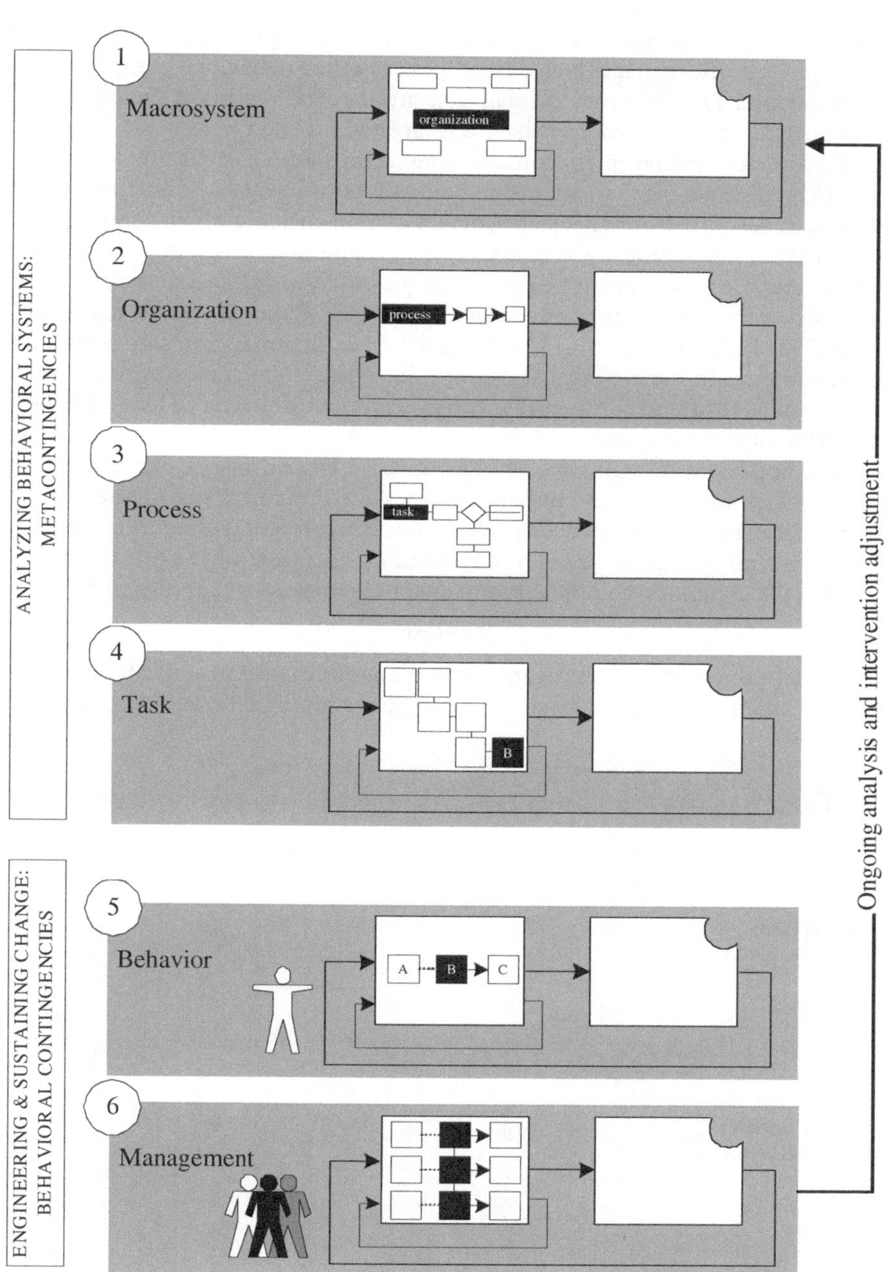

The sixth component refers to engineering interlocking performance contingencies at all levels of management that ultimately support the target behaviors for change. The contingencies are interlocked because a component of the behavioral contingency of the manager is also a component of the behavioral contingency of the performer. The performance managers are those who control the behavioral consequences for those whose behavior is targeted for change.

Performance management consists of replacing ineffective existing contingencies with effective performance management contingencies. Sometimes it is possible to design performance management contingencies in which consequences are delivered automatically. For example: a computer program that delivers consequences contingent on responses only – such as immediate feedback for practice test answers – without the need of managers. Other automatic contingencies include the ability to enter a building only if an identification card is scanned at the entrance. In the majority of organizational situations, however, someone is needed who consistently ensures that consequences are delivered. That someone is the performance manager.

It is important to maintain the behavior of the performance manager. If the manager does not implement the contingencies, it is difficult to sustain the targeted behavioral change. Maintenance of behavioral change requires ongoing feedback (a control system) on implementation and results. The interventions have to constantly adjust to the dynamics, complexity, and chaos organizations typically go through.

Review

Specify the existing contingency and the performance management contingency to change a specific behavior of interest in your organization. Use Figure 9-11.

Figure 9-11. Exercise on Existing and Performance Management Contingencies

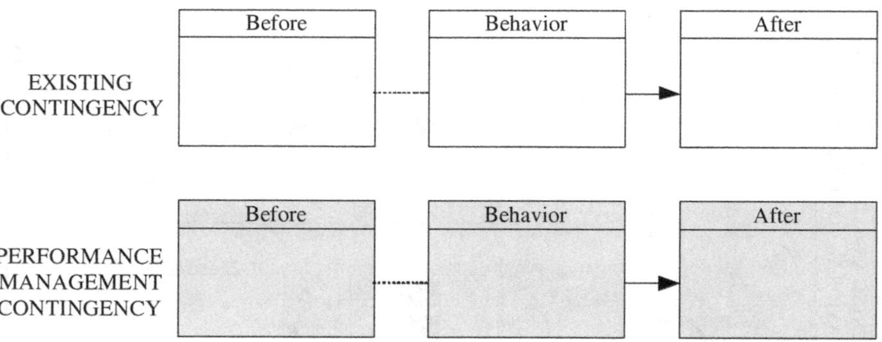

Identify the management contingencies at various levels that will support the behavior change of the target participant. Use Figure 9-12 in the analysis.

Figure 9-12. Interlocking Behavioral Contingencies at Various Management Levels

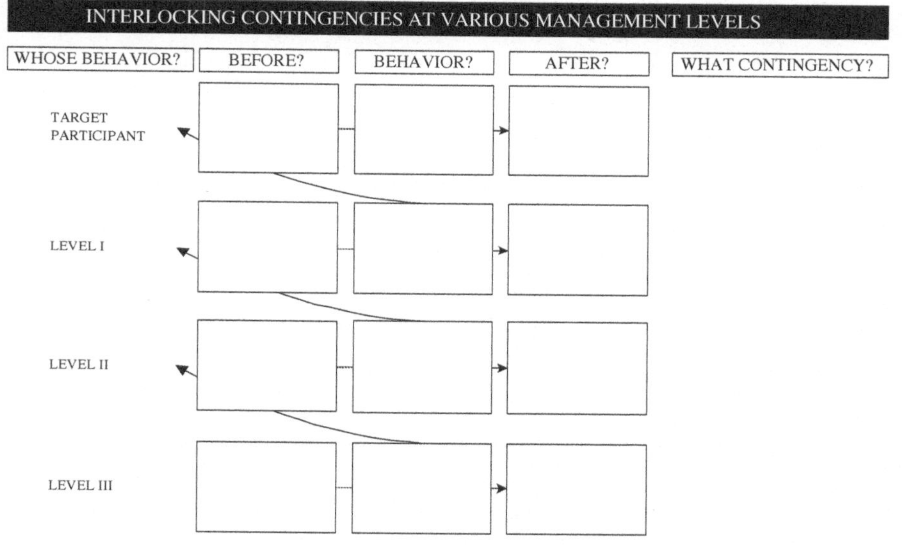

Chapter 10
Behavioral Systems Engineering

CHAPTER 10
BEHAVIORAL SYSTEMS ENGINEERING MODEL[1]

The "sane" man is not the one who has eliminated all contradictions from himself so much as the one who uses these contradictions and involves them in his work.

Maurice Merleau-Ponty (1908–1961)[2].

The Vicious Cycle

Next slide please, Don says. Jay, the consultant, advances the next slide while the vice president of Operations continues with his presentation about the "manufacturing of the future" program... the latest and hottest change initiative.

There are 24 people in the conference room. They nod their heads and smile here and there. *Can't Don and Jay see how they are putting the audience to sleep?* Kim wonders.

The speakers, exchanging positions at the podium, shift gears and begin acting like cheerleaders – rallying their fans with promises. *"Manufacturing of the future" will help us improve performance over the competition ... excel in our customer's eyes... reduce turnover...*

How many times have I heard this before? Kim asks herself. In her 20 years on the job, she's sat through countless flashy initiatives like this. Sighing quietly, she thinks *it's just the same old stuff, over and over again.*

Gerard, the company's new president, is alarmed about the $40 million remaining in inventory at year-end and he pressures Don for a solution. Gerard has never run a plant and has no clue as to what really goes on or what it takes to change the company. He delegates two or three initiatives per week: each with the same sense of priority.

Excuse me, someone from the audience says. *Will I have to work longer hours to keep this program going?* Jay – with enthusiasm that seems clearly forced – smiles and says, *not much!* Wrong answer. The person who asked the question continues with a chain of complaints. *NOT MUCH? You're asking a lot! How can you ask us to work harder without taking away any other responsibilities?*

[1] *For an alternative view to organizational reengineering, see Hammer, 1997; Hammer & Champy, 1993; Hammer & Stanton, 1995.*
[2] *French existentialist philosopher.*

Jay, not knowing how to handle the complaints, turns to the group. *Can anyone address those points?* he asks. Avoiding a direct answer has paid off for him before. Let someone else take the heat.

Karen raises her hand. Most of those in the audience anticipate her typical tell-the-bosses-what they-want-to-hear comments. She concludes her own session of corporate cheerleading by saying, *We can do it!* Feeling in safe territory once more, Jay says, *Excellent points.*

As usual, the challenger is stigmatized as a *complainer* and his valid points are ignored. Everyone pretends that good attitude alone can change the company's numbers, without giving it any further thought.

Kim knows what will happen. Karen will be the first one to jump overboard once the new program is launched. Those that do try to keep the ship afloat will do so at the expense of failing to focus on scrap rate reduction, production quality, and other critical processes: key areas for the company. Eventually, someone will call a meeting – in this same conference room – to launch yet another new change initiative that will focus on one of the neglected processes. And the game will go on. In the end, everyone will feel victimized by their own actions, overwhelmed by the demands; and frustrated by the lack of real progress.

Breaking the Vicious Cycle

Many change initiatives are a vicious cycle. These initiatives get launched, people are mobilized, resources allocated, and energy invested. Soon afterwards, other demands take over and attention, resources, and commitment go elsewhere. When no real change occurs, justifications for failure emerge and the same problems resurface. All that is left are partial records and distorted memories of how the initiative began, developed, and died. Same initiatives take new names, new sponsors, new players, and the same vicious cycle continues.

> *Concept 10-1. Vicious Cycle of Organizational Change – change is approached superficially to resolve crisis, but the underlying problems are not resolved and they resurface. When that happens, new superficial solutions are attempted.*

In this chapter, I bring all the pieces of the Behavioral Systems Engineering Model from previous chapters together and explain how the Model addresses the constant, simple, and orderly aspects of the paradox of organizational change. In other words, I will explain how to stop the vicious cycle.

We have to start by appreciating the paradoxical nature of change. Change involves inherent contradictions. Consider, for instance, a system for a figure skater to win a short-program competition in the Olympics. A technical program only lasts two minutes and 40 seconds. To get the highest score, all aspects of performance count: proper posture, balance, length of glide, and speed.

In order to compete well, the skater must practice the same short routine thousands of times. And each instance of the performance is unique; it cannot be replicated. Why? Because a short routine is complex and depends on many factors that affect each other. Audience reactions affect emotional conditions, practice affects skill, the position of the arms affects the ability to gain speed, and speed varies with distance.

Because studying performance in the existing environment is complex, training interventions must be adjusted to variables such as the type of competition, skill of the skater, previous injuries, skill level, and performance of other competitors. A rigid training program will not produce consistently great performance because it will not suit all of the changing environmental conditions.

The conditions affecting the skater's performance might seem chaotic, but the shaping of a professional skating repertoire is a systematic and orderly process. Ultimately, performance will be improved as a result of changes in the behavioral contingencies affecting each precise movement in the short program. Each single movement in the program is different from the one performed in previous program practices (for instance, each triple turn is slightly different), but the functional relationship between each movement and its consequences remains constant.

Many change initiatives fail because they are approached as if change were simple and accomplished with permanent solutions or inflexible interventions. We produce things and those things – the training, the process, the technology – are sold as if they were fixed solutions. But fixed solutions never work. For example, a rigid diet often fails. Unless the diet is adapted to changing conditions, such as travel schedules, available foods, social circumstances, physical health, and exercise routine, the diet (intervention) will be unsuccessful in the long run.

In this book, I have presented a method that breaks the vicious cycle of typical organizational change: a method that generates *real* change with dynamic and evolving interventions that produce meaningful results. This method is founded on the principles that govern change – derived from the scientific study of behavior and the dynamics of behavioral systems – and in the units or components of change. The remainder of the book addresses the foundation and method of changing behavioral systems. (See Table 10-1.)

Table 10-1. Orderly, Simple and Constant Aspects of the Change Process

Orderly Simple, and Constant Aspects of the Change Process		
Principle	**Units**	**Method**
Environmental selection: -Cultural Selection - aggregated product demand alters interlocking behavioral contingencies -Selection by consequences- consequences alter future behavior	-Behavioral system -Metacontingency -Behavioral contingency	-Analyzing behavioral systems through metacontingencies (macrosystem, organization, process, tasks) -Engineering and sustaining behavioral change (behavior, management)

The foundation

The basic principle underlying change is environmental selection. Environmental demands ultimately select organizational practices. For instance: manufacturing practices are driven by customers' product specifications, retailing product mix is determined by trends in consumers' buying habits and, services are improved as the demands of clients/consumers increase. These environmental demands shape cultural practices within the organization. And cultural practices are made up of many behaviors.

Just like the environment selects future practices of complex systems (cultural selection), the consequences of behavior select future behavior (law of effect). When rewarding consequences follow behavior, that behavior will more likely occur in the future (e.g., rewarding consequences for work discussions will probably increase participation). When aversive consequences follow behavior, that behavior will *less* likely reoccur (e.g., written warnings for arriving late to work will probably decrease late arrivals).

Environmental selection is best expressed through the units of organizational analysis – the behavioral system, the behavioral contingency, and the metacontingency. We use the behavioral system, to define the scope of the system we are analyzing; the behavioral contingency, to analyze the behavior of single individuals; and the metacontingency, to analyze complex systems involving the behavior of multiple individuals affecting each other.

Behavioral System

A behavioral system is one that contains the behavior of its participants and their interaction with the resource, which generates a product that has a receiver. Total Performance System (TPS) is the analysis tool that helps to illustrate how a behavioral system interacts with its environment. It has the following components: an ultimate mission, a product, receiving system, receiving system feedback, processing system, processing system feedback, resources, and competition.

Behavioral Contingency

A four-year-old boy's temper tantrums – every time his parents went out for the evening – drove his distraught parents to seek the advice of a psychologist. The child cried, moaned, and screamed so hard that they no longer had a social life. The psychologist, one of my colleagues, asked the couple if he could interview the child alone. *Danny, your parents say that when they are about to leave you cry and scream really hard, is that true?* Danny nodded his head in affirmation. *And why is that?* my friend asked. *Because when I do, they stay,* Danny said.

Danny's disruptive behavior paid off. When he threw a temper tantrum, his parents would not leave. This same effect happens at all levels in organizations – consequences affect the future probability of behavior. Arriving on time to work is maintained if it prevents disciplinary action; checking a particular computer screen increases if the needed information is reliably there; participation in decision making increases if it is supported. (Chapters 7, 8 and 9 detail how consequences affect future instances of behavior.)

The behavioral contingency is the smallest unit of analysis of a behavioral system. It involves the behavior of one individual and its consequences (given specific conditions). We engineer behavioral change at the level of the behavioral contingency by affecting the frequency of behavior or generating new behavior.

Metacontingency

A metacontingency involves a conglomerate of interlocking behavioral contingencies containing the behavior of multiple individuals, which generates a product that has a demand. The metacontingency of telegraph development two centuries ago involved a complex set of interlocking behavioral contingencies, the behavior of countless individuals in all systems and subsystems of the telegraph industry); an aggregate product, the transmission of messages intercity, transcontinental and transoceanic; and the demand of the receiving systems – railroad companies and newspapers – both of which became primary users of telegraphs.

To understand how environmental determinism works at the complex levels of the metacontingency, we should understand three critical components of the metacontingency: interlocking behavioral contingencies, aggregate product, and receiving-system demand.

Interlocking behavioral contingency

"An interlocking behavioral contingency involves the behavior of at least two participants, where any components of the behavioral contingency or the behavioral product of one participant interacts with the behavioral contingencies or products of other participants" (Glenn, 1988, p. 167).

For instance, consider an assembly line. A single part is assembled by one individual, the assembled part is given to another person who labels it, the labeled part is received by another individual who wraps it, the wrapped product is given to another line worker who boxes it ... and so forth.

The dynamics of organizations are not as linear as the preceding assembly-line example. Instead, they involve convoluted interlocking behavioral contingencies. For instance, person A makes a request to person B; the request causes person B to search for a file; person B looks at the clock, realizes it is lunch time, and leaves; person C looks up, notices that person B has left, and stops his or her work to make a phone call ...

It is impossible, impractical, and unnecessary to study all behavior that occurs in organizations. To narrow down the set of interrelated behavior that makes a difference for an organization, we focus on interrelationships that generate relevant aggregate products for the success of the organization. For instance, we might not be interested in learning about every single telephone call people make or every employee interaction throughout the workday.

Aggregate product

An aggregate product is the result of the behavior of multiple individuals. Aggregate products might be the daily newspaper, the monthly flight schedule of an airline, the daily electricity delivered in a community.

Because each organization has an incalculable number of contingencies, we need a way to identify those that are worth analyzing. A practical way to start sorting the relevant metacontingencies is by identifying the aggregate products critical for the organization's survival. If an aggregate product does not meet needed standards, then we should study metacontingencies involving aggregate sub-products.

For instance, we might start with the final product of an organization: the plastic parts of an injection molding company. If the aggregate product does not meet quality standards, we might analyze the metacontingencies that produce aggregate subproducts indispensable to the production of plastic parts – molds, dried plastic, molding specifications, packaging, and shipping. If the molds are damaged too often, we might study aggregate sub-products involved in the handling process: set up, delivery, and storage.

The analysis of metacontingencies is like peeling an onion. The more complex layers involve aggregate products with the largest number of individuals and interlocking behavioral contingencies; whereas, the least complex metacontingency involves the aggregate product generated by two individuals. At the heart is the behavioral contingency that maintains the behavior of each individual. Each layer is contained in the next layer.

Receiving system demand

A set of interlocking behavioral contingencies will continue to exist only if their aggregate product has demand from the receiving system. The receiving system demand determines survival of an organizational practice. Here lies the principle of cultural selection.

For instance, the receiving-system demand for telegraphic services revolutionized the way organizations communicated at the beginning of the 1800s and caused substantial change in the telegraph-industry metacontingency. Many new telegraph companies emerged, others consolidated, and upgraded technology was developed. The whole industry changed as consumer demand changed. If there were no demand for its services, the telegraph industry would not have developed.

Likewise, less complex metacontingencies, such as those contained in internal organizational processes, change, and adapt to the demands of receiving systems. I once worked for an injection molding company that produced plastic components for telecommunication devices. The production metacontingency dramatically changed with the placement of a *single order* from a manufacturer of health products: molded blood conductors for heart transplants in infants. Because the stakes were so high – a contaminated part could result in the loss of an infant's life – we increased safety standards, determined additional quality control procedures, designed a pollution-free environment, and redesigned the layout of the plant.

But not all receiving-system demand generates adaptive changes. Because millions of behavioral contingencies and metacontingencies form an organization, some of its receiving systems could generate dysfunctional processes. Consequently, organizations could evolve until reaching the point of self-destruction.

Dysfunctional organizational growth is like cancer. A healthy human body is composed of 30 trillion cells, all of which are constantly dying and reproducing. In a cancerous cell, permanent gene alterations, or *mutations*, cause the cell to malfunction. These mutations may take many years to accumulate and can go unnoticed. But cancerous cells can form secondary growths by extending to neighboring tissue. The dysfunctional cells eventually break through nearby blood vessels – entering the circulatory system – and invade the rest of the body. The result can be deadly. When dysfunctional cells enter the respective receiving systems, the systems break down and facilitate additional dysfunctional growth.

> *Concept 10-2. Dysfunctional Organizational Growth – receiving system demand can shape and maintain metacontingencies harmful for the long-term survival of an organization.*

Utilizing the concept of "serendipitous architecture," a city planner illustrated for me the dysfunctional growth of human systems outside the capital city of a Latin-American country. People with the least amount of resources move from marginal zones in the country to the outskirts of the capital, looking for better living opportunities. Initially, their situation shows little improvement. As generations evolve, however, the economic condition of the family improves. They acquire access to electricity, build additional rooms onto their homes, and begin to prosper. Sections of the various neighborhoods develop, meeting the demands of each family. But the whole grows by accidental conditions – in a serendipitous fashion – without a systematic plan. Eventually, the entire system may collapse as the marginal neighborhoods outgrow the supplies of water and electricity and fail to sustain its weak physical, economic, and social infrastructure.

Organizations often evolve in a serendipitous manner without an integrated plan. If dysfunctional growth gets out of control and is not properly corrected, it may eventually erode the organization to the point of collapse. We need a process of change that helps organizations to correct dysfunctional evolution, adapt, and survive.

The method

The change model proposed in this book consists of implementing modifications that have survival value for the organization and help it to avoid serendipitous evolution. The model has two components: (1) the analysis of behavioral systems with metacontingencies and (2) behavioral engineering to sustain behavioral change. Figure 10-1 shows a summary of the model presented in this book.

Figure 10-1. Behavioral Systems Engineering Model

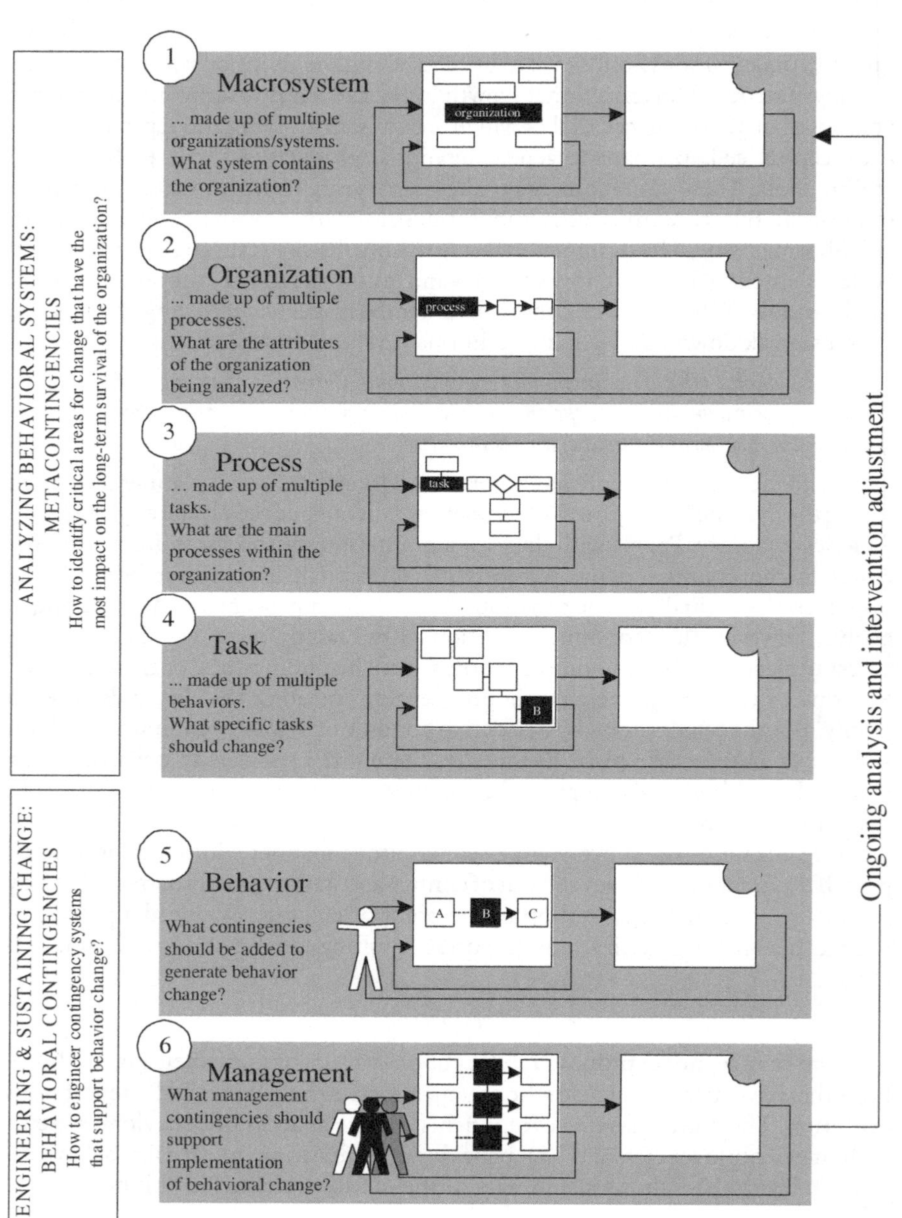

Analyzing behavioral systems with metacontingencies

Too often, those in positions of power – the board of directors, senior vice presidents and business owners – make change decisions without the benefit of an objective analysis. It is not always clear how many of those decisions are the product of ignorance (simply not knowing what it really takes to implement change) or pretentious (people intuitively *knowing what's best*). In any event, impulsive decisions result in incidents like the one experienced by the corporate president – at the beginning of this chapter – who overwhelmed his team with requests for change. Those asking for change might not realize the feasibility and consequences of their requests; for instance, the impact that a 10 percent sales increase will have on margins, inventory management, or labor demands.

Change cannot be taken lightly. Systems analysis with metacontingencies allows us to study the complexity of organizations and determine what is worth changing, which battles to fight, what is the impact of change on other processes, competitiveness, and long-term survival. Systems analysis requires order, research, and measurement at various levels: macrosystem, organization, process, and tasks.

Macrosystem

The study of how an organization operates within its macrosystem begins by answering the following questions: *How is the industry performing? What are the consumer trends? What are the conditions of the economy?* (See chapter 3.) If we ignore the macrosystem, we could end up deceiving ourselves. For example, the company that celebrates increased sales while its market share remains low. If the whole industry is selling more, an increase in sales does not reflect progress – especially if the organization's sales are decreasing in proportion to that of the competition.

Organization

An understanding of the macrosystem gives direction to the study of the organization as a whole. At all organizational levels of analysis, we assess improvement priorities by objectively responding to questions like the following: *What aspects of the product need improvement, based on customers' feedback? What process in the organization is directly responsible for that improvement? How is the company positioned in relation to the competition?* (See Chapter 4.)

Process

By establishing priorities at the organizational level, we set parameters for studying the critical processes necessary for overall success. We ought to determine how the core processes of the organization perform and whether support and integrating departments contribute to that core. (See Chapter 5.)

Organizational change needs to be driven by the core of the organization, the processes that generate the product ultimately responsible for revenue. Unfortunately, most organizations – from manufacturing to service, communications, and retail – have similar functional problems. The work is driven by department structure (administrative structure) rather than by integrated processes, and every department acts as if it were the core. Furthermore, departments at the core do not work cooperatively: support departments do not assist core departments and integrating departments work independently. Personnel lose sight of their department's purpose. They do not understand the importance of their function to critical issues of the business. As a result, core departments have no support and must do much of the work that other departments *should* do for them. They acquire too many responsibilities to do a good job; therefore, they end up overwhelmed and ineffective.

Tasks

In order to fully comprehend a process, we have to understand the tasks involved – what each individual does, uses, and produces. (Chapter 6 explained how to study tasks within processes.) By studying the tasks, we realize that processes cannot have departmental walls. For instance, a production process starts when the order gets into the system and ends when the consumer receives his or her product. People from all departments have something to do with the process. Salespeople receive the specifications of the order, purchasing acquires the raw materials, and engineering provides the equipment. The actions of each participant are important, no matter what department he or she works in.

The analysis of tasks ends with the identification of the critical behaviors. It is like sorting the wheat from the chaff – much of the behavior occurring in organizations is irrelevant to success. We should limit our focus to the following: behavior essential for the production of critical tasks; tasks essential for critical processes, and processes essential for the organization to satisfy a need of the macrosystem.

Engineering and sustaining behavioral change

Systems analysis through metacontingencies helps us to identify interlocking behavioral contingencies that need improvement. The transition from the analysis of interlocking behavioral contingencies to behavioral contingencies is in identification of detailed tasks. Detailed tasks involve the behavior of a single individual. Ultimately, we identify the target behaviors worth changing within a task. Engineering helps us to design interlocking behavioral contingencies that generate and maintain the desired target behavioral change.

> *Concept 10-3. Behavioral Engineering – application of the science of behavior to design environments that generate and sustain desired behavior.*

Engineering behavioral systems is like constructing a building. The basic elements of building involve (but are not limited to) the foundation, which supports the building and provides stability; the structure, which supports all the imposed loads and transmits them to the foundation; and control systems, including the heating, lighting, and acoustical systems. In behavioral systems, the foundation consists of the interlocking behavioral contingences of the performers directly responsible for the process; the structure consists of the supporting body of contingencies at various level of management; and the control system consists of the ongoing feedback and improvement of supportive contingencies and aggregate results.

Behavior

The foundation of behavioral systems engineering is the design and implementation of behavioral contingencies for the performers directly responsible for the processes.

Concept 10-4. Performer – individual responsible for the tasks involved on the front line of the process.

Just like we need to understand ground conditions before laying a building's foundation, we need to understand why the performers act the way they do – analysis of the existing behavioral contingencies – before we can effectively engineer new behavioral contingencies.

Effective contingencies involve consequences that are sizeable, probable, and consistently delivered: contingent upon the target behavior. For instance, we encourage workers to use safety glasses in a plant. If compliance has significant consequences, like getting work-schedule privileges, workers will wear the glasses. If consequences are not maintained, compliance more likely will not be maintained either. (Analysis and design of behavioral contingencies were detailed in Chapters 7 and 8.) Therefore, to sustain compliance, we ought to affect the management structure of the organization.

Management

Engineering a well-designed system requires much thought, creativity, and skill. It is like setting up a structure and control systems in the construction of a building. The structure consists in designing metacontingencies involving behavioral contingencies at all levels of management that ultimately support the target behavior of the performer. (See Chapter 9.) The consequences of the performer's contingencies, the foundation of the behavioral engineering system, are delivered by the manager level one. The contingencies for the behavior of manager level one are delivered by manager level two, and so forth.

For example, consider a system where a sales representative of a pharmaceutical company who visits high profile physicians gets positive feedback from the district manager. High profile physicians have the highest number of patients and therefore the highest opportunity to prescribe drugs. In order to maintain the contingency for the sales representative, we ought to design behavioral contingencies for the district director to provide feedback to the performer; for the regional director to provide feedback to the district director; and for the vice president of sales to provide feedback to the regional director. If well designed, the system of performance management contingencies ought to generate the expected aggregate product –

increased sales – which ought to be in demand by the rest of the company. (See Figure 10-2 for an illustration.)

Figure 10-2. Interlocking Behavioral Contingencies at Multiple Management Levels

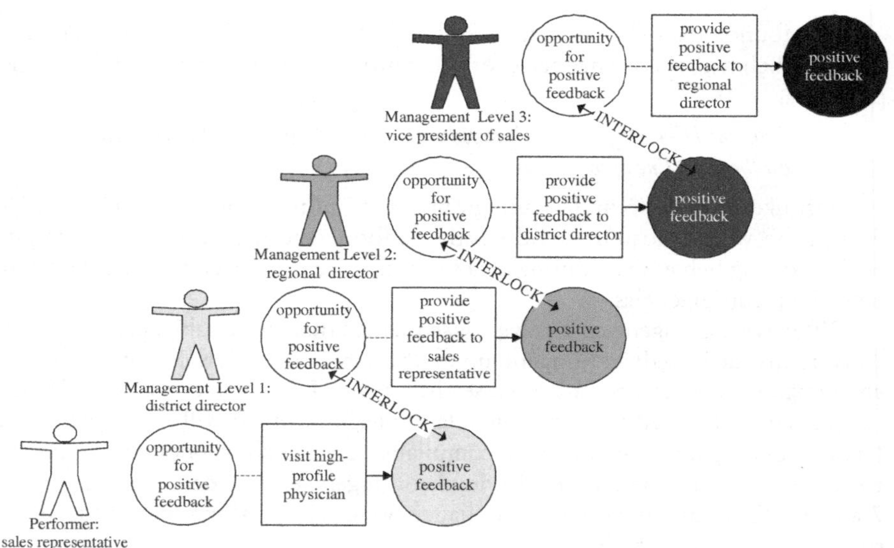

A control system is needed in order to maintain multiple levels of performance management contingencies. It provides information to evaluate whether contingencies are maintained and expected aggregate results are obtained. This information is needed to fine-tune behavioral contingencies.

The engineering of behavioral contingencies should be ongoing. Just like the systems we are trying to change are constantly evolving, the fine-tuning of contingencies must continually change: at all levels of management.

Throughout each component of the model, various analyses and change tools were presented to assist those attempting to change organizations. Table 10-2 shows a summary of the levels of analysis, the questions asked, and helpful tools.

Table 10-2. Levels of Analysis and Tools for Systematic Organizational Change

Level of Analysis	Questions	Analysis Tools
Macrosystem and Mission (Chapter 3)	- What macrosystem are we analyzing - What is the product of the macrosystem? - What is the macrosystem receiving system? - What is the macrosystem receiving system feedback? - What is the processing system of the macrosystem? -What is the macrosystem processing system feedback? -What is the ultimate mission of the organization?	- Guide for formulating the mission - Analysis of the macrosystem as a total performance system (TPS)
Organization (Chapter 4)	- What objective measurements answer the following questions? - What is the difference between the mission and the products of the organization? - Who are the clients that receive the products? - What is the clients' feedback in relationship to the products? - What process transforms the resources into products? - How do we know if the process is functioning well? - What resources are necessary to generate the products? - Who competes for resources and clients in the organization?	Analysis of the organization as a total performance system
	Strategic Plan: - What are the three-year goals of the organization, with respect to the mission, products, clients, process, resources, and competition? - What strategies will be implemented to achieve the goals of the strategic plan in three years?	Strategic planning framework

Level of Analysis	Questions	Analysis Tools
Process (Chapter 5)	- What is the summary of the administrative organizational chart? - How do we understand the organization as a process where some departments' output serve as input for other departments? - What are the aggregate products, responsibilities, and measurements of each department or function? - What are the core, support, and integrating departments? - How can you graphically represent the relationship between the department functions?	-Structural analysis -Department-function analysis -OUGHT TO BE analysis of departments
Task (Chapter 6)	Summarize a process: - What process are we analyzing (identification)? - Where does it begin and end (scope)? - What are the subprocesses? - Which units participate? - How many participants does it include? - What are the general tasks? - What are the main aggregate products? - What is the sequence of general tasks? - What components make the process unique? - How long does it last?	Summary map
	-How is the relationship between the tasks and products of the participants graphically represented in the process?	Detailed process map
	-What are the indispensable tasks? -Which can be modified? -Which can be eliminated? -Which could be added? -Which databases, operational systems, and applications do the participants use? -What is the impact of task optimization?	Map of existing technology infrastructure

Level of Analysis	Questions	Analysis Tools
Behavior (Chapters 7 and 8)	-What behavior is under analysis? -How often does it occur? -Whose behavior is under analysis? -Is the consequence a reinforcer, an aversive condition, or a neutral stimulus? -What are the antecedent stimuli (i.e., before condition, establishing operation, discriminative stimulus)? -Does the contingency directly control behavior? -What are the dimensions of the consequence: immediate or delayed, probable or improbable, significant or too small? -Is the contingency direct-acting, indirect-acting or ineffective? -Is the relationship between the behavior and the consequence presentation, removal, or avoidance? -What type of contingency is it? Choose one of the following: -Is the contingency reinforcement, punishment, penalty, or escape? -Is the contingency avoidance? If so, is it by the prevention of an aversive stimulus, by the prevention of the removal of a reinforcer? -Is the behavior extinction.	Functional Assessment
Management (Chapter 9)	-What are desired change interventions for the performer's behavior? -What are the levels of management needed to support the change interventions? -What is the system of contingencies that supports the change interventions? -What control system facilitates the implementation of engineered interlocking behavioral contingencies?	Interlocking behavioral contingencies at various levels of management

Conclusions

Organizational change is paradoxical because it involves contradictions between the nature of the environment where change takes place and the process that causes the change. The environment where change occurs is dynamic, as it evolves over time; however, the process of change is constant because the dynamic relationship between behavior and environment does not vary. The environment of change is complex, but the components are simple, having only one essential part – the behavioral contingency. The environment appears chaotic, unsystematic, and unpredictable. Yet the way that environment gets to be chaotic is orderly, systematic, and predictable.

Change interventions that do not adapt to the intricacies, complexity, and dynamics of organizations do not make a difference in the long term. The actions of a production worker depend on many variables, such as the state of technology, customer demands, equipment, conditions of the plant, other aspects of his or her job, the job of others, and much more. All of those variables are constantly affecting each other.

Throughout this book, I described the orderly, simple, and constant aspects of the change process. Those consist of the principle, the units of analysis, and the method of change.

The principle consists of the underlying law or assumption in change, that is, environmental selection or determinism. At the metacontingency level, environmental determinism is expressed through cultural selection – the demands of an aggregated product alters the interlocking behavioral contingencies that produce it. At the behavioral contingency level, environmental determinism is expressed through selection by consequences – the consequences of behavior alters future occurrences.

Units of analysis are the parts in which a system can be analyzed. I used three units of analysis: the behavioral system, the metacontingency, and the behavioral contingency. The behavioral system helps to define the system being analyzed. The metacontingency is a complex unit; it consists of the demand for an aggregate product generated by the behavior of at least two individuals affecting each other. The behavioral contingency is the simplest unit; it consists of the relationship between behavior and its antecedents and consequences.

The method is a systematic and orderly procedure used to alter organizations. The method consists of the behavioral systems engineering model presented in this book, which helps to break the vicious cycle of organizational change that produces no results. This model has three primary components: analyzing behavioral systems with metacontingencies and engineering, sustaining change by manipulating behavioral contingencies, and ongoing analysis and intervention adjustment.

Review

- What is the paradoxical nature of change?
- What are the two main units of analysis in organizational change?

- Describe the three components of metacontingencies:
    - Interlocking behavioral contingencies
    - Aggregate product
    - Receiving system demand
- What is the rationale for the components of the behavioral systems engineering change model:
    - Macrosystem
    - Organization
    - Process
    - Tasks
    - Behavior
    - Management

GLOSSARY

Concept 1-1.	Dynamic vs. Constant Contradiction – the environment where change occurs is dynamic, as it evolves over time. But the process of change is constant because the dynamic relationship between behavior and environment is always present
Concept 1-2.	Change – the product of alteration, variation, or modification.
Concept 1-3.	Change Process – a series of actions that result in alteration, variation, or modification.
Concept 1-4.	Complex vs. Simple Contradiction – the environment of change is complex because it occurs in the midst of multiple and convoluted interactions. It is simple because there is only one essential process that accounts for the evolution of organizations – the functional relationship between the behavior and the environment.
Concept 1-5.	Closed System – group of interrelated components that do not interact or evolve with changes in the environment. Closed systems eventually die.
Concept 1-6.	Chaotic vs. Orderly Contradiction – organizations are seemingly unpredictable, but the process through which they change can be systematic and predictable.
Concept 1-7.	Open System – a group of interrelated components that adapt to complexity, dynamics, and chaos in the environment.
Concept 1-8.	Paradox of Change – change involves contradictions between the environment where change occurs and the process of change: dynamic vs. constant, complex vs. simple; chaotic vs. orderly.
Concept 2-1.	Organizational Victim Blaming – unjustly assuming that those who suffer the consequences of a poor functioning system are responsible for the system's flaws.
Concept 2-2.	Environmental Selection – the underlying principle of change: the conditions that precede and follow the behavior of individuals affect how they behave in the future.
Concept 2-3.	Cultural Selection – cultural practices that produce material gains for a culture tend to survive.
Concept 2-4.	Law – affirmation of an invariable order or relationship that occurs under specific conditions.
Concept 2-5.	Law of Effect – under constant conditions, the future probability of the behavior increases when rewarding consequences follow it. The future probability of the behavior decreases when aversive consequences follow it.
Concept 2-6.	Behavioral Selection – behavior that produces rewarding consequences for the individual tends to reoccur.

Concept 2-7.	Units of Analysis – parts in which a system can be analyzed: behavioral system, behavioral contingency, and metacontingency.
Concept 2-8.	Behavioral System – a group of interrelated elements that form an entity.
Concept 2-9.	Total Performance System – an analysis tool of an organization which includes the mission, product, receiving system, receiving system feedback, processing system, processing system feedback, resources, and competition.
Concept 2-10.	Interlocking Behavioral Contingency – involves the behavior of at least two participants, where any component of the behavioral contingency or product of one participant interacts with elements of the behavioral contingency or product of other participants.
Concept 2-11.	Behavioral Product – results after the behavior occurred.
Concept 2-12.	Aggregate Product – compounded result of multiple behavioral products.
Concept 2-13.	Metacontingency – a conglomerate of interlocking behavioral contingencies containing the behavior of multiple individuals, which generates a product that has a demand.
Concept 2-14.	Performance – behavior and its product.
Concept 3-1.	Macrosystem – the system that contains the organization we are analyzing.
Concept 3-2.	Mission – the ultimate goal of the organization.
Concept 3-3.	Mission-Driven Organizations – define the ultimate mission of the organization in its macrosystem and design contingencies that facilitate the achievement of the intermediate and ultimate objectives.
Concept 3-4.	Organizational Myopia – to lose sight of the dynamics of the macrosystem and mission.
Concept 3-5.	Activity Trap – focus on the activity, losing sight of the mission.
Concept 3-6.	Micro Management – excessively checking on others' activities rather than delegating responsibilities and holding others accountable, losing sight of the main objective.
Concept 3-7.	Guide for Formulating the Mission – the mission of the organization is stated in terms of the product, receiving system, and feedback from the receiving and processing systems of the macrosystem.
Concept 4-1.	Basic Elements of Measurement – type of measure (nature of the measure), unit of measurement (expression of the measure), standard (quantitative performance expectation).
Concept 4-2.	Volume – quantity or rate.
Concept 4-3.	Quality – essential properties or precision.
Concept 4-4.	Timeliness – ability to meet deadlines.
Concept 4-5.	Duration – quantity of time invested.

Concept 4-6. Cost – value defined in terms of money or effort invested.
Concept 4-7. Receiving System – customers who receive an organization's products and services.
Concept 4-8. Market Strategy – method of taking an organization's products and services to the potential market.
Concept 4-9. Receiving System Feedback – data or customer information that reflects the evaluation of the organization's products and services.
Concept 4-10. Process – systematic tasks that transform an organization's resources into products and services.
Concept 4-11. Organizational Structure – administrative-reporting between departments within organizations.
Concept 4-12. Organizational Chart – graphic representation of the organizational structure.
Concept 4-13. Sub-Optimization Principle – optimization of a subsystem does not result in the optimization of the whole system.
Concept 4-14. Feedback of the Processing System – evaluation of how a system functions.
Concept 4-15. Resources – indispensable means to generate the organization's products; for example, personnel, services, information, materials, and equipment.
Concept 4-16. Competition – organizations that offer products or services to the same potential customers and that use the same resources to generate their products.
Concept 4-17. Strategic Plan – specifying the organization's activities that ensure future competitive advantage and profitability.
Concept 5-1. Process – series of actions and their aggregate products directed to a particular purpose.
Concept 5-2. Function – purpose of one action or group of actions that generates an aggregate product.
Concept 5-3. Department – section of one organization generally separated by different administrative lines that generates a main aggregate product.
Concept 5-4. Structural Analysis – study of the administrative reporting lines.
Concept 5-5. Department-Function Analysis – study of the main functions or responsibilities of the departments, the interactions between departments and measures of success.
Concept 5-6. Core Departments – the motor of an organization, departments directly responsible for business income.
Concept 5-7. Support Departments – provide specific products and services to other departments.
Concept 5-8. Integrating Departments – receive and provide information across all the departments of the organization.

Concept 6-1.	Process Executive Summary – graphic outline of the process. Includes identification, scope, subprocesses, units, general tasks, aggregate products, participants, uniqueness, and duration.
Concept 6-2.	Identification – a description of the process metacontingency being analyzed and where it fits into the overall functioning of the organization.
Concept 6-3.	Scope – the limits of the process metacontingency, where it begins and where it ends.
Concept 6-4.	Subprocesses – the main component metacontingencies of a larger process, listed in the order of occurrence.
Concept 6-5.	Units – departments or groups of individuals that participate in the process.
Concept 6-6.	Participants – individuals that play a role in the process and whose behavior are part of the interlocking behavioral contingencies being analyzed.
Concept 6-7.	General Task – a summary of a metacontingency that forms part of a process; that is, a group of interlocking behavioral contingencies carried out by different individuals, the resulting aggregate product, and the source of receiving system demand.
Concept 6-8.	Uniqueness – variations of single processes.
Concept 6-9.	Specific Task – an individual's action or set of actions and the resulting behavioral product.
Concept 6-10.	Task Analysis Guide – a tool for analyzing specific tasks within a process. It provides answers to the following questions: Who executes it? What does it consist of? How long does it last? What does it produce? What are the indispensable resources? Who receives the products?
Concept 6-11.	Detailed Process Map – graphic representation of the relationship between specific tasks and products among individuals and units involved in a process.
Concept 6-12.	Computer Program Application – list of instructions in a programming language that tells a computer to perform a certain task and allows the user to manipulate information.
Concept 6-13.	Database – systematically arranged collection of computer data, structured so that it can be automatically retrieved or manipulated.
Concept 7-1.	Functional Assessment – a study of the environmental relations that maintain behavior.
Concept 7-2.	Dead Man Test – if a dead man can do it, it is not a behavior.
Concept 7-3.	Behavior – an organism's action.
Concept 7-4.	After Condition – the consequence of behavior; in other words, a stimulus, event, object, or condition that is presented contingent on behavior.

Concept 7-5. Reinforcer – a stimulus, event, object, or condition that when presented immediately after the behavior, increases its future likelihood.

Concept 7-6. Aversive Consequence – a stimulus, event, object, or condition that, when presented immediately after the behavior, decreases its future likelihood.

Concept 7-7. Generalized Conditioned Reinforcer – a stimulus, event, or object that has acquired reinforcing properties for most individuals through pairing with other reinforcers (e.g., attention and money).

Concept 7-8. Teleology – the cause for an action is in the future.

Concept 7-9. Antecedent Condition – a stimulus, event, object, or condition that precedes the response.

Concept 7-10. Before Condition – a condition that exists before the behavior occurs. The contrast between the before and the after conditions helps to define the behavioral contingency.

Concept 7-11. Behavioral Contingency – a casual relationship between the behavior and its consequences, given specific antecedent conditions.

Concept 7-12. Establishing Operation – environmental event, operation, or stimulus condition that affects an organism by momentarily altering (a) the reinforcing effectiveness of other events and (b) the frequency of occurrence of the type of behavior that had been consequated by those events.

Concept 7-13. Discriminative Stimulus (SD) – a stimulus in the presence of which a contingency is in effect.

Concept 7-14. SD – a stimulus in the presence of which the contingency is not in effect.

Concept 7-15. Direct-Acting Contingency – contingency that involves a consequence that is immediate, probable, and sizeable that directly increases or decreases the future likelihood of the behavior that precedes it.

Concept 7-16. Dimensions of a Consequence – temporality, probability, and size.

Concept 7-17. Contingency with Delayed Consequences – the consequence is presented more than 60 seconds after the behavior.

Concept 7-18. Contingencies with Improbable Consequences – the behavior's consequence may or may not occur.

Concept 7-19. Contingency with Small Consequences – the consequence of behavior is so small that only the cumulative effect of repeated incidents of that behavior have a significant effect.

Concept 7-20. Indirect-Acting Contingencies – contingencies that involve delayed, though probable and sizeable, consequences. They control behavior through additional processes other than the contingency itself.

Concept 7-21. Ineffective Contingencies – do not control behavior because they involve a consequence that is too small or improbable.

Concept 7-22. Rule – verbal description of a contingency.

Concept 8-1. Neutral Stimuli – do not have any influence on behavior.

Concept 8-2. Reinforcement – stimulus, event, object, or condition that when presented immediately after the behavior increases its future likelihood.

Concept 8-3. Escape – aversive stimulus, event, or condition that when removed immediately after a behavior increases the future likelihood of that behavior.

Concept 8-4. Punishment – aversive stimulus, event, or condition that when presented immediately after a behavior decreases the future likelihood of that behavior.

Concept 8-5. Penalty – stimulus, event or condition that when removed immediately after a behavior decreases the future likelihood of that behavior.

Concept 8-6. Avoidance Contingency – the behavior prevents the presentation of an aversive stimulus or the removal of a reinforcer.

Concept 8-7. Resistance to Extinction – when the reinforcement contingency is not in effect, the behavior's frequency increases temporarily and then decreases until the behavior ceases to occur.

Concept 8-8. Extinction – procedure in which reinforcement of a previously reinforced behavior is discontinued. In the extinction procedure, the before and after conditions are the same.

Concept 8-9. Stimulus-Response Chain – a sequence of discriminative stimuli and responses in which each response, except for the very last one in the chain, serves as a discriminative stimulus for the following response.

Concept 8-10. Analog to Stimulus-Response Chain – sequence of stimuli and responses in which one response may serve as an antecedent stimulus for another response, with the exception of the last one. The sequence between the components of the chain is not continuous and it involves indirect and ineffective contingencies.

Concept 9-1. Existing Contingency – a contingency that maintains behavior before a performance management intervention.

Concept 9-2. Performance Management Contingency – an artificial contingency used as an intervention to alter a target behavior not supported by existing contingencies.

Concept 9-3. Performance Manager – one who is in charge of delivering the consequences when implementing performance management contingencies.

Concept 9-4. Management of the Manager – contingencies that maintain the behavior of the manager implementing consequences for the behavior change of others.

Concept 9-5. Interlocking Behavioral Contingencies at Various Levels of Management – design behavioral contingencies at all levels of management that ultimately support the targeted behavior change. The interlock consists of a manager delivering the consequences for the contingencies of those in the level below.

Concept 9-6. Control Systems for Behavioral Engineering – provide information to evaluate the implementation of behavioral contingencies at multiple management levels and the accomplishment of expected aggregate results.

Concept 10-1. Vicious Cycle of Organizational Change – change is approached superficially to resolve crisis, but the underlying problems are not resolved and they resurface. When that happens, new superficial solutions are attempted.

Concept 10-2. Dysfunctional Organizational Growth – receiving system demand can shape and maintain metacontingencies harmful for the long-term survival of an organization.

Concept 10-3. Behavioral Engineering – application of the science of behavior to design environments that generate and sustain desired behavior.

Concept 10-4. Performer – individual responsible for the tasks involved on the front line of the process.

REFERENCES

Abernathy, W. B. (1996). *The sin of wages.* Memphis, TN: PerfSys Press.

Aguirre Serena, M. E. (1998). *Aplicación del sistema de supervisión de tesis en la línea de investigación curricular en la Facultad de Psicología y Educación de la Universidad Veracruzana de la Región de Veracruz.* Unpublished master's thesis, Universidad Veracruzana, Veracruz, Mexico.

Alarcón Urdapilleta, A. F. (2001). *Un modelo organizacional aplicado a la normatividad de la Universidad Pedagógica de la Universidad Veracruzana.* Unpublished master's thesis, Universidad Veracruzana, Veracruz, Mexico.

Alvarado Ruíz, S. E. (2000). *Propuesta de un sistema de supervisión para incrementar la titulación de alumnos de psicología.* Unpublished master's thesis, Universidad Veracruzana, Veracruz, Mexico.

Bacon, F. (1956). *The advancement of learning and New Atlantis.* London: Oxford University Press.

Baldwin, J. D., & Baldwin, J. I. (1998). *Behavior principles in every day life* (3rd ed.). Upper Saddle River, NJ: Prentice Hall.

Bellamy, E. (1967). *Looking backward, 2000-1887.* Cambridge: Belknap Press of Harvard University. (Original work published 1888)

Berry, R. D., & Geller, E. S. (1991). A single-subject approach to evaluating vehicle safety belt reminders: Back to basics. *Journal of Applied Behavior Analysis, 24,* 13-22.

Bicycle helmet use in British Columbia: Effects of the helmet use law. (2000, April.) Chapel Hill, NC: University of North Carolina Highway Safety Research Center.

Brethower, D. M. (1972). *Behavioral analysis in business & industry.* Kalamazoo, MI: Behaviordelia.

Brethower, D. M. (1993a). Strategic improvement of workplace competence I: Breaking out of the incompetence trap. *Performance Improvement Quarterly, 5*(2), 29-42.

Brethower, D. M. (1993b). Strategic improvement of workplace competence II: The economics of competence. *Performance Improvement Quarterly, 5*(2), 29-42.

Brethower, D. M. (1995). Specifying a human performance technology knowledge base. *Performance Improvement Quarterly, 8*(2), 17-39.

Brethower, D. M. (1999). Specifying a human performance technology database. In P. J. Dean (Ed.), *Performance Engineering at Work* (pp. 17-142). Washington, DC: International Society for Performance and Instruction.

Brethower, D. M. (2000). A systemic view of enterprise: Adding value to performance. *Journal of Organizational Behavior Management, 20*(3/4), 165-190.

Brethower, D. M., & Smalley, K. (1998). *Performance based instruction.* San Francisco, CA: Jossey-Bass Pfeiffer.

Campanella, T. (1981). *The city of the sun: a poetical dialogue*. Berkeley: University of California Press. (Original work published 1623)

Carver (Jr.), N. F. (1981). *Iberian villages*. Kalamazoo, MI: Documan.

Carver (Jr.), N. F. (1987). *Japanese folk houses*. Kalamazoo, MI: Documan.

Carver (Jr.), N. F. (1993). *Form & space in Japanese architecture*. Kalamazoo, MI: Documan.

Carver (Jr.), N. F. (1995). *Italian hill towns* (2nd ed.). Kalamazoo, MI: Documan.

Case, J. (1995). *Open-book management*. New York: Harper Business.

Chenier, T. C., & Evans, L. (1987). Motorcyclist fatalities and the repeal of mandatory helmet wearing laws. *Accident Analysis and Prevention*, *19*, 133-139.

Covey, S. R. (1990). *The seven habits of highly effective people*. New York: Simon & Schuster.

Daniels, A. C. (1989). *Performance management* (3rd ed.). Tucker, GA: Performance Management Publications.

Daniels, A. C. (1994). *Bringing out the best of people*. New York: McGraw-Hill.

Daniels, A. C. (2000). *Other people's habits*. New York: McGraw-Hill.

Darwin, C. (1979). *The origin of the species*. New York: Gramercy. (Original work published 1859)

Dean, P. J. (1999a). Performance engineering. In P. J. Dean (Ed.), *Performance engineering at work* (pp. 3-26). Washington, DC: International Society for Performance and Instruction.

Dean, P. J. (1999b). Tom Gilbert, engineer of worthy performance. In P. J. Dean (Ed.), *Performance engineering at work* (pp. 27-40). Washington, DC: International Society for Performance and Instruction.

Diamond, J. (1997). *Guns, germs, and steel*. New York: W. W. Norton.

Encarta. (2003). *World English Dictionary*. [Computer software]. Redmond, WA: Microsoft Corporation.

Evans, L. (1991). *Traffic safety and the driver*. New York: Van Nostrand Reinhold.

Faigin, B. M. (1991). The costs of motor vehicle injuries. *Auto & Traffic Safety*, *1*, 2-10.

Garlock, M. M. (2001). Distilling the need for process-driven change. In L. Hayes, R., Fleming, J. Austin, & R. Houmanfar (Eds.), *Organizational change* (pp. 321-323). Reno, NV: Context Press.

Geller, E. S., & Lehman, G. R. (1991). The buckle-up promise card: A versatile intervention for large-scale behavior change. *Journal of Applied Behavior Analysis*, *24*, 91-94.

Geller, E. S., & Ludwig, T. D. (1990). A behavioral change taxonomy for improving road safety. *Proceedings of the International Road Safety Symposium* (pp. 41-45). Copenhagen, Denmark.

Geller, E. S., Rudd, J. R., Kalsher, M. J., Streff, F. M., & Lehman, G. R. (1987). Employer-based programs to motivate safety belt use: A review of short-term and long-term effects. *Journal of Safety Research*, *18*, 1-17.

Gilbert, T. F. (1996). *Human competence: Engineering worthy performance.* Amherst, MA: HRD Press. (Original work published 1978)

Gilbert, T. F. (1999). A question about performance. In P. J. Dean (Ed.), *Performance engineering at work* (pp. 41-60). Washington, DC: International Society for Performance and Instruction.

Gilbert, T. F., & Gilbert, M. B. (1999). Performance engineering: Making human productivity a science. In P. J. Dean, *Performance engineering at work* (pp. 61-74). Washington, DC: International Society for Performance and Instruction.

Glenn, S. S. (in press). Culture and its origins. In K. A. Lattal & P. N. Chase (Eds.), *Behavior theory and philosophy.*

Glenn, S. S. (1991). Contingencies and metacontingencies: Relations among behavioral, cultural and biological evolution. In P. A. Lamal (Ed.), *Behavioral analysis of societies and cultural practices* (pp. 39-73). New York: Hemisphere.

Glenn, S. S. (1986). Metacontingencies in Walden Two. *Behavior Analysis and Social Action, 7,* 1-7.

Glenn, S. S. (1988). Contingencies and metacontingencies: Toward a synthesis of behavior analysis and cultural materialism. *The Behavior Analyst, 11*(2), 161-179.

Glenn, S. S., & Field, D. P. (1994). Functions of the environment in behavioral evolution. *The Behavior Analyst, 17(2)*, 241-259.

Glenn, S. S., & Madden, G. J. (1995). Units of interaction, evolution, and replication: Organic and Behavioral Parallels. *The Behavior Analyst, 18*(2), 237-251.

Glenn, S. S., & Malott, M. E. (2001, May). *Units of selection in organic behavioral and cultural domains.* Paper presented at the annual meeting of the *Association for Behavior Analysis*, New Orleans, LA.

Guthrie, R. (1989). *Nicholas Mukomberanwa.* Zimbabwe, Harare: Z.P.H.

Hagenzieker, M. P. (1991). Enforcement or incentives? Promoting safety belt use among military personnel in the Netherlands. *Journal of Applied Behavior Analysis, 24,* 23-30.

Hammer, M. (1997). *Beyond reengineering.* New York: Harper Business.

Hammer, M., & Champy, J. (1993). *Engineering the corporation.* New York: Harper Business.

Hammer, M., & Stanton, S. A. (1995). *The reengineering revolution.* New York: Harper Business.

Harris, M. (1964). *The nature of cultural things.* New York: Random House.

Harris, M. (1974). *Cows, pigs, wars and witches.* New York: Random House.

Harris, M. (1977). *Cannibals and kings: The origins of cultures.* New York: Random House.

Harris, M. (1979). *Cultural materialism: The struggle for a science of culture.* New York: Random House.

Harris, M. (1981). *Why nothing works.* New York: Simon & Schuster.

Harris, M. (1986). *The sacred cow and the abominable pig.* New York: Simon & Schuster. (Originally published as Good to Eat)

Heylighen, F. (1992). Evolution, selfishness and cooperation, *Journal of Ideas*, *2*(4), 70-76.

Johnson, D. M., & Bell, D. A. (1995). *Metropolitan universities: An emerging model in American higher education*. Denton, TX: University of North Texas.

Jonah, B. A., & Grant, B. A. (1985). Long-term effectiveness of selective traffic enforcement programs for increasing seat belt use. *Journal of Applied Psychology*, *67*, 89-96.

Jonah, B. A., Dawson, N. E., & Smith, G. A. (1982). Effects of a selective traffic enforcement program on seat belt usage. *Journal of Applied Psychology, 67*, 89-96.

Keller, F. S., & Schoenfeld, W. N. (1950). *Principles of psychology*. New York: Appleton-Century-Crofts.

Khan, C. H. (1979). *The art and thought of Heraclitus*. New York: Cambridge University.

Krause, T. R. (1997). *The behavior-based safety process* (2nd ed.). New York: Van Nostrand Reinhold.

Lattal, K. A., & Perone, M. (1998). The experimental analysis of human operant behavior. In K. A. Lattal & M. Perone (Eds.), *Handbook of research methods in human operant behavior* (pp. 3-14). New York: Plenum.

Lavarreda Martinez, K. (2001). *Efectos de la implementación de un modelo organizacional en la Universidad Pedagógica Veracruzana*. Unpublished master's thesis, Universidad Veracruzana, Veracruz, Mexico.

Lincoln, J. F. (1951). *Incentive management*. Cleveland, OH: The Lincoln Electric.

Lincoln, J. F. (1961). *A new approach to industrial economics*. New York: The Devin-Adair.

Ludwig, T. D., & Geller, E. S. (1991). Improving the driving practices of pizza deliverers: Response generalization and moderating effects of driving history. *Journal of Applied Behavior Analysis*, *24*, 31-44.

Lund, A. K., Stuster, J., & Fleming, A. (1989). Special publicity and enforcement of California's belt use law: Making a "secondary" law work. *Journal of Criminal Justice*, *17*, 329-341.

Machado, A. R. (1969). *Antología poética*. Madrid, Spain: Editores Salvat.

Malott, M. E. (1992). Planning the well-being of a culture: An analysis of the Cuban experiment. *Behavior and Social Issues*, *2*(2), 99-118.

Malott, M. E. (1998). Misión universitaria: Calidad de vida a través de la educación superior. *Agenda Académica*, *5*(2), 3-12.

Malott, M. E. (1999). Creating lasting organizational changes. *Performance Improvement*, *38*(2), 33-36.

Malott, M. E. (2001, May). Finding and counting the needles in the haystack. Paper presented at the annual meeting of the Association for Behavior Analysis. New Orleans, LA.

Malott, M. E. (2001a). Putting the horse before the cart. In L. Hayes, R., Fleming, J. Austin, & R. Houmanfar (Eds.), *Organizational change* (pp. 297-320). Reno, NV: Context Press.

Malott, M. E. (2001b). *Paradoja de cambio organizacional* [Paradox of organizacional change]. México: Trillas.

Malott, M. E. (in press). Enforcement of seat-belt laws. In M. Sato, N. Sujiyama, & M. Boyle (Eds.), Theoretical and applied issues of behavior analysis. Osaka, Japan: Niheisha.

Malott, M. E., & Glenn, S. S. (2001, May). *Is the metacontingency greater than the sum of behavioral contingencies?* Paper presented at the annual meeting of the *Association for Behavior Analysis*, New Orleans, LA.

Malott, R. W. (1988). Rule-governed behavior and behavioral anthropology. *The Behavior Analyst, 11*, 181-203.

Malott, R. W. (1992). A theory of rule-governed behavior and organizational behavior management. *Journal of Organizational Behavior Management, 12*(2), 45-65.

Malott, R. W., & García, M. E. (1987). A goal-directed model for the design of human performance systems. *Journal of Organizational Behavior Management, 9*, 125-159.

Malott, R. W., & Malott, M. E. (1990). Role of private events in rule governed behavior. In L. J. Hayes & P. N. Chase (Eds.), *Dialogues on verbal behavior* (pp. 237-258). Reno, Nevada: Context Press.

Malott, R. W., & Whaley, D. L. (1976). *Psychology*. Kalamazoo, MI: Behaviordelia.

Malott, R. W., Malott, M. E., & Shimamune, S. (1992a). Comments on rule-governed behavior. *Journal of Organizational Behavior Management, 12*(2), 91-102.

Malott, R. W., Malott, M. E., & Shimamune, S. (1992b). Rule-governed behavior and organizational behavior management. *Journal of Organizational Behavior Management, 12*(2), 112-116.

Malott, R. W., Malott, M. E., Trojan, E. A. (2000). *Elementary principles of behavior* (4th ed.). Upper Saddle River, NJ: Prentice Hall.

Martin, G., & Paer, J. (1996). *Behavior modification: What it is and how to do it* (5th ed.). Upper Saddle River, NJ: Prentice Hall.

McSween, T. E. (1995). *The values-based safety process*. New York: John Wiley & Sons.

Michael, J. L. (1993). *Concepts and principles of behavior analysis*. Kalamazoo, MI: Association for Behavior Analysis.

Miller, L. K. (1997). *Principles of everyday behavior analysis*. Pacific Grove, CA: Brooks/Cole.

Molina Candiani, E. (1997). *Efecto de un sistema de supervisión en la calidad de las actividades para la elaboración de tesis*. Unpublished master's thesis, Universidad Veracruzana, Veracruz, Mexico.

More, T., Sir (1999). *Utopia*. Oxford, New York: Oxford University Press. (Original work published 1516)

National Highway Traffic Safety Administration. (2000). *Traffic safety facts 1999*. (NHTSA Publication No. DOT HS 809 100). Washington, D.C.: U.S. Department of Transportation.

Nava Bustos, M. A. (2001). *Un modelo para evaluar la licenciatura en educación física de la Universidad Pedagógica Veracruzana.* Unpublished master's thesis, Universidad Veracruzana, Veracruz, Mexico.

O'Brien, R. M., Dickinson, A. M., & Rosow, M. P. (1982). *Industrial behavior modification: A management handbook.* New York: Pergamon Press.

Odiorne, G. S. (1974). *Management and the activity trap.* New York: Harper & Row.

Peter, L. J. (1993). *Peter's Quotations: Ideas for our time.* New York: Morrow, William.

Peter, L. J., & Hull, R. (1976). *The Peter Principle: Why things always go wrong.* New York: Morrow, William.

Plato. (2000). *The Republic.* (T. Griffith, Trans.) Cambridge, New York: Cambridge University Press. (Original work published 380 AC)

Ragnarsson, R. S., & Bjorgvinsson, T. (1991). Effects of public positing on driving speed in Icelandic traffic. *Journal of Applied Behavior Analysis, 24,* 85-88.

Rothengatter, T. (1991). Automatic policing and information systems for increasing traffic law compliance. *Journal of Applied Behavior Analysis, 24,* 53-88.

Rummler, G. A., & Brache, A. P. (1995). *Improving performance: How to manage the white space on the organizational chart.* San Francisco, CA: Jossey-Bass.

Serrano Solis, R. (2001). *Evaluación de un modelo organizacional en el area administrativa de la Universidad Pedagógica Veracruzana.* Unpublished master's thesis, Universidad Veracruzana, Veracruz, Mexico.

Skinner, B. F. (1953). *Science and human behavior.* New York: Macmillan.

Skinner, B. F. (1957). *Verbal behavior.* Englewood Cliffs, NJ: Prentice-Hall.

Skinner, B. F. (1974). *About behaviorism.* New York: Knopf.

Skinner, B. F. (1976). *Walden Two.* New York: Macmillan.

Sleet, D. A. (1987). Motor vehicle trauma and safety belt use in the context of public health priorities. *The Journal of Trauma, 27,* 695-702.

Smith, P. (1990). *Killing the spirit.* New York: Penguin Books.

Stack, J. (1992). *The great game of business.* New York: Doubleday.

Stein, S. J. (1994). *The Shaker experience in America: A history of the united society of believers.* New Haven, CT: Yale University.

Sulzer-Azaroff, B. (1998). *Who killed my daddy?* Boston, MA: Cambridge Center for Behavioral Studies.

Sulzer-Azaroff, B., & Mayer, G. R. (1991). *Behavior analysis for lasting change.* New York: Harcourt Brace Jovanovitch.

Thompson, D. C., Rivara, F. P., & Thompson, R. S. (1996). Effectiveness of bicycle safety helmets in preventing head injuries: a case-control study. *JAMA, 276*(24), 1968-1973.

Thorndike, E. L. (1898). Animal intelligence. An experimental study of the associative processes in animals. *Psychology Monograph, 2*(8), 36-40.

Thorndike, E. L. (1911). *Animal intelligence: Experimental studies.* New York: Macmillan.

Wells, H. G. (1933). *The shape of things to come.* New York: Macmillan.

Williams, A. F., & Lund, A. K. (1986). Seat belt use laws and occupant crash protection in the United States. *American Journal of Public Health, 76,* 1438-1442.

Williams, A. F., Lund, A. K., Preusser, D. F., & Blomberg, R. D. (1986). Results of a seat belt use law enforcement and publicity campaign in Elmira, New York. *Accident Analysis & Prevention, 19*, 243-249.

Williams, A. F., Preusser, D. F., & Lund, A. K. (1990). *Evaluation of a program to increase belt use on the New York thruway*. Arlington, VA: Insurance Institute of Highway Safety.

Williams, A. F., Preusser, D. F., Blomberg, R. D., & Lund, A. K. (1987). Seat belt use law enforcement and publicity in Elmira, New York: A reminder campaign. *American Journal of Public Health, 77*, 1450-1451.

Williams, A. F., Wells, J. K., & Lund, A. K. (1987). Shoulder belt use in four states with belt use laws. *Accident Analysis & Prevention, 19*, 251-260.